BOLSHEVIK VISIONS

First Phase of the Cultural Revolution in Soviet Russia

Part 1
The Culture of a New Society:
Ethics, Gender, the Family, Law, and
Problems of Tradition

Edited by William G. Rosenberg

Second Edition

Ann Arbor Paperbacks

THE UNIVERSITY OF MICHIGAN PRESS

Copyright © by the University of Michigan 1990
First published 1984 by Ardis Publishers
All rights reserved
Published in the United States of America by
The University of Michigan Press
Manufactured in the United States of America

2002   2001   2000   1999   6   5   4   3

Library of Congress Cataloging-in-Publication Data

Bolshevik visions : first phase of the cultural revolution in Soviet
  Russia / edited by William G. Rosenberg. — 2nd ed.
     p.   cm.— (Ann Arbor paperbacks ; [AA201–AA202])
    Translations from the Russian.
    Reprint. Originally published : Ann Arbor, MI : Ardis, c1984.
    Includes bibliographical references.
    ISBN 0-472-09424-6 (v. 1). — ISBN 0-472-06424-X (v. 1, pbk.).
    — ISBN 0-472-09425-4 (v. 2). — ISBN 0-472-06425-8 (v. 2, pbk.)
    1. Communism and culture—Soviet Union. 2. Communism and society.
  3. Soviet Union—Social conditions—1917–   I. Rosenberg, William G.
  HX523.B65   1990
  306'.345'0947—dc20
                                             90-10958
                                              CIP

Cover illustration from a fashion magazine cover design by L. Popova, 1924.

To My Parents

ACKNOWLEDGMENTS

Several people have participated in preparing these volumes, and I only hope they have enjoyed it as much as I have. Robert Gorlin, a wayward Russianist now practicing law in Detroit, helped in its conceptualization and in the early selection of materials. Initially we had hoped to edit the volume together. He also did some of the first draft translations, along with myself and Kira Stevens, who gave up time from her interesting study of the eighteenth century Russian grain trade to help. The translations were reviewed by Nina Lifshits and Ann Ellen Akeley, who worked skillfully together to assure their accuracy, and to help render versions as close to the originals as possible, whatever their grammatical or stylistic weaknesses. Final responsibility is, of course, mine. Anne Bobroff assisted with the bibliography.

Generous support for this volume has come from the Center for Russian and East European Studies at the University of Michigan. Carl and Ellendea Proffer and their remarkable institution, Ardis Publishers, were patient and supportive throughout the preparation of the first edition, and Ardis has graciously given permission for republication. Mary Erwin of the University of Michigan Press has been instrumental in the preparation of this revision, and I appreciate Jane Burbank's helpful comments as well. Anatole Senkevitch, Jr., has generously assisted with materials on architecture and city planning.

The book is dedicated to my parents, Constance and Gordon Rosenberg, who have long had their own admirable vision of what society "ought to be like."

ГОСКИНО произвводство ГОСКИНО

КИНО ГЛАЗ

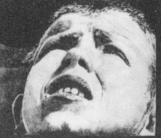

6 СЕРИЙ

РАБОТА
ДЗИГИ ВЕРТОВА
ОПЕРАТОР
КАУФМАН

CONTENTS OF PART 1

xi

ILLUSTRATIONS IN PART 1

под редакцией ЭЛ ЛИСИЦКОГО и ИЛЬИ ЭРЕНБУРГА

GEGENSTAND
INTERNATIONALE
RUNDSCHAU
DER KUNST
DER GEGENWART

ВЕЩЬ

МЕЖДУНАРОДНОЕ
ОБОЗРЕНИЕ
СОВРЕМЕННОГО
ИСКУССТВА

OBJET
REVUE
INTERNATIONALE
DE L'ART
MODERNE

№ 3

БЕРЛИН
МАЙ
1922

PUBLIÉE SOUS LA DIRECTION DE EL LISSITZKY ET ELIE EHRENBURG

BERLIN, MÜNCHENER STRASSE 16 — TELEPHON: KURFÜRST 47-68.

1 ИСКУССТВО И ОБЩЕСТВЕННОСТЬ

LOCOMOTIVE CHASSE-NEIGE

ПАРОВОЗ-СНЕГООЧИСТИТЕЛЬ

K. MALEVITSCH   К. МАЛЕВИЧ
1914

изображать машину — все равно
что писать ню

человек не является разумным
творцом своего тела

машина — урок ясности и экономии

ТЕХНИЧЕСКАЯ ВЕЩЬ
÷ ЭКОНОМИЯ

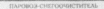

СУПРЕМАТИЧЕСКАЯ
ВЕЩЬ

INTRODUCTION TO THE SECOND EDITION

When the Politburo of the Soviet Communist Party elected Mikhail Sergeevich Gorbachev General Secretary on March 11, 1985, few Western observers imagined he would launch one of the most dramatic efforts at social and political transformation in modern history. The new fifty-four-year-old leader seemed relatively untested at the high levels of Soviet politics. Little in his background suggested bold vision. Born into a peasant family in the village of Privolnoe, near Stavropol, Gorbachev had grown up in the countryside, driving farm machinery as a teenager at a local machine-tractor station. In the 1950s he studied law in Moscow, but returned after his graduation to Stavropol as an organizer for the Young Communist League, a typical post for fledgling party professionals. In 1962 he was promoted to party organizer for collective and state farms; and in 1966, Leonid Brezhnev rewarded him with an appointment as the Stavropol region first secretary. In all apparent respects his career trajectory resembled that of countless other party functionaries, even after Brezhnev brought him to Moscow in 1978 as a party secretary for agricultural administration, and Yuri Andropov assured his further ascendency to the Politburo in 1980.

By the time he replaced the aged and ailing Konstantin Chernenko in 1985, however, Gorbachev clearly recognized the need for radical change. Major problems existed in the Soviet economy. His own area of specialization in particular, collectivized agriculture, remained woefully unable to meet the basic consumption needs of increasing numbers of Soviet citizens. Imports of a commodity as basic as grain were rapidly draining the Soviet treasury of precious hard currency reserves. With inadequate levels of savings, capital formation also remained a serious problem and so, consequently, did future economic development. Worker productivity was estimated to be less than half that of Western Europe and the United States, and was even lower in comparison to Japan; many in white collar jobs often seemed to do next to nothing. Planning, distribution, and especially research and development suffered from archaic methods and entrenched procedures, particularly in the crucial area of technology.

Increasing urbanization was also severely straining Soviet social services. Virtually every major city and town desperately needed new housing. Population growth was also affecting educational opportunities, health care delivery, and transportation services. Popular morale was low. Television and tourism made it painfully apparent that especially in comparison to Western Europe, East Asia, and North America, but also to parts of East Europe, Soviet socialism was lagging far behind. On the streets, Soviet youth displayed patent alienation and resentment.

Alcoholism was a major problem; drug use was increasing. In Moscow and Leningrad, black-marketeering was a common after-school activity.

Many in the West saw the root of these problems in the very nature of Soviet socialism and the Communist party itself. Entrenched in archaic bureaucratic routines, tolerant of corruption, the party represented stagnant patterns of behavior and outlook. Apparatchiki seemed to strangle any efforts at change. To press for reform would not only threaten many comfortable careers, but would also confront such deeply institutionalized systems of behavior that most observers thought reformers would themselves be quickly smothered or swallowed into the bureaucratic morass. Socialism itself seemed to signify bureaucracy, ineptitude, and stagnation. As Thomas J. Watson, Jr., the former U.S. ambassador to Moscow observed to the *New York Times* on March 12, 1985, as Gorbachev came to power, "The government of the USSR is a very solid, firmly-in-place bureaucratic government . . . I don't think the United States should expect any real change. . . . Occasionally, there are some freedom moves but such activity is very minimal. I think the impact of [Gorbachev's appointment] will be zero."

Within months, of course, the extent to which the new Soviet leader was dedicated to change was evidenced by the emergence of two new words into the English lexicon: *perestroika* and *glasnost'*. To the astonishment of observers like Ambassador Watson, virtually every major aspect of Soviet politics and society soon came under review. The evidence quickly mounted that Gorbachev intended a thorough overhaul of the most fundamental components of Soviet Russia's economic and political order. Most startling, the key to change seemed to be frank discussion and openness. Intellectuals and writers were soon encouraged to speak out. Dramatically, the dissident physicist Andrei Sakharov returned from exile. Prepublication censorship was eliminated. Surprising articles began to appear in Soviet journals and newspapers, including *Pravda,* criticizing current conditions and raising questions about the past. Soviet television introduced new programming, and evening news shows were soon offering their unaccustomed viewers truly startling depictions of Soviet reality.

That the watchwords of Brezhnev's and Chernenko's successor soon became "honesty," "openness," "democracy," and "the human factor" was not simply the boldest element of *perestroika,* but also the one least expected by Western observers accustomed to associating Soviet Marxism with intellectual regimentation. Indeed, by past Soviet standards the freedom that emerged in 1986 and 1987 to publish or otherwise articulate critical and harsh analyses of Soviet society was extraordinary. And so, for the Soviet intelligentsia, was the challenge to think constructively and creatively, to participate in this remarkable, even revolutionary, process of social and cultural transformation.

Why was "new thinking" the foundation of *perestroika?* First, clearly, to expose ineffective and corrupt aspects of Soviet society and politics and discredit practices contributing to economic stagnation. Second, to enlist the intelligentsia itself, at once the most alienated and critical group in society, behind the tasks of reconstruction. Especially important here was to capture the support of Soviet Russia's young technological intelligentsia and its well-educated middle-level managers. Gorbachev and his supporters understood the relationship between technological innovation and social progress, between knowledge and change, between honesty, exposure, and reform. And they recognized first and foremost the degree of alienation felt by those most needed for their efforts at change. Critical thinkers in every area of intellectual life simply had to be brought to support a new vision of Soviet socialism if the impediments to revolutionary social transformation were to be overcome. Thus, self-confident Western assumptions about the permanence of Soviet stagnation and intellectual repression proved as unwarranted as corresponding assumptions about the absolute conservatism of Soviet politics.

This was not the first time in Soviet history, however, that diverse elements of the Soviet intelligentsia were challenged to define the principles and visions of a new socialist order, to create a new and transformational political culture. As the materials collected in this volume indicate, "new thinking" in many areas was a vibrant part of the Bolshevik revolution and early Soviet power. It was clear by the spring of 1989, moreover, that Gorbachev and others defined their current tasks not so much in terms of emulating the West, as Western analysts and news media frequently assumed, as in terms of realizing their own notions of what the founding moment of Soviet power, the October Revolution, actually meant: "a revolution of the people, of every individual, for his emancipation and development," as Gorbachev himself described it. During the dramatic election campaign for a new Soviet congress in March and April, 1989, for example, the banners raised by Yuri Afanasyev, one of the best known critics of the contemporary order, were "Land to the Peasants!" "Factories to the Workers!" and "Power to the Soviets!"— precisely the Bolsheviks' slogans in 1917. That many Westerners failed to see these connections reflected as much a misperception of Gorbachev's own underlying system of values as it did a limited understanding of the Russian revolution and early Bolshevik visions.

Although the preconditions for the remarkable upheaval of 1917 were well set even before the war, the "path toward October," as Soviet historians have frequently described it, began in February when massive strikes and demonstrations by Petrograd workers and garrison soldiers brought down the three-hundred-year-old Romanov dynasty. Within weeks of the tsar's abdication on March 2, the liberal Provisional Government, which took power in the name of long-sought Western democratic principles, found itself under attack for defending "bourgeois" values. Moderate socialists in various workers' councils (soviets) challenged the government's war aims, insisting on peace "without annexations and indemnities." Radicals attacked the liberals' defense of private property. In the countryside, peasants began to seize landlords' estates in defiance of government law, rejecting pleas that reforms be postponed until after democratic national elections. In cities and towns, workers struck for higher wages to meet a galloping inflation, and when managers responded by closing their shops, sequestered plants to keep them going or demanded government nationalization. By late spring a coalition regime had been formed, forcing moderate soviet spokesmen to assume some responsibility in official government affairs, but this only sharpened the attack of radicals like Lenin, who accused the moderates of selling out workers' interests.

In June, the Provisional Government launched a new military offensive under the socialist war minister Kerensky, linking coalition government, moderate socialism, and "bourgeois" values with the continuation of the increasingly unpopular war. Within weeks the troops faltered badly. As a disillusioned Right began to muster forces of its own to "restore order and discipline," Bolshevik popularity grew. By late summer, Lenin's supporters had majorities in the soviets of Moscow and Petrograd. The cry "All Power to the Soviets" was now heard as often as "Peace, Land, and Bread." When Moscow and Petrograd workers took up arms to defeat a counterrevolutionary attack by General Kornilov, it was relatively easy for Trotsky and others to organize Military Revolutionary Committees, and mobilize workers' Red Guards for an armed Bolshevik insurrection; and when Lenin took power in October, many regarded this second revolution as simply one more episode in the long process of Russia's political disintegration.

It was not, of course, but for many students, political "disintegration" and Lenin's "seizure of power" *are* the Russian revolution, just as *perestroika* is often viewed simply in terms of Kremlin politics, rather than as a broad engagement with entrenched social relations and the culture of stagnation. The events of 1917 are understood in terms of the "political vacuum" created by the collapse of tsarist autocracy, and the successive inability of weak democratic regimes to restore order. October is a "coup d'etat." Lenin takes power "illegally," but succeeds through authoritarian politics to maintain his position, restoring indirectly a form of Russian autocracy. Through a long civil war, the new communist "autocracy" is buffeted first by internal opposition and then by powerful anti-Bolshevik armies and Allied intervention. Anarchist peasant uprisings occur in the Ukraine, Tambov, and Siberia, lashing out at both "Reds" and "Whites," while catastrophic shortages of food and supplies in areas under Bolshevik control prompt strikes, requisitioning, new dissidence, and new repression.

But compared to its opposition, the Bolshevik party is well organized and well disciplined. Political power is assured because the Bolsheviks are determined to rule, and willing to apply forceful practical measures.

The problem with this view is not so much its focus on Bolshevik authoritarianism or even its de-emphasis of revolutionary communist ideology, but rather the way in which its excessive concentration on politics obscures crucial social and cultural changes, which may ultimately have been even more important than politics in securing Bolshevik hegemony. The weakness of the Provisional Government in 1917, like that of the autocracy it replaced, was not its unwillingness to use forceful political measures, but its inability, which stemmed from mass disaffection from the values and institutions it represented. The condition of "dual power" reflected in the liberal regime on one hand and the soviet network on the other in 1917, was at the same time an expression of profound social and cultural polarization. As peasants seized the landlords' land, as workers took over factories and shouted "Down with the War," they implicitly rejected Russia's traditional system of social estates, as well as the system of law designed to protect hierarchical social interests and even the treasures of art and literature so deeply revered by Russia's upper classes. Paintings were burned with manor houses; crockery was smashed; fine furniture split into kindling. The anger and alienation of workers and peasants had little to do with representative government, trial by jury, national elections, or freedom of speech. And the Bolsheviks came to power not only because they identified with militant workers and peasants in rejecting the premises of liberal rule, but also because they associated themselves directly with mass social and cultural aspirations.

After October, Russia's social revolution continued unabated. The expropriation of the gentry was extended to cities and towns, where factory owners, managers, financiers, and other elements of the "bourgeoisie" found their assets confiscated, their apartments requisitioned to house the poor and homeless. Tens of thousands fled abroad. Others refused for a time to cooperate with the new Bolshevik regime, paralyzing commercial and government institutions, and then joined the Whites in South Russia and Siberia. Social leveling thus brought incredible chaos and intense class conflict.

But it also brought opportunity: the chance to establish new social and cultural relations theoretically free from the exploitative, hierarchical characteristics of prerevolutionary society. As the Bolsheviks came to power, a deep belief in the oppressive nature of "bourgeois" social values and cultural norms became the foundation of a new revolutionary assault, one which mobilized a cultural radicalism in an effort to "build a new life." Bolshevik power was to become the basis for new social values as well as revolutionary social relations, and the stimulus for radically new proletarian cultural forms.

It thus developed that in the midst of incredible destruction, unspeakably brutal warfare, massive hunger, and the imposition of the draconian, dictatorial policies of "war communism," there also emerged a period of remarkable cultural creativity in Russia, both in terms of artistic expression and in the broader sociological sense of institutional forms and social relations. On one hand, cultural revolutionaries hoped to produce a new type of person in Soviet Russia, just as the dictatorship of the proletariat was to produce a new socioeconomic order: the selfless, dedicated party member, the nurturant parent, the compassionate judge, the honest and uncorruptible "new man" and "new woman." These attributes were seen both as natural derivatives of a new nonexploitative Soviet socialism. They were also considered necessary and appropriate modes of behavior for Soviet Russia's new political leaders, "conscious" Bolsheviks whose actions had to serve as encouraging models until socialism was fully developed and natural processes worked freely. In ways that contradicted the materialist foundation of rigid Marxist outlooks, many early Bolsheviks took an anthropological view of the problems of social and political transformation, recognizing the centrality of cultural change. Seventy years later, it was precisely this perspective and these values that linked *perestroika* with the Bolshevik past.

On the other hand, this early cultural revolution also aimed at new artistic achievements: new theater and music, new films, and other forms of artistic creativity. "Bourgeois" art, designed for the pleasures of a social elite and reflecting its values, would yield to proletarian socialist art, both richer in its aesthetic content and technical mastery, and broadly accessible. Theaters would become truly public institutions; the pleasures of artistic creativity would be cultivated within all social strata. At the same time, cultural institutions like schools would shed their functions as training centers for social elites and become places of universal proletarian enlightenment. Social services would be modernized, expanded, and made broadly accessible as hospitals and health care facilities were "proletarianized," their resources increased, their benefits universally shared. During this first phase of cultural change in Russia, when elitist institutions and "bourgeois" cultural values were to be smashed, there seemed virtually no limit to range or radical cultural innovation available to the Bolsheviks and their supporters. Here, too, there are parallels to *perestroika,* not so much in content as in the very openness and freedom of aesthetic expression.

The materials collected in parts 1 and 2 of *Bolshevik Visions* document these early efforts at cultural change in Soviet Russia, and reveal the values and principles on which they were based. While their specific relevance to the tasks of *perestroika* may be doubtful, the search for new principles itself links these periods together. The materials here also indicate the ways in which struggles for new cultural norms are invariably fraught with contradictions. The very question of what a communist "ought to be like," for example (part 1, chap. I), raised the issue for many Marxists of whether communist ethics can be prescriptive ideals, or whether, as "superstructural" elements, they are necessarily derivative of material conditions and not susceptible to abstract formulations. Such questions were not simply grist for philosophical mills. The effort to smash bourgeois institutions and values lies at the heart of Russia's revolutionary process in 1917, but once this destructive phase had run its course, Bolsheviks faced a real need to establish rules and norms of behavior. Few in the party doubted the appropriateness of Leninist pragmatism, but decisions about modes of behavior still had to be made in terms of achieving practical goals. Was Red Guard brutality functional in the class struggle? Was terror? Did workers require strict rules in shops and factories to help them overcome bourgeois habits (indifference, lateness, low productivity), or were there better forms of motivation and mobilization? Even the absence of a formal party decision on these matters was, in effect, a decision by default. It was also obvious that bourgeois habits and values were deeply ingrained in Russian society, even among politically conscious proletarians, just as it was clear in the 1980s that loyal and honest Soviet citizens were nonetheless accustomed to patterns of thought and behavior inimical to social progress or adequate economic growth. Better, therefore, to face these issues head on, as Krupskaya and Solts argue in part 1, chapter I, and as Gorbachev has insisted in virtually every one of his major speeches.

Russia's bourgeois legacy after 1917 was problematic in other ways as well. If socialist freedom meant the end of class exploitation in socioeconomic terms, it also had to involve the end of exploitative attitudes and habits. Gradually, of course, a socialist mode of production would generate collectivist outlooks. Exploitative relationships between men and women, institutional sexism, even the proprietary "bourgeois" attitudes of parents toward children would yield to a range of open, genuinely supportive and fraternal patterns. In the meantime, however, the habits of bourgeois individualism could seriously weaken the young socialist state. Concern for self could manifest itself in a variety of damaging ways, undermining the tasks of collective achievement (and the willingness for collective sacrifice) on which the revolution's fate depended. Here, too, consequently, an activist front had to be created.

For some in the party, as the materials in part 1, chapter II indicate, these issues were most important in terms of sex roles, marriage, and the family. Socialism would mean very little, in Kollontai's view, if constraining male prejudice about inappropriate roles for women was not radically altered. Involved here were not only the issues of equal career opportunities for professionals or the elimination of parasitic bourgeois life-styles on the part of wives of successful men, but a revolutionary

7

assault on the caste attitudes of Moslems and other borderland people under Soviet control, and a forceful effort to transform proletarian marriages and families from loveless institutions serving bourgeois values and production interests to places of genuine nurturance. Materials in part 1, chapters III and V show as well how antisocialist habits in other areas could similarly weaken the tasks of building a new life. Religious beliefs undermined Marxist rationalism; language patterns reinforced bourgeois social stratification, particularly in the use of familiar verb forms (*thee*/*thou*) to indicate respect and subservience. Prostitution also seemed to some a dangerous, exploitative legacy of Russia's bourgeois past.

Thus the early years of Bolshevik power witnessed a profusion of articles and essays on cultural attitudes in the broad sense, seemingly far from the central issues of politics and social organization, and enormously interesting to present-day Soviet as well as Western readers, particularly considering their suppression during the intervening decades. Perhaps equally important to efforts at legitimizing the policies of *perestroika,* however, is the simple fact that there were major differences of opinion among the early Bolsheviks over these matters, including serious questions about their importance and about their appropriate resolution. Was prostitution, for example, really a "bourgeois" habit? Was it "immoral," according to some abstract code of communist ethics, or even a crime? And were "bourgeois" sexual constraints really antisocialist, or (to put the matter conversely), were uninhibited sexuality, casual relationships, even postcard divorces really equivalent to political radicalism? Also, what about a revolutionary offensive on these fronts, which effectively alienated masses of potential Bolshevik supporters: religious factory workers, for example, or poor peasants; Red Army men and women who found their spouses unwilling to wait for them; students, particularly women, who found themselves challenged every time they rejected a comrade's advances? "These issues do not have one tenth the importance some people ascribe to them" Vinogradskaya writes in a selection included in part 1, chapter II; energy spent here diverted the party from more serious matters. Such a view can readily be found among the detractors of Gorbachev.

For others, however, the resolution of such issues was inseparable from the very fate of the revolution, just as the survival of Soviet Russia after Brezhnev as a viable socialist order seemed for many to depend on its fundamental transformation. If early Bolsheviks could not succeed in smashing bourgeois attitudes and habits, could not succeed in ending oppressive patterns of behavior and erecting a new set of social relations, even a radical socioeconomic transformation would not produce a new historical order. And if *perestroika* were to leave entrenched behavior and attitudes intact, Soviet Russia's future would necessarily resemble its past.

In some ways, the goal of revolutionary institutional change in cultural areas was (and is) even more radical than the struggle for a new communist man and woman, as the materials included here on social welfare, law, and education suggest. In the first months of Soviet power a new system of public health care forced a radical reorientation of the medical profession, for example, away from the treatment of an elite, using relatively advanced methods and intensive care facilities, to a mass clinical system based on prophylaxis rather than cure. The Commissariats of Health and Welfare were themselves radical innovations, preceding the establishment of a comparable institution in the United States by some thirty-five years. And while *zemstvo* medicine was itself a form of public health service in Russia before 1917, as the Introduction of part 1, chapter III indicates, the effort to refocus the entire institutional framework of medical care had no historical precedent.

The area of judicial reform was similarly innovative (part 1, chap. IV). The effort of Commissar of Justice Stuchka and others not only involved the creation of new "Revolutionary Tribunals" and "Peoples' Courts," modeled to some extent on Western European revolutionary precedents, but the formulation as well of new principles of criminal law and Marxist jurisprudence, and the revamping of the entire system of nonpolitical criminal justice. Traditional notions of "crime" and "punishment," with their moral and ethical overtones, were to give way to nonretributive concepts of "socially harmful act" and "penalty." Rehabilitation, rather than punishment, became the institutional goal of imprisonment. As Stuchka himself argues in one of the selections included here, the laws of the new society would be founded on its socioeconomic relations, rather than the other way around, as in bourgeois states. It is true, of course, that law and the courts very quickly became a means of political repression. But for a while, at least, the effort to restructure Russia's criminal justice system in the direction of social reconstruction and rehabilitation evoked a series of radical measures and interesting, progressive principles, many of which have subsequently been adopted in the West.

Russia's educational network was similarly assaulted. Here, Lunacharsky, Krupskaya, and others worked at replacing "bourgeois" institutions, which emphasized individual achievement, competition, and intellectual (as opposed to physical) labor, and which served a social elite, with "proletarian labor schools," integrating knowledge with ordinary life activities. As the materials in part 2, chapter I suggest, there was a remarkable optimism in Bolshevik educational outlooks: "freedom" under socialism meant consciousness and awareness; ignorance was a means of oppression. The institutional goals of Soviet education were thus designed to "enlighten" as well as to "educate," to integrate a collectivist order rather than to stratify social elites, and to develop bold new programs to bring rudimentary educational skills to Russia's mass of illiterate workers and peasants. Such goals led as well to remarkable educational experimentation, much of it in conditions of incredible social dislocation

9

and political chaos. But here, as several of the selections in that chapter indicate, the very dislocation of the civil war period in some ways actually facilitated radical change. In most places, for example, it was necessary, not simply pedagogically desirable, for students to work if their schools were to be heated and clean; and dislocation of traditional educational systems helped provide a pool of selfless instructors, willing to work in "workers' faculties" and other similar mass education experiments.

In each of these areas of cultural innovation and change, the fledgling socialist order encountered enormous practical and even political difficulties. The first phase of Russia's "proletarian cultural revolution," lasting more or less until the new radical transformations of the 1928–32 period, was a time of limitless expectations and circumscribed possibility. Setting goals and laying out principles in the midst of a devastating civil war meant that every cultural innovation necessarily had political connotations. Resources were either limited or nonexistent, and the practical benefits of every cultural activity had to be weighed against the alternative gains to be had if energy and resources went in different directions. It is not surprising, therefore, that social welfare reforms were frequently ineffective, that boycotting physicians occasionally forced local Bolsheviks to abandon plans for institutional change, that judicial reforms were frequently ignored, or even that a regime desperate for skilled and educated personnel should follow a policy of tolerance for a while toward universities, the Academy of Science, and similar centers of higher learning. But meager results should not obscure heroic efforts. Nor should the prominence of politics and economics in Russian revolutionary transformation obscure the imagination and creative experimentation present in these cultural arenas.

Imagination and creativity also characterized the final areas of cultural revolution touched in these volumes, that of filmmaking, theater, music, literature, architecture, and the arts. Here the vibrant tendencies of a strong prerevolutionary avant garde set the stage for a remarkable period of artistic experimentation, legitimized in theoretical terms as appropriate and necessary to a new stage of historical development. Artists like Malevich and Lissitzky, film makers like Eisenstein, architects like Tatlin, and others were joined not so much by their views about what proletarian art itself might be, but by their conviction that "bourgeois" art, defined rather loosely as the cultural products of bourgeois society, had no place in a proletarian dictatorship. The quest for a definition of proletarian art, in fact, led in every conceivable new direction: mass, open-air theaters; constructivist posters and the manifestoes of "futurists" denouncing artistic conservatism; architectural experiments like Tatlin's "Monument to the Third International," which would send a technological marvel soaring into the Moscow skies (part 2, chaps. II, III, and IV).

Here, too, there were important questions of attitude, as well as

10

problems of institutional change. Asking whether art in a proletarian society had to be comprehensible to the masses raised issues of aesthetics as well as cultural elitism. What role would be left to radical innovators if the norms of quality were defined by acceptance? Was proletarian art necessarily utilitarian? And how could cultural institutions like the Bolshoi Theater become practically accessible to any but an urban elite? As the selections throughout part 2 indicate, arguments over these and other issues raged intensely in the first years of Soviet power, and in some ways, as readers will see, tendencies toward artistic repression (in the name of mass acceptance, utilitarianism, and ideological conformity) began to emerge early even from within the artistic community itself. As in so many other areas, the distance between imagination and creativity and the demands of Bolshevik dictatorship rapidly widened. It was not very long before the excitement of this early period had vanished, along with most of its participants.

Here, too, however, there is an important resonance with the late 1980s. The very notion of *glasnost'* venerates imagination, as well as openness; and in evoking the wide diversity of opinion, outlook, and aesthetic form under Gorbachev, many Soviet writers and artists looked quite consciously to the early 1920s, partly in an effort to demonstrate the degree to which Stalinist perversions destroyed genuine socialist aesthetics and ideals. On November 10, 1988, for example, the first comprehensive exhibit ever of the works of Kazimir Malevich, now hailed as one of the greatest innovators in art of the twentieth century, opened in Leningrad. Included in the exhibition catalog were the artist's own notes on architecture and painting, reflecting many of the views expressed in part 2, chapters III and IV.

It should be emphasized, however, that the materials in these books are about visions, not realities; about the hopes, partly utopian, of artists, educators, and jurists, not the actualities of Bolshevik practice. Nor were they collected because of their relationship to the perspectives and cultures of *perestroika* and *glasnost'*. The materials were assembled, simply, to help illuminate an exciting and neglected area of Russia's revolutionary experience. The very disparities between vision and reality, in fact, which are quite well known (and both shocking and depressing), tend in some ways to distort our historical understanding of what much of the revolution seemed to be about to many of its participants. In the aftermath of 1917, as in the 1980s, attitudinal change mattered greatly. So did a reconstruction of Russia's social relations, habits, and cultural institutions. Whether there was merit in these first visionary efforts to "build a new life," and whether they offer possibilities for the present generation, is for readers to judge for themselves.

Ann Arbor, July, 1989

11

NOTE ON TRANSLITERATION

The system of transliteration used in the text is that of the Library of Congress, modified in accordance with the recommendations in J. Thomas Shaw, *The Transliteration of Modern Russian for English-Language Publications* (Madison: University of Wisconsin Press, 1967). In the Notes and Suggested Readings sections the Library of Congress system has been used without modification for titles of publications and most proper names.

I. WHAT A COMMUNIST OUGHT TO BE LIKE

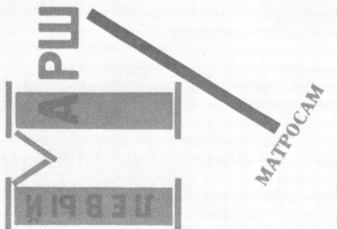

МАТРОСАМ

Разворачивайтесь в марше!
Словесной не место кляузе.
Тише, ораторы!

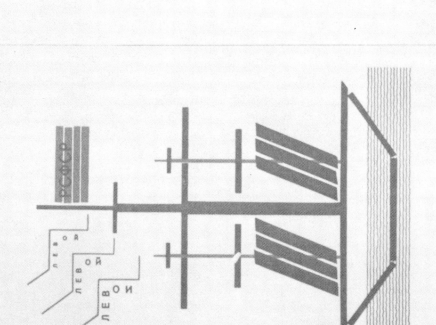

INTRODUCTION

What ought a communist be like? What ethical standards ought to govern his or her behavior, what code of conduct? "There are no questions which have been worked on so little as these," Emilyan Yaroslavsky, secretary to the Bolshevik Central Committee wrote shortly after the revolution, "nor any whose resolution matters so much to the successful upbringing of a new generation."[1]

Western students familiar with early Soviet history might be surprised at the importance Yaroslavsky attributes to these issues. "Morality," Lenin declared in a celebrated phrase, "is what serves to destroy the old exploiting society and to unite all the working people around the proletariat, which is building a new, communist society."[2] What is ethical, in other words, is what advances the Bolshevik cause. Means and ends are inextricably fused in a perspective justifying any behavior which advances or strengthens Bolshevik power. "We have finished, thank goodness, with purely theoretical debates, quarrels about general issues, endless resolutions about principles," Lenin told the Ninth Party Congress in 1920, seemingly rebutting Yaroslavsky. "That is a stage we have passed, that task was settled yesterday and before. Now we must go forward, we have to realize that practical tasks lies ahead...."[3]

But *how* should practical tasks be carried out, once the Bolsheviks had achieved power? And what sort of behavior *would* "unite all the people around the proletariat"? Despite Lenin's wish to be done with "theoretical debates," the question of Bolshevik conduct became an issue of serious practical importance in the months following the 1917 revolution, perhaps even determinant in structuring the future development of the party.

This was so for two reasons. First, the period immediately after the October revolution, from 1918 through the spring of 1921, was one of unspeakable brutality in Soviet Russia, as the Bolsheviks fought a deadly war for survival against the Whites and their interventionist allies. Scarcities of food and supplies pushed Lenin's party into the radical measures of "war communism," which involved seizing grain from poor as well as wealthy peasants, and imposing a range of tight controls over workers and industrial production. Labor discipline and even "militarization" were introduced, which allowed local party committees to mobilize workers for special tasks or reassign them from factory to factory; and strict new controls were placed over trade unions and other workers' organizations, including the factory committees and workers' control organizations which played such an important role in bringing the party to power. As those familiar with this period are well aware, strong opposition

15

to these measures developed within Bolshevik ranks. "Democratic Centralists" and members of the "Workers' Opposition" group, led by T. V. Sapronov, V. V. Osinsky, Vladimir Smirnov, Alexandra Kollontai and A. G. Shlyapnikov, the first Commissar of Labor, accused the Central Committee majority of violating fundamental communist principles concerning party democracy and worker participation in their own affairs. Bolsheviks were creating a dictatorship *over* the proletariat, rather than a proletarian dictatorship.

Whether or not they agreed with Opposition criticism over the *measures* of War Communism, many in the party recognized the validity of their attack as it pertained to the *style* of Bolshevik rule. Lenin's followers were in grave danger of alienating even their active supporters among rank and file workers and poor peasants because their behavior often seemed arbitrary, capricious, and coldly bureaucratic. *Proizvol,* the Russian word used critically to describe the wanton behavior of tsarist officialdom, re-emerged in the Civil War, as Kollontai argued: appointed party officials were "surrounded by an atmosphere of officialdom, servility, and blind subordination, which infects all subordinates and discredits the party... Every comrade can easily recall scores of instances when workers themselves attempted to organize dining rooms, day nurseries, transportation of fuel, etc., and when each time a lively immediate interest in the task died from red tape, interminable negotiations with various institutions that brought no results, or refusals, new requests, etc...."[4] Equally important, the behavior of party officials towards each other was producing serious problems. "The initiative of party members is restricted. Every independent attempt, every new thought that has not passed through the censorship of our center is considered a 'heresy,' a violation of party discipline."[5] In this regard, the party's Control Commission and even its secret police, the Cheka, needed clear guidelines. Those Bolsheviks whose actions and behavior was not "serving to unite all working people" or otherwise advancing the Bolshevik cause had to be purged from party ranks, but to do this effectively, cadre needed clear ideas of what a communist ought to be like.

The second reason why this issue was one of practical importance had to do with the need to formulate new goals for social institutions like the schools and the courts, new outlooks and habits in the areas of family life and relations between men and women, and the desirability of formulating some kind of proletarian aesthetic, although not necessarily one to be rigidly imposed in all areas of artistic creativity. The broad corpus of Marxist writings itself provided very little assistance in these spheres. Ethics and aesthetics both were derivative of material conditions in the Marxist view, aspects of the "superstructure" which reinforced in some way the basic socio-economic relationships characteristic of a particular "base." In modern capitalist society, Engels wrote, each class—the aristocracy, the

16

Could use for counter-argument that socialist thought ill of human nature in how they hated "bourgeoisie." But it was in how they believed that to be learned through culture that was money.

bourgeoisie, and the proletariat—had a morality of its own, from which one could only conclude "that men, consciously or unconsciously, derive their ethical ideas in the last resort from the practical relations on which their class position is based—from the economic relations in which they carry on production and exchange."[6] It made no sense to prescribe transcendent ethical absolutes, since such ideals simply did not exist independent of material reality; and the "codes of conduct" by which capitalist societies claimed to be governed, and which ostensibly lay at the core of Western religion, were actually no more than ideological justification for exploitative social relations.

Thus Marx's own writings contain no explicit condemnation of capitalism on moral grounds, although the history of human development he charts is essentially a moral drama. Humankind liberates itself from various stages of oppression, working teleologically towards conditions of absolute good. Communism is "just," not because it conforms to some ideal notion of "right," but because it eliminates exploitative social relations. And the revolutionary process which creates a communist order is not the result of ethical prescriptions, but the consequence of fundamental social antagonisms, contradictions between the production and distribution of wealth under capitalism which bring about its destruction from within.

But if Marxist ethics were not prescriptive, if moral behavior could not be determined in some ideal or absolute way, how could the Bolsheviks determine clearly what a communist ought to be like? What was an appropriate, proletarian social consciousness, which would reflect the morality of communist society? These issues became the focus of genuine concern in the early years of Bolshevik rule, as the selections in this chapter indicate, but the very effort to formulate answers caught party figures in the contradiction between ethical relativism, consistent with Marxist materialism, and the insistence both of the moral superiority of Bolshevik rule, and of discernable principles of communist ethics. Thus Bukharin considers the term "communist morality" itself to be "incorrect" in the selection below, and worries about the "fetishism" involved in subordinating human behavior to "some authority, the sources of which are actually unknown." But at the same time , he insists from "an absolutely sober, realistic, and materialistic" point of view that "rules of behavior" are necessary, and "must exist."

Perhaps because of this contradiction, the Bolsheviks refrained at first from establishing a formal moral code, as they were later to do under Stalin and Khrushchev (and incorporate into the 1961 Party Program as a separate chapter).[7] Instead, the issue was frequently approached negativistically, by identifying and rejecting "bourgeois" morality, and condemning traits among party comrades which resembled those of the prerevolutionary order. Thus Lenin's wife Krupskaya explains the purge of

human nature is derived by money. So just taking money away would solve everything? I'll no has no human money so do w/ human nature.

17

& they give negative spins on these things

"undesirable" party figures in her *Yuny Kommunist* (*Young Communist*) article (below) by indicating they possessed "coarse manners," "self-conceit," and "insincerity," as well as standing "well apart from the masses" and "putting their personal interests above the communist cause." These "bourgeois" characteristics also indicated the grave danger of harnessing pre-revolutionary experts and specialists to Soviet institutions, as Kollontai and others argued in these years: their influence would perpetuate a set of outlooks and attitudes antithetical to the goals for which the revolution had been fought. And if bourgeois morality was derivative of exploitative social relations, the Bolsheviks' failure to root it out would signify the ultimate failure of the revolutionary struggle itself. Thus the issue of moral values, however problematic, was "often raised," as Bukharin noted, and "occupied a very large place in our party organization," as A. A. Solts told students at the Sverdlov Institute (below).

The selections which follow represent both the diversity of opinion on this question and its contradictory aspects, as well as indicate the broad importance of "communist ethics" in the creation of a proletarian culture. Lenin's speech at the Third Congress of the Communist Youth League (Komsomol) in 1920 is the Bolshevik leader's fullest statement on the issue. It clearly rejects moral principles as "commandments," and lays out the Marxist notion of functional relationships between ethical behavior and social organization. "One cannot become a communist from books," Lenin argues, or by "assimilating slogans." An awareness of ethical behavior derives from consciousness of exploitation and participation in the struggle for a new life. For all its subsequent citation, however, the speech reveals as much through omission as it does through direct statement. How does struggle inculcate virtues, and which virtues, exactly? Lenin shows a genuine pessimism when he suggests that even Russia's workers, brought up under capitalism, can only "accomplish the task of destroying the capitalist way of life," and only lay the political foundations for communism, since they retain in manners and outlook much of what they absorbed in the bourgeois world. But how, then, will communist morality emerge without prescription from above? And what principles will party organizations like the Control Commissions use to weed out "undesirables"?

Bukharin and Krupskaya both suggest answers. Although representing what might be called a "moderate left" viewpoint within the party at the time, one concerned with arbitrariness on the part of local cadre and the desire to "clean up" Bolshevik behavior, Bukharin opts in a straightforward way for "rules of behavior." Never mind that establishing rules seems very much like raising moral "commandments," the very fetishism Bukharin himself rejects. "Rules on the wall are a positive thing," since they "remind comrades what they must be reminded about." Bukharin even lapses into one of his "bourgeois" analogies, which would later get him into

18

so much difficulty, comparing Bolshevik precepts with capitalist advertisements. "We must learn something from the capitalists," he argues, in the methodology of salesmanship.

One can see clear Stalinist tendencies in Bukharin's resolution of the issue, and also in his injunctions against alcohol, tobacco, and sexual dissoluteness. His stress on honor and competition invokes notions of individual (rather than collective) striving, precisely what communism was to replace; and the process of setting rules clearly suggests a special place for the rule-setter. What is interesting, however, is not only the way Bukharin outlines palpably "bourgeois" resolutions to the problems of ethics (forecasting in the process several prominent characteristics of contemporary Soviet society), but the logic of his conclusions, given the difficulties of ascertaining what ethical behavior for a communist actually is.

Krupskaya's article reflects these difficulties. She insists "social instincts" be developed among workers, meaning a consciousness of social class and a sense of solidarity. "Instinct" is an important word for her, since it suggests the naturalness of moral behavior; but in actually describing Bolshevik ethics, Krupskaya, like others, approaches the question in a negative way, condemning those who place personal interests above social ones, who are distant or indifferent towards the "masses," who are not "respected" or "loved," or who display coarse manners and insincerity. One might wonder how this differs significantly from Christian ethics; and in any event, while Krupskaya stresses the importance of educational institutions in bringing up the new generation, her essay lays out little in the way of practical guidelines.

The need for such guidelines is reflected clearly by A. A. Solts, the chairman of the party's Central Control Commission. Charged with purging undesirables from party ranks, and beset both by protests from those losing their positions (which sometimes resulted in the suicides he discusses) and oppositionists demanding high ethical standards, Solts travels a narrow line between prescription and spontaneity. Discipline is essential, he argues, but it must come voluntarily, from within, rather than in the form of formal codes. At the same time, drunkenness, political "scheming," excessive complaining, sexual libertarianism, personal striving and enrichment, even marriage to members of "alien" social groups are definitely to be avoided. One cannot separate one's private life from one's party life, he argues, although asceticism, like Tolstoyism (an individualist solution to social problems), must be avoided. Solts was tough-minded as Control Commission chairman, and a dedicated Leninist. (He perished for his commitment during Stalin's blood purges in the 1930s.) His essay is particularly interesting as a comprehensive statement on the question of ethics, as well as for its recognition of the dangers in the New Economic Policy (NEP) in terms of reinforcing bourgeois legacies (a process he calls

19

NEP-ification). Noteworthy as well is his location of the source of "political scheming" within the party in the very act of struggling for power.

The final essay, by P. I. Lebedev-Polyansky, touches the issues of proletarian values more broadly, in the area of literature and the aesthetic arts. Lebedev-Polyansky was president of the Proletarian Cultural Organization (Proletkult) between 1918 and 1920, while also serving in the Commissariat of Education and as head of Glavlit, the Soviet censorship board. But despite his government and party positions, he insists here on the independence of culture from politics, and opposes arguments in favor of merging (and subordinating) Proletkult groups to party organs. Later, he would retract these views, become an ardent Stalinist, and secure a comfortable position for himself as head of the Leningrad Institute of Literature; but in 1918 his stress on the collective, creative essence of proletarian culture helped set conditions for the exciting burst of artistic innovation which accompanied the Bolsheviks coming to power. Soviet socialism represented a new epoch in human development. Its cultural forms were unclear, except that they were not bourgeois forms, and hence any artistic expression reflecting the ethical and moral essence of proletarian labor qualified as aesthetically appropriate. The general issues Lebedev-Polyansky raises in this 1918 speech to the first Proletkult Congress will be discussed more fully by others in subsequent chapters.

TASKS OF THE YOUTH LEAGUES
(BOURGEOIS AND COMMUNIST MORALITY)
V. I. Lenin

I first of all shall deal here with the question of communist ethics.

You must train yourselves to be Communists. It is the task of the Youth League to organise its practical activities in such a way that, by learning, organising, uniting and fighting, its members shall train both themselves and all those who look to it for leadership; it should train Communists. The entire purpose of training, educating and teaching the youth of today should be to imbue them with communist ethics.

But is there such a thing as communist ethics? Is there such a thing as communist morality? Of course, there is. It is often suggested that we have no ethics of our own; very often the bourgeoisie accuse us Communists of rejecting all morality. This is a method of confusing the issue, of throwing dust in the eyes of the workers and peasants.

In what sense do we reject ethics, reject morality?

In the sense given to it by the bourgeoisie, who based ethics on God's commandments. On this point we, of course, say that we do not believe in God, and that we know perfectly well that the clergy, the landowners and the bourgeoisie invoked the name of God so as to further their own interests as exploiters. Or, instead of basing ethics on the commandments of morality, on the commandments of God, they based it on idealist and semi-idealist phrases, which always amounted to something very similar to God's commandments.

We reject any morality based on extra-human and extra-class concepts. We say that this is deception, dupery, stultification of the workers and peasants in the interests of the landowners and capitalists.

We say that our morality is entirely subordinated to the interests of the proletariat's class struggle. Our morality stems from the interests of the class struggle of the proletariat.

The old society was based on the oppression of all the workers and peasants by the landowners and capitalists. We had to destroy all that, and overthrow them but to do that we had to create unity. That is something that God cannot create.

Speech delivered at the Third All-Russian Congress of the Young Communist League (Komsomol), October 2, 1920. From *Collected Works* (4th ed.), Vol. 31, Moscow, 1966, pp. 290-96. First published in *Pravda*, Oct. 5, 6 & 7, 1920.

This unity could be provided only by the factories, only by a proletariat trained and roused from its long slumber. Only when that class was formed did a mass movement arise which has led to what we have now—the victory of the proletarian revolution in one of the weakest of countries, which for three years has been repelling the onslaught of the bourgeoisie of the whole world. We can see how the proletarian revolution is developing all over the world. On the basis of experience, we now say that only the proletariat could have created the solid force which the disunited and scattered peasantry are following and which has withstood all onslaughts by the exploiters. Only this class can help the working masses unite, rally their ranks and conclusively defend, conclusively consolidate and conclusively build up a communist society.

That is why we say that to us there is no such thing as a morality that stands outside human society; that is a fraud. To us morality is subordinated to the interests of the proletariat's class struggle.

What does that class struggle consist in? It consists in overthrowing the tsar, overthrowing the capitalists, and abolishing the capitalist class.

What are classes in general? Classes are that which permits one section of society to appropriate the labour of another section. If one section of society appropriates all the land, we have a landowner class and a peasant class. If one section of society owns the factories, shares and capital, while another section works in these factories, we have a capitalist class and a proletarian class.

It was not difficult to drive out the tsar—that required only a few days. It was not very difficult to drive out the landowners—that was done in a few months. Nor was it very difficult to drive out the capitalists. But it is incomparably more difficult to abolish classes; we still have the division into workers and peasants. If the peasant is installed on his plot of land and appropriates his surplus grain, that is, grain that he does not need for himself or for his cattle, while the rest of the people have to go without bread, then the peasant becomes an exploiter. The more grain he clings to, the more profitable he finds it; as for the rest, let them starve: "The more they starve, the dearer I can sell this grain." All should work according to a single common plan, on common land, in common factories and in accordance with a common system. Is that easy to attain? You see that it is not as easy as driving out the tsar, the landowners and the capitalists. What is required is that the proletariat re-educate a section of the peasantry; it must win over the working peasants in order to crush the resistance of those peasants who are rich and are profiting from the poverty and want of the rest. Hence the task of the proletarian struggle is not quite completed after we have overthrown the tsar and driven out the landowners and capitalists; to accomplish that is the task of the system we call the dictatorship of the proletariat.

The class struggle is continuing; it has merely changed its forms. It is

22

the class struggle of the proletariat to prevent the return of the old exploiters, to unite in a single union the scattered masses of unenlightened peasants. The class struggle is continuing and it is our task to subordinate all interests to that struggle. Our communist morality is also subordinated to that task. We say: morality is what serves to destroy the old exploiting society and to unite all the working people around the proletariat, which is building up a new, a communist society.

Communist morality is that which serves this struggle and unites the working people against all exploitation, against all petty private property; for petty property puts into the hands of one person that which has been created by the labour of the whole of society. In our country the land is common property.

But suppose I take a piece of this common property and grow on it twice as much grain as I need, and profiteer on the surplus? Suppose I argue that the more starving people there are, the more they will pay? Would I then be behaving like a Communist? No, I would be behaving like an exploiter, like a proprietor. That must be combated. If that is allowed to go on, things will revert to the rule of the capitalists, to the rule of the bourgeoisie, as has more than once happened in previous revolutions. To prevent the restoration of the rule of the capitalists and the bourgeoisie, we must not allow profiteering; we must not allow individuals to enrich themselves at the expense of the rest; the working people must unite with the proletariat and form a communist society. This is the principal feature of the fundamental task of the League and the organisation of the communist youth.

The old society was based on the principle: rob or be robbed; work for others or make others work for you; be a slave-owner or a slave. Naturally, people brought up in such a society assimilate with their mother's milk, one might say, the psychology, the habit, the concept which says: you are either a slave-owner or a slave, or else, a small owner, a petty employee, a petty official, or an intellectual—in short, a man who is concerned only with himself, and does not care a whit for anybody else.

If I work this plot of land, I do not care a whit for anybody else; if others starve, all the better, I shall get the more for my grain. If I have a job as a doctor, engineer, teacher, or clerk, I do not care a whit for anybody else. If I toady to and please the powers that be, I may be able to keep my job, and even get on in life and become a bourgeois. A Communist cannot harbour such a psychology and such sentiments. When the workers and peasants proved that they were able, by their own efforts, to defend themselves and create a new society—that was the beginning of the new and communist education, education in the struggle against the exploiters, education in alliance with the proletariat against the self-seekers and petty proprietors, against the psychology and habits which say: I seek my own profit and don't care a whit for anything else.

23

That is the reply to the question of how the young and rising generation should learn communism.

It can learn communism only by linking up every step in its studies, training and education with the continuous struggle the proletarians and the working people are waging against the old society of exploiters. When people tell us about morality, we say: to a Communist all morality lies in this united discipline and conscious mass struggle against the exploiters. We do not believe in an eternal morality, and we expose the falseness of all the fables about morality. Morality serves the purpose of helping human society rise to a higher level and rid itself of the exploitation of labour.

To achieve this we need that generation of young people who began to reach political maturity in the midst of a disciplined and desperate struggle against the bourgeoisie. In this struggle that generation is training genuine Communists; it must subordinate to this struggle, and link up with it, each step in its studies, education and training. The education of the communist youth must consist, not in giving them suave talks and moral precepts. This is not what education consists in. When people have seen the way in which their fathers and mothers lived under the yoke of the landowners and capitalists; when they have themselves experienced the sufferings of those who began the struggle against the exploiters; when they have seen the sacrifices made to keep what has been won, and seen what deadly enemies the landowners and capitalists are—they are taught by these conditions to become Communists. Communist morality is based on the struggle for the consolidation and completion of communism. That is also the basis of communist training, education, and teaching. That is the reply to the question of how communism should be learned.

We could not believe in teaching, training and education if they were restricted only to the schoolroom and divorced from the ferment of life. As long as the workers and peasants are oppressed by the landowners and capitalists, and as long as the schools are controlled by the landowners and capitalists, the young generation will remain blind and ignorant. Our schools must provide the youth with the fundamentals of knowledge, the ability to evolve communist views independently; they must make educated people of the youth. While they are attending school, they must learn to become participants in the struggle for emancipation from the exploiters. The Young Communist League will justify its name as the League of the young communist generation only when every step in its teaching, training and education is linked up with participation in the common struggle of all working people against the exploiters. You are well aware that, as long as Russia remains the only workers' republic and the old, bourgeois system exists in the rest of the world, we shall be weaker than they are, and be constantly threatened with a new attack; and that only if we learn to be solidly united shall we win in the further struggle and—having gained strength—become really invincible. Thus, to be a Communist means that

24

you must organise and unite the entire young generation and set an example of training and discipline in this struggle. Then you will be able to start building the edifice of communist society and bring it to completion.

To make this clearer to you, I shall quote an example. We call ourselves Communists. What is a Communist? Communist is a Latin word. *Communis* is the Latin for "common". Communist society is a society in which all things—the land, the factories—are owned in common and the people work in common. That is communism....

utopian

this part of the human nature theory is correct. This is why the Soviet Union is able to last so long, because it was paranoid of outsiders, paranoid of attack. This is an enormous contradiction. Under their utopian vision, shouldn't people just fall in line live peacefully?

25

WHAT A COMMUNIST OUGHT TO BE LIKE
N. Krupskaya

[handwritten margin note: Could be counter-argument here →]

A communist is, first and foremost, *a person involved in society,* with strongly developed social instincts, who desires that all people should live well and be happy.

Communists can come from all classes of society, but most of all they are workers by birth. Why? Because the conditions of workers' lives are such as to nurture in them social instincts: collective labor, the success of which depends on the separate efforts of each; the same conditions of labor; common experiences; the common struggle for humane conditions of existence. All this brings workers closer together and unites them with the bonds of class solidarity. Let us take the capitalist class. The conditions of life for this class are completely different. Competition forces each capitalist to see another capitalist primarily as an opponent, who has to be tripped up. In the worker the capitalist sees only "worker's hands" which must labor for the creation of his, the capitalist's, profits. Of course, the common struggle against the working class unites capitalists, but that internal unity, that formation into a collective which we see among workers—they have nothing to divide among themselves—does not exist in the capitalist class, where solidarity is corroded by competition. That is why in the working class the person with well-developed social instincts is the rule, while among the capitalists such a person is the exception.

Social instinct means a great many things. Often it offers a clue for finding a way out of a situation, for choosing the correct path. That is why during the purge of the RKP [Russian Communist Party], attention was paid to whether this or that member of the party had been born in a working family or not.[8] He who comes from a worker's background will more easily straighten himself out. The Russian intelligentsia, seeing how easily a worker, thanks to this class instinct, comprehends that which an intellectual, for example, perceives only with great difficulty, was inclined, in the end of the nineties and in the first half of the first decade of the twentieth century (1896—1903) to exaggerate the significance of class

---

From the journal *Iunii Kommunist,* No. 8–9, 1922. Republished in E. Yaroslavsky, ed., *Kakim dolzhen byt' kommunist,* Leningrad, 1925, pp. 14–18, and N. K. Krupskaya, *Pedagogicheskie sochineniia,* Vol. 2, Moscow, 1958, pp. 121-26. Krupskaya, Lenin's wife and closest friend, played an active role in educational and cultural matters at the time of the revolution, and for a brief period was Deputy Commissar of Education. See Robt. H. McNeal, *Bride of the Revolution: Krupskaya and Lenin,* Ann Arbor, 1972.

instinct. *Rabochaya Mysl'* [*Workers' Thought*], one of the underground Social Democratic newspapers, even came to the conclusion that no one other than people from workingman backgrounds could be accepted as socialists. Since Marx and Engels were not workers, *Rabochaya Mysl'* wrote "We don't need Marx and Engels!"

Class instinct, which among workers coincides with a social one, is a necessary condition for being a communist. Necessary, but not sufficient.

A communist must also *know* quite a lot. First, he must understand what is happening around him, and must gain an understanding of the existing system. When the workers' movement began to develop in Russia, Social Democrats were concerned from the very first with the widespread distribution of such pamphlets as Dikshtein's "Who Lives by What," "Worker's Day," etc. But it is not enough to understand the mechanics of the capitalist system. The communist must also study the laws of the development of human society. He must know the history of the development of economic forms, of the development of property, of division into classes, of the development of state forms. He must understand their interdependence and know how religious and moral notions will develop out of a particular social structure. Understanding the laws of the development of human society, the communist must clearly picture to himself where social development is heading. Communism must be seen by him as not only a desired system, where the happiness of some will not be based on the misfortune of others; he must further understand that communism is that very system toward which mankind is moving, and that communists must clear a path to this system, and promote its speedy coming.

In workers' circles at the dawn of the workers' movement in Russia, commonly studied courses were, on the one hand, political economy, which had the aim of explaining the structure of contemporary society, and the history of culture (the history of culture was usually opposed to the regular exposition of history, which often presented just a set of heterogeneous historical data). That is why in the circles of those days they read the first volume of Marx's *Capital* and F. Engels' *The Origins of the Family, Property and State*.

In 1919, in one of the villages of Nizhny Novgorod province, in the village of Rabotki, I happened to come across this phenomenon. Teachers told me that in the intermediate school they taught political economy and the history of culture; that the students unanimously demanded the introduction of these subjects into the curriculum of the intermediate school.

Where could such a desire, and such a definitely formulated one, have come from among peasant youth in a Volga village whose population was occupied exclusively with Volga river trades and agriculture? Obviously, interest in political economy and the history of culture was brought into

27

Rabotki by some worker, who at one time had attended some circle and who explained to the children what they needed to know.

However, at the present moment the Russian communist must know not only that. The October Revolution opened for Russia an opportunity for widespread building in the direction of communism. But in order to utilize these possibilities it is necessary to know what one can do at the moment in order to make at least one first step toward communism, and what one cannot, and it is necessary to know how to build a new life. It is necessary first and foremost to know thoroughly that sphere of work which you have undertaken, and then to master the method of a communist *approach* to the matter. Let us take an example. In order to organize correctly medical affairs in the country, it is first necessary to know the situation itself, secondly, how it was organized earlier in Russia and is currently organized in other states, and thirdly, how to approach the problem in a communist manner, namely, to conduct agitation among wide strata of workers, to interest them, to attract them to work, to create with their efforts a powerful organization in regard to medical affairs. It is necessary not only to know how to do all this, but to be able to *do* it. Thus it follows that a communist must know not only what communism is and why it is inevitable, but also know his own affairs well, and be able to approach the masses, influence them, and convince them.

In his personal life, a communist must always conduct himself in the interests of communism. What does this mean? It means, for example, that however nice it might be to stay in a familiar, comfortable home environment, that if for the sake of the cause, for the success of the communist cause, it is necessary to abandon everything and expose oneself to danger, the communist will do this. It means that however difficult and responsible the task the communist is called upon to perform, he will take it upon himself and try to carry it out to the best of his strength and skill, whether it is at the front, on a "subbotnik,"[9] during the confiscation of valuables, etc. It means that the communist puts his personal interests aside, subordinates them to the common interest. It means that the communist is not indifferent to what is happening around him and that he actively struggles with that which is harmful to the interests of the toiling masses, and that he on the other hand actively defends these interests and makes them his own. . . .

Who was discarded during the purging of the party? (a) the self-seekers and their adherents, that is, those who put their personal interests above the communist cause; (b) those who were indifferent to communism, who did nothing to help it make headway, who stood far from the masses and made no efforts to draw closer to them; (c) those who did not enjoy the respect and love of the masses; (d) those who were distinguished by a coarse manner, conceit, insincerity and other such characteristics.

Thus, in order to be a communist: (1) it is necessary to know what is bad about the capitalist system, where social development is heading and how to promote the speediest coming of the communist system; (2) it is necessary to know how to apply one's knowledge to the cause; and (3) it is necessary to be spiritually and physically devoted to the interests of the working masses and to communism. . . .

COMMUNIST ETHICS
A. A. Solts

Comrades! First of all I would like to tell you that on such a question as party ethics, we must conduct discussions and not hear reports with accompanying resolutions or some such thing.

It seems that the question of party ethics has in recent times occupied a very large place in our party organization. But I contend that this in no way can be understood to be some sort of militant campaign on this question, the result of the party being convinced of or seeing some elements of corruption, some trouble in party life in connection with which it has initiated a campaign. I think that all comrades, having dealings with members of the party, even with those who have made some mistakes, if they raised the question of party ethics at the last plenary session of the TsKK, [Central Control Commission] it was on entirely different grounds. In the party a more or less intensified interest in these questions has been noticed, and the plenum of the TsKK put this question on its agenda. The reasons for this are the following: in the last year many members of the party have come to us from the working class environment. For these persons, in light of the fact that we are going through a period when direct active struggle is not being conducted, the questions of how a member of the party should act, of what he should do in his everyday life, play no minor background role; and this interest is increasing everywhere and we cannot pass over it. But this issue need not be viewed as some sort of urgent question, which should be resolved quickly and on which the party should pass a definite resolution and then rest.

Comrades, it is not for nothing that we say party ethics, and not communist ethics. We are saying that a member of the party must have an opinion and work out for himself a general view on what it is to be a member of the party, on how a member of the party must behave, and not on how to behave in a communist system, since communist ethics require a communist system, and we are still far from that. We are going through a transitional period, in which ethics for us must be examined from two sides. What are ethics? They are the sum of the customs and habits which are accepted in a given society. Their violation is not prosecuted by law, but

Speech given at Sverdlov University, 1922 (?), published in E. Yaroslavsky, ed., *Kakim dolzhen byt' kommunist*, Leningrad, 1925, pp. 84-98. At the time this speech was given, Solts was Chairman of the Central Control Commission, the party organ charged with purging Bolshevik ranks of undesirable elements.

their observance is obligatory without punitive sanction. And in today's discussion the question [is not] why it might be necessary to expel a member from the party, or pronounce some sort of sentence, i.e., not the ethics of members of the party working in the KK [Control Commission]. Perhaps we can also talk about this, but for now I am going to talk about how ordinary members of the party must behave.

The basis for our behavior rests on the fact that although we are going through an epoch of construction, a supposedly peaceful epoch, we remain at posts appropriate to members of a fighting revolutionary party, for whom the interests of struggle, the interests of revolution are, so to speak, the measure by which we evaluate whether we are conducting ourselves well or badly. Everything which facilitates our struggle, everything which strengthens us as fighters, everything which helps us in this struggle is to be considered ethical and good. It is from this point of view that any deed must be evaluated, that is, whether it helps us in this struggle or is harmful in all respects.

There is one very interesting question which has to be answered, first of all, for the sake of these ordinary party members. It is the question of the formation of public opinion on behavior not only of party members, but also of those who follow behind them. We conceive of ourselves—we are certain of it—as the vanguard of the toiling classes, i.e., of the enormous mass of the population, and thus we find ourselves in the fortunate position where we can decide questions not only for ourselves, but can establish, so to speak, the mode, the norm by which society must live. We are the ruling class here, in our country, and life will be constructed according to us. It is according to how we live, dress, value this or that relationship, according to how we behave that customs will be established in our country.

It is necessary to say that in addition to external obstacles, an enormous obstacle for us is the fact that we bear a very large capitalist hump which we acquired while living in a capitalist society. After all, the communist party did not come up with its ideas and aims out of the clear blue sky. It lived and grew up in a capitalist system; it acquired all the habits characteristic of that system. About such a system it is said that only by proceeding from personal interests is it possible to create anything, and that beyond this, people are not able to do anything. We are being brought up in different conditions, but are still forced to live in such a way that personal interest plays a colossal role. One of the features of liberation from the capitalist hump will be the establishment of a new evaluation of good and evil, of what is acceptable and not acceptable in a given society. By our behavior the construction of a new life is beginning, since this is the only country where we, as the ruling class, can cultivate these habits in the new younger generation and even in the mass of the older. We know, for example, that our revolutionary holidays are gradually becoming simply national holidays, because, after all, a great number were such holidays.

31

Earlier, for example, the population, when it celebrated one or another of the holidays, did not connect it at all with whatever it was created for, but knew that visits with comrades took place on these days, that on these days they ate better, etc. When new holidays are created, when there is a new tone of life among those who are the rulers in the building of a new class, when they create new norms, then the masses will get used to evaluating life and separate actions according to these norms. Before us stands the task of preserving ourselves as fighters, and in accordance with this, to form our morals and customs and to lead a new order. It is from this point of view, and in light of the fact that we cannot make claims to any absolute ethical norms, that we must approach anything which interferes with the establishment of the new order. From the point of view of ethics we must create such public opinion as will lighten this task.

I now pass to—not what I would call illnesses of the party, since by illness is meant something which is abnormal and evidence of some sort of incorrect growth of our party—it would be better to say: to those shortcomings which manifest themselves in our life, in our statements, in our struggle and which must be understood by us and eradicated as much as possible.

Since we did not come from some perfect world, it is natural that we manifest a whole series of those characteristics which are inevitable in a growing society, developing under the colossal difficulties which face us and will continue to face us.

I will touch first of all on comradely mutual relations. The existence of party discipline is the greatest foundation and achievement of our party. Why? Because what existed earlier in theory, when the founders of the party spoke of the necessity of military discipline, of the solidarity of all forces for the attainment of a quicker victory, now has received corroboration in life, and has become apparent to everyone. Undoubtedly it was precisely the creation of such a party, united, with a single will, which facilitated the possibility of victory for us and secured success for us in the struggle with hostile forces. In the revolutionary epoch we were the only organized party with a single will which firmly knew what it wanted, what it was striving for, and for whom words were not divorced from deeds. Our favorite slogan was "Not in words, but in deeds." In each of his addresses, Vladimir Ilich literally repeated it. The value of discipline found its justification not in words, but in acts, because we considered ourselves the only party which had to make the revolution, and it was possible to make it only with great and conscientious discipline. Of course we are not speaking of the kind of discipline under which a person does something with which he does not agree. Voluntary discipline, the awareness of its necessity and value, must be for us the first foundation of our work.

Can there be voluntary discipline when there are not sufficiently good comradely mutual relations? No. In that situation discipline can only be coercive. Only when we look at one another as comrades, united for a single definite active task, can that discipline be created which extricated us from all misfortunes. The further our party grows, the more difficult it is to preserve those comradely relations, which were created on the soil of mutual struggle, and the more necessary it is that comrades feel and recognize strongly what is required for such voluntary discipline. It is easier to preserve good comradely relations when we are a group of twenty people, than when there are eighty thousand of us, as in the Moscow organization. The needed comradely relations—love and friendship towards a comrade—can be strengthened by an awareness of the fact that, after all, he is my helpmate, through him I hold on to all that is dear to me, in whose name I am a member of the party.

I will touch, for example, on a contentious question in the Control Commissions. If comrades sometimes make mistakes in one or another instance, if they act in an inappropriate way, what must a comrade, a member of the party who notices this, do? If he has good relations with him, if he considers him his co-member, with whom he works, he will try to settle the matter in private. But among ourselves we have enthusiastically taken to dragging a member of the party to the KK for any trifle. This is evidence of the fact that among the members of the party comradely mutual relations are not sufficiently developed. After all, for example, if your brother, your wife, your close comrade makes a mistake, I am convinced that you would not drag him off to the KK, but rather would attempt to eliminate the misunderstanding in private, since it would certainly be strange for a son to drag his father off to the KK or to a judicial institution. They would try to do everything possible to overcome it. Among ourselves this is not happening, because we have formal relationships, and many members of the party consider it their communist duty to inform to the KK on the sins of one or another comrade. As is probably well known to all of you, it happens among us this way: comrades gather together, drink together, and then one after another they go to the KK and complain, and a dispute occurs—who drank the most, who the least. Could such a thing really happen if there were comradely mutual relations? Such a state of affairs can only exist when people wish to scheme. This striving to scheme has as its source the struggle for power. We must not close our eyes to this. We are the ruling party, and the fact that we are the ruling party undoubtedly affects us badly in a certain way. But we are after all a fighting party and as the foundation of our life we put, not holiness, but rather the interests of struggle, and therefore we will never reject power in the name of holiness, since for us struggle and success are more important than holiness, which in its absolute form brings more harm than good to the struggle. If there would appear among us the tendency to speak exceptionally much about personal behavior, about personal sanctity, then I would even begin to worry and would say, "There is something unhealthy

33

in our party. We ceased being fighters and became interested in personal life." What is Tolstoyism? It is a movement which renders one powerless to fight in the name of the establishment of a good system and says, "Go into yourselves and preserve your own personal sanctity." This testifies to a rejection of struggle; it expresses disappointment with the revolution and with struggle. If such moods begin to predominate in our party, it will bring the end. We know that it is in the interests of the working class that we, a healthy fighting party, have power. As Marxists we know that power corrupts and from time to time we carry out a purge, review our ranks, have Control Commissions which expel from the party that member who has been corrupted, who has ceased to be a fighter, who has stopped taking part in our struggle. We break with such members of the party. And it is in this very struggle that the elements of intrigue, the elements of self-promotion take a place. We need to create in the party a public opinion which will forbid the doing of certain things, which will forbid intrigue among comrades, and under which it would be the obligation of each comrade, even in the cell, not to discuss these questions because there we find a formal attitude toward the behavior of comrades, but rather, as often as possible, to eliminate the faults of various party members by way of personal friendly relations. Then it will be much easier for my department; there will be less work for the KK, and the party will live more easily, because as we know, the punitive system itself never achieves the aim of general correction. It only assists in removing that which is harmful, but from the correctional point of view it gives no positive results.

We have at present a rather great number of suicides. Comrades, that need not cause us any panic. It is natural and understandable. We are going through an era where the nerves of a very great number of people have been so tested, have endured so much, that they no longer have the strength to do further that which is demanded of them by the party. There are young party members who have already survived the civil war, who were on all the fronts, who worked in our punitive organs of the GPU, etc., and who completely overstrained themselves, since a colossal steadfastness was demanded from them. And to the least steadfast among them, it seemed that here, with this last effort, he will enter the communist paradise, and when he sees that the matter is more serious and that more prolonged work is required, he begins to feel disappointment, searches for a way out. When he encounters a formalistic attitude, not even a friendly approach among members of the party, but even there a dense wall of formalistic relations, he cannot take it any longer and commits suicide. The fact that he commits suicide says that he has some kind of wormhole, that he is a bad member of the party, since we demand from our party members steadfastness, the ability to evaluate events and the ability to struggle with those obstacles encountered along the route. After all, every suicide, when he decides the question of his suicide, comes to the conclusion that there is no way out.

34

These are abnormal feelings and these people are always mistaken in their evaluation of the situation. I can point to such a person as Maksim Gorky, who, before he became a famous writer, on one fine day attempted to end his own life. Fortunately he did not succeed. But at that moment it seemed to him that there was no way out of the situation. This speaks of a collapse of will, of mood, which gives him a bad mark as a fighter. Among us it often happens that when members of the party receive the decision of the KK as to their expulsion, they declare, "Well comrades, I have only one recourse, suicide." "How," he says, "can I go on living when my party has expelled me?" I think that in such situations it is necessary to answer thus—and this is how I personally answer and I think it is how other comrades must answer and most likely do answer—that you are a bad member of the party and the KK did not make a mistake. The KK is made up of people who can make mistakes and might expel one who need not have been expelled, who at worst deserved only a scolding, instruction, or comradely persuasion. Now just because one or another organ or control commission is bad, is it necessary to commit suicide? No, you must prove to the party and the KK (especially to the KK) that it made a mistake. How can you prove this? By a resolve of the will and by such behavior, by such work, as would convince us, because if the KK expels someone from the party, and after half a year, the comrade through his cell or workers' circle proves that he works well, then I in the name of the KK must say that there is no greater pleasure for the KK than to be convinced of its own mistakes, for the matter is not at all in proving one's absolute infallibility. What kind of KK would it be if it thought its opinion was always irrefutably correct? On the contrary, the more prodigal sons return to the party after finding in themselves the strength to overcome everything, the better. We have forbidden all Control Commissions to pass resolutions on permanent expulsion. There is no person about whom it can be said that he is unable to reform. Such a thing cannot be, and sometimes the very reverse happens. Sometimes it is possible that a member of the party who in a certain situation must be expelled can, after a year, if he overcomes everything—and several comrades will confirm this—become a better party member than those so-called irreproachable party members, for there are no irreproachable members of the party. We are all living people and from time to time make mistakes. But when is this possible? When might such a situation occur? When we have comradely mutual relations, but often in these situations, when a comrade who had earlier been expelled is restored by us, we ruin him because we do not have friendly comradely relations. When we restore him, the cell sometimes says that the Central Control Commission is kind, that it restored him, but the sin remains over him and he is brought to account for any trifles. If the comrades looked upon this question as they should, that the Central Control Commission rehabilitated him, that he is an equal member of the party, and if he were to encounter a thoughtful

35

attitude just as before, then of course everything would be all right. The reverse of this also occurs: a party member is restored, his case having been reexamined. He comes back and says, "Here, you see, although you expelled me from the party, the Central Control Commission has restored me and therefore I spit at everyone but the Commission." Thus the reverse situation is created; there is here no comradely desire to improve oneself. The Central Control Commission must act carefully, because we are the last resort, and naturally we have a great responsibility, for one has nobody to complain to about us, so in the latter instance people might think, "We will expel him to make sure, in order to purify our party, and if we are wrong, the Central Control Commission will reinstate him; let them check him." We, in the latter instance, must approach matters more carefully. Comrades there think that he cannot reform himself, but we hope that he can. But the comrade who thinks he has come out of it as a fair-haired boy just because the Central Control Commission restored him, and that he will spit on his own cell, such a comrade will not do at all. Then it will turn out that the lower cell which expelled him was right. Only when we have comradely mutual relations, only when everyone understands for what reason they are members of the party, when that conviction becomes the dominant element in how we relate to one another, then every problem will not be dragged off to the Control Commission.

Passing now to other developments within our party, to what comrade Yaroslavsky has called "nepification,"[10] i.e., to that nasty influence which has been noticed among some party members who are insufficiently firm, insufficiently steadfast—the consequence of our contact with alien elements—with class enemies, with those who are building their lives outside of soviet construction, acting only from personal interests. I must confirm that there must be a certain number of such people and that we must free ourselves from them. We need to know that contact with this NEPist order cannot fail to have a harmful influence on insufficiently staunch party members, and we need to distinguish that period or moment when a person has basically ceased to be our comrade and must be dropped from the party. What takes place here, particularly from the viewpoint of our primary need, the preservation of the fighter? Such a comrade ceases to be a fighter, from the point of view of "fashion," he interferes with our leading such a form of life which corresponds to our new construct, our new aesthetics, our beauty. Aesthetics says that beauty consists of full correspondence between external and internal content. When the class of exploiters created fashion, it was natural that any external distinctions showing successes in life as a representative of this capitalist system were valuable. So dress, manners, appearance were considered beautiful, aroused envy, the desire to imitate, because they testified to success in life, to the fact that one was really a representative of this same ruling class. And what about for us? We are not only a workers' government, but for us all

36

forms of life are grounded on respect for labor, on a striving to place workers ahead of everything. We say that among us, labor occupies the primary place. If the external appearance of a party member testifies to a full rift with working life, then that must be ugly, and it must encounter such an attitude as to make the party member not wish to dress in such a way and have an external appearance which the class of workers condemns, which arouses resentment among workers. Such a comrade thinks that there exists some sort of personal life in which he is completely free to follow his own tastes, and his tastes are such that he wants to imitate that which bourgeois society considers elegant, to have an appearance which speaks of a different party, of other norms, of a different evaluation of man. If we do not have such an attitude toward appearances which arouse condemnation in the working masses, in the mass of workers, and if a person outwardly is sharply deviant from the masses which he represents, then we ourselves will make the struggle more difficult and will lengthen the time for the implementation of our ideas into reality. Some will ask venomous questions concerning my statement: And what do you think? Must one be dirty, slovenly? Is it best to go about in rags? Of course very literate cultured people normally raise such questions, people who think, you see, that here perhaps I am speaking this way on the question of external appearance because I am a big slob myself and wish to serve as a model. I am far from that. I am not at all preaching that my path be followed. One may dress beautifully, even well, but beauty must be of a different sort.

I consider it ugly for a person to wear rings, bracelets, gold teeth. In my view that must arouse aesthetic indignation.

Not long ago I was at a meeting in the Rogozhsko-Simonovsky district where I observed new forms of beauty, new pleasures, because I again say that ours is not a party of hypocrites, that it is not necessary to reject all the pleasures of life, and this I must repeat. Mikhailovsky, although a Narodnik, noted very well that among the Protestants there are libertarians and ascetics. There are two types of people who protest against the existing system. One says, "The popular masses do not have the possibility for rejoicing, so let us also deny ourselves the pleasures of life; as a protest let us become fasters, let us observe holiness. And if all people will be like us, then in the end everything will be fine." And there are less restricted people, who say, "Life is given to us for pleasure, we must take all available pleasures from life and must expand life so as to receive the most pleasure possible." The Bolsheviks adhere to the free-thinkers and not to the ascetics. Of course we are not against joys and pleasures, but we are against the distribution of them in such a way that half of the day is spent in the role of devout party member and the other half spent living one's personal life. One cannot separate private life from party life. It is the good member of the party for whom party work and struggle give, in any case, greater joy and personal satisfaction than what under the capitalist system was called private life. Earlier each worker who entered the party, who fought, knew that personally he would receive very little. Each person wishes to live in order to express openly what he is striving for. In a revolution, he desires the system in whose name he is fighting and this struggle brings him delight. That is clear. Can one really say that a visit to the theatre is personal life and work in a circle or lectures is public life? If a person feels no personal satisfaction, but rather performs his public work as a formal obligation, then he will force himself, he will carry this burden on himself, as a party member. "There is no choice," he says, "I have to do it!" But if he is personally pleased, then it does not turn out this way; it means that he is a whole-hearted person. "Nepification" must be met with condemnation. The striving of members of the party and of the class whose representatives we are to imitate, even in external life, all that the class which we have defeated considered beautiful and good, and in which it found satisfaction, must be condemned. It is from this point of view that we must look at a whole series of our actions. I will touch first of all the family question.

The family question asks how a party member must live in his own family. N. K. Krupskaya has spoken on this subject better than anyone else. It is from her that I first heard this successful, so to speak, formulation, that the family of the party member must in a certain sense be a cell of cooperation. It must be a grouping of comrades where one lives in the family approximately like one lives outside the family, and all members of the family through their work and life must be conceived as something resembling a cell of cooperation. It is that toward which we must strive. What is it that must meet exceptionally severe condemnation in this area? I am not talking of those acts which encounter the condemnation of any society, and which amount to crimes prosecuted by the court, for, of course, that is neither your nor my business, and, of course, you are not interested in hearing about what is punishable by the courts. It is clear that a party member cannot do that which, if done by a non-member, would be punishable. This is clear. You know that there are very many party members who refuse to maintain their children. This is already in the sphere of the criminal. But among us this question is arising first of all because a rather significant number of party members, occupying more or less responsible positions, have taken wives from an alien class. I am approaching this question first of all from the viewpoint of aesthetics, from the viewpoint of beauty, and I find that these people have very bad taste. This bad taste shows itself in the fact that this must all be seen just as the marriage of a count to a chambermaid was earlier perceived in the former society. Society was horribly scandalized: "He betrayed our tradition, it's disgusting, after all, it's something to be ashamed of!" Such was the attitude. Now we are the ruling class, and among us the same attitude must prevail. Intimacy with a member of a camp hostile to us when we are the ruling class—this must encounter such public condemnation that a person will think it over thirty times before making such a decision. Of course, any feeling is an individual one, and one cannot always interfere in personal life, but we can condemn this, just as former society condemned it when a member of society refused to submit to its demands. We call this prejudice, but for the preservation of one's identity it was not prejudice at all. One must repeatedly think it through before deciding to take a wife from an alien class.

In regard to this it is necessary to note that I use the phrase "hostile class" in its literal meaning, and that we members of the party must not regard ourselves with communist conceit as chosen people. No, we are representatives of the workers, and, of course, to separate ourselves from the masses and to hold ourselves out as a downright aristocracy which does not wish to mix with anyone is of course forbidden, it is wrong. To say that it is forbidden to drink water with a non-party person because he is non-party is not to be allowed. We are not talking here of the workers, of that mass of the population whom we represent, but rather of that element hostile to us, because a conquered class naturally looks for possibilities of fortifying itself, and marrying a commissar is rather flattering. Through him a connection is brought about with this society, relatives are set up, etc. If this encounters sharp condemnation among members, it will not happen often.

The old society held that the family had to be formed primarily according to the principle of property, in order to concentrate property in definite hands. In England among the aristocracy this reached the point where all property was passed into the hands of the eldest son. The strength of the marital tie was considered a fundamental principle. As representatives of the minority, they strove of course to influence the majority by means of deception. Marriage was cloaked with a sort of sanctity, the participation of supernatural, godly forces. This was necessary for them, since their ethics had to take cover under hypocrisy and deception. For ethics is that which is accepted in a given living society. When the minority wishes to lead the majority for its own purposes, it must conceal its true face. We do not have this need and therefore need not lie and say that in marriage, in the sexual intimacy of people any supernatural forces take part. But when we took power, we found ourselves carried away in the opposite direction. An opinion was formed that from the viewpoint of the communist party struggling at a given moment, there were no family problems at all, and that each day one might change and diversify one's family relations. This already closely relates to the sex issue in general. There are two sides to this which we must look at first of all. First, a disordered sex life undoubtedly weakens each party member as a fighter, and second, despite the fact that this is a fully lawful area, that we are not ascetics preaching abstinence and a rejection of all the pleasures of life, we

39

still say that we must observe some proportion in it, so that one still remains a fighter, and that great variety in this area will take too much energy, feeling and intellect from a person. Excepting those cases when sexual relations are grounded purely on physiological needs, and this already shows a certain humility of man (for man in this respect differs somewhat from the animal, since he seeks more refined forms of pleasure)—if we discard this, then everything which remains requires a greater amount of energy, emotion, nerves, etc. And looking for diversity in this area demonstrates that this area of life is taking up too much of a person's time and strength and that his head is occupied more with this side of life than with the interests of the struggle.

It is from this point of view that we must approach the problem of drunkenness. In the old society the question of drunkenness was also understood as a violation of certain norms established from above. Why are we also struggling against drunkenness? First of all, drunkenness weakens us as fighters; overindulgence in drinking undoubtedly weakens the will, and a person cannot answer for himself. Undoubtedly the drinker is more subject to every other element of decay in the sphere of crime and more easily deserts to the side of the former rulers, and therefore this should be met with every possible condemnation. But what makes a man need to drink? Comrades, life used to be boring. We were slaves. The absolute majority of the population executed, so to speak, only the will of the ruling classes. There was no hope in life. But a person wants joys, and if real life does not give them to him, he will at least look for the illusions of these joys. When a person drinks, life seems better and people seem better than they really are. Nerves are excited and he, so to speak, takes a rest from that boring life which he must live. And it is out of this that this habit of some of our comrades originated. Of course, it is difficult for them to break it. It must encounter criticism, but when we decide the question what kind of a party member a person is, we cannot, of course, base our judgment exclusively on whether or not he drinks, because in general, when evaluating a person, you cannot proceed formalistically from an act which he has committed. A person is not measured by separate acts. It is necessary to know the entire person and what he has amounted to. If he has maintained himself as a fighter, then it is necessary only to point to the misdeed which he has done. We are the builders of life. Life is being built in our way, and now such a miraculous life is being built, we live in such an epoch, the epoch of the greatest creativity of mankind, that if a person gives himself the chance and time to think about this, he will find such a mass of outlets for his energies, his nerves, for the striving to show his worth, that he will need no illusions. Why have illusions, when life is so fine? Why should a party which is creating such enormous things and about which legends will be told have illusions? People are such that they get used to whatever miraculous things are being accomplished around them. Here an airplane

40

flies in the sky; a person looks once and then is too lazy to raise his head again. We cannot fully realize the value of these new forms, this new life which we are creating. Members of the party living in such a period, living in such a country, working, are in the most favorable position for affirming and developing that which they undertake. When they can do all this with united forces, then why create illusions and seek oblivion? We live at a time when there is no need to seek oblivion, but, on the contrary, must remember and remember where and when we are living, and in this find great pleasure. And we are especially interested in giving to the younger generation such a life and raising it in such conditions that, with the approach of old age, it will not search for reveries. We are the party which creates the pattern. If we do not drink, then all will reject it, but if we do drink, if communists who have an opportunity to show their worth, for whom all possible amusements are available, such as clubs, such as the chance to speak openly—if they look for reveries, then what will the others do? So then, is it preordained for man? Nonsense. It is a certain historical legacy which exists in Russia and which it is necessary to be rid of.

In my view it is not worth talking about economic accumulation. Economic accumulation—it is the conversion of a person into someone for whom a significant part of their efforts go towards personal enrichment. Of course it is impermissible; of course, he then ceases to be a party member. But it is necessary to see how this happens in real life. We must mark off the boundaries. We know that at this moment we do not yet have a communist system, and that it is impossible to require equality. The working class itself has gradations in payment for labor. But we must say, "You have to live within such and such bounds, you are in the seventeenth rank." If he receives more, then he is subject to special demands; some return will be exacted of him. It is only literary work which is paid outside of any limits. Why is this done? Because it is still difficult to reach the situation where communist writers write just as cheerfully for nothing as for pay, and we are forced to make this concession. But we must have a public opinion which will not allow anyone, in any field, to receive more than a certain maximum permissible wage. When we have created such a public opinion, the writer will be ashamed to receive more. We must create within the party the opinion that a communist cannot live in a manner too different from that of the class he represents, for that would create a gap not only from the masses, but from the party, because we cannot tolerate a situation where our lives as representatives of the working class significantly differ from that of the class itself. We require that in your habits and morals you be close to the mass which you represent. Once you have another life, then you are infected, and you must leave the party.

I will also say a few words on religious rites. Just a few words because it is perfectly clear that a party member must not perform religious rites under any circumstance. Why? First, it shows a divorce between words and

41

deeds. Sometimes comrades say, "But I am not religious, and what difference will it make if I get married in church or baptize the children, because my wife wants it?" It is not permissible because it makes our anti-religious propaganda difficult, for, I repeat, we are creating a standard. What kind of propaganda can there be if in the countryside the peasant-communist gets married in church and then goes out to agitate against the priests? All workers act according to our standard. What is this party member who performs religious rites? In the countryside, for example, he must know that from the party point of view, he is inflicting enormous harm when he gets married in church. But when we come to discuss an already accomplished act, we need particular care. There are those circumstances where the peasant communist has no way out because of the backwardness of the peasantry. He needs a woman, a head of the household, but the woman, the mistress of the house, considers that their marriage will be strong only after a church ceremony, and she will not agree otherwise. So each situation, from the viewpoint of what it reveals about the party member, must be looked at separately, must be considered in terms of when he did it and under what circumstances. Even having kept him in the party, it is necessary that everyone recognize that the comrade has committed a serious party misdemeanor. But as I have already said, a person is not measured by separate faults, but is measured in his entirety. That must be the approach.

This is what I wished to speak about, comrades. It is extremely important that we exchange opinions here, because we must create public opinion and not only listen to reports.

BRINGING UP THE YOUNG GENERATION
N. Bukharin

The question of so-called communist morality is often raised. I consider such terminology and such an approach to be incorrect. As is known, by morality is always meant that norm or rule of behavior which has about it something of a fetish. They say "You must do so and so"—and nothing more. And quite naturally you will meet up with bourgeois morality, and bourgeois morality—its very heart—consists in this fetishism, this norm, which involves the subordination of human behavior to some authority, the sources of which, as well as the reasons for having to obey it, being quite unknown. It is this very thing which quite naturally evokes a protest, and therefore the most common and usual attitude to this problem—as soon as you begin speaking about such things—is the rather lighthearted "Oh, these sermons, the same old story!"

There is, of course, something healthy in this protest. It plainly shows that any fetishism for the working class and working youth must be eliminated. We must not tolerate what neither we nor anyone else can understand. We must destroy everything which goes beyond the bounds of rational cognition. From this point of view the fetishistic norms being foisted on us by the past must be destroyed. But on the other hand, I hold that the working class, and especially the working youth, need some rules of behavior. I think that these differ from morality in that they are not supported by some unknown and inexplicable norm.

I look upon this question of norms very simply and, it seems to me, very reasonably. For example, if we wish to achieve some aim (and we have until now proceeded from the assumption that we wish to achieve socialism), then in order to accomplish that aim we must undertake certain actions and not undertake others. If a joiner or carpenter has to make a stool, then he must perform certain definite body movements, he must plane, discard shavings, and not dance the "trepak." If he dances the

---

Speech delivered to the Fifth Komsomol Congress, Oct. 11-19, 1922, as published in *Piatyi vserossiiskii s"ezd RKSM 11-19 oktiabria 1922 goda. Stenograficheskii otchet.* Moscow-Leningrad, 1927, pp. 113-23. Bukharin's style reflects some of the worst elements of early "Commissar writing," and is difficult to translate. We have preserved here the convolutions of the original wherever this did not seriously affect the English meaning. Regarded by many as the Bolshevik party's leading theorist, Bukharin, an editor of *Pravda,* took Lenin's seat on the Politburo after the latter's death, and at the time this speech was given, was a leading party spokesman. See Stephen F. Cohen, *Bukharin and the Bolshevik Revolution,* New York, 1971.

"trepak," then he will not make stools. It is necessary to do one and not the other. It is the same thing in social life. If you wish to make socialism your aim, then you must construct this socialism, and in exactly the same way do just this one thing, and not another. If you do something which is called harmful, malicious, base, etc., then you will be like the joiner who dances, and does not build anything. You will be destroying and not building. Therefore it is natural that there must be certain definite rules of behavior for the working youth. If there are no such norms and rules, there will be nothing at all. We feel this at every turn. What is party discipline? It is a rule of behavior. But no one has gotten around to calling the rules of party discipline morals in the same way that the regulations of a cooperative store are not labeled as morals, although these are the norms which regulate the behavior of people. If we look at the question in this way (which I know many of the old and young comrades will not agree with, but I am only laying the theoretical foundations for what I will speak about later), then it follows that we are destroying fetishism and soberly going about our business. Do we wish to achieve socialism? Yes, we wish it. Then let's act in a way to achieve it. What about this is incomprehensible? . . .

It is from such a non-fetishistic, absolutely sober, realistic and materialistic statement of the question that there follows the necessity of rules of behavior. They must exist. I protest against any moral trappings, but at the same time declare categorically that there must be rules for the working class, the proletarian party, especially for those still uncomplicated individuals, the working youth. It is perfectly natural that the significance of these rules must be intensified when we are surrounded by enemies. Overall, it is that which ties and binds and makes it possible to preserve an inner unity and to be a striking iron fist We know that in the conditions of the new economic policy, where there exist stores, taverns, etc., etc., the danger of dissolution or demoralization is extremely great, but it is similarly clear that some group or entity like your Union of Youth can be counterposed to this phenomenon, thanks to its unusually strong unity.

If cohesion is so important in the period of socialist revolution, then it is two times, four times, even ten times more indispensable during a period in the life of the working class and working youth when they find themselves in a petty-bourgeois environment, in a predatory capitalist encirclement . . .

It seems to me that as a transition point in this area it is necessary first of all to clarify the question of the adoption of the socialist ideal. We speak too little about socialism in its full meaning. For more coldly analytical thinkers, for more mature people, this is not so necessary; first, because they know what socialism is, and second, because they do not need that additional injection of inspiration to attune themselves to socialism. But for the more emotional youth, it is necessary to give more distinct expressions of full-scale socialism, to display the emotional side of the struggle for socialism and the socialist ideal in all its fullness, from the viewpoint of art, from the viewpoint of culture, from the viewpoint of the entire complex of human emotions. I repeat, the older comrades will smile about this, because they have gone through it all already. They have already eaten their fill and they forget that they have absorbed it, that it has penetrated their flesh and blood. In contrast, for the young, this side of the matter must be developed and cultivated just as the other side must be, which also proceeds along the lines of normative relations and along the lines of relations among people.

It is necessary to nurture an absolutely instinctive reaction of passionate hatred toward our class opponents. On the one hand, hatred of our enemies, on the other, a depiction of the socialist ideal as an immense unity. This must be the starting point in our work, which determines the rules of human behavior.

I ought to state further that it is necessary to cultivate various methods when you portray socialists. Here there should be rational proofs, as well as direct pictorial artistic portrayals. It is completely clear that from this should flow the unconditional necessity of all possible types of comradely solidarity. In order not to be limited by this general aim which the Komsomol has set forth, it is necessary, moreover, to nurture the feeling of comradeship in general. It is perfectly natural that the Union as a whole cannot meet this petty demand. We must advocate within the Union a system of all possible associations, circles, etc., which would themselves cultivate a feeling of comradeship and would be somewhat of an intermediate link between the person of a single Komsomol member on the one hand, and the entire mass of members of the organization of the RKSM on the other hand. It seems to me that enormous significance must be attached to all the rules, that is to say, the "precepts" of the Komsomol. I know very well that this will encounter quite a few enemies among young people. They will say, "Why fix, why write and advance external signs, written precepts?" I hold that this is a prejudice. . . . I maintain that slogans which contain the rules of behavior and precepts which are put up on the walls are a positive thing, because they constantly remind us and constantly will agitate for and speak about that which we must be reminded of. I will allow myself a comparison, which at first glance does not seem to have any connection with this matter, a comparison with capitalist advertisement. Explain to me why it is that capitalists who desire to capture the market for their firms put their trade-mark on every kitchen pot? Why does this go on? It goes on because it is extraordinarily useful. The same with us. We must learn something from the capitalists. We have a whole series of rules of behavior which we wish to inculcate. And there is nothing wrong with this fixation, because otherwise we cannot acquire new personnel. What is surprising about this? What is bad about it? If we have such fixed rules, we

45

will have more intensive work. We will have more intensive independent activity in all the basic parts of our organism. There will be a more conscientious attitude toward work.

Let us proceed to the issues of tobacco and alcohol. Here too stand a series of ancient prejudices.

Among us it is considered obligatory that every member of the Union goes around with four cigarettes at once, and responds scornfully toward anti-alcohol and anti-tobacco propaganda. I believe that this is a big mistake. I remember in the old days, when I studied in the gymnasia, we smoked as a form of demonstration, and it was even an established norm of behavior, which was useful from the social point of view, since by this small deed we destroyed the discipline of the old system. This was a protest against the organization of the school, a protest which carried over to the organization of all society. It was a rational means then: it was pleasant to pass under the nose of the supervisors with a cigarette in one's mouth, and therefore all that was revolutionary in the old school supported this habit, mischievous as it might be. Socially it was a positive phenomenon, and therefore it was necessary to regard it with some respect. This triviality led to various revolutionary movements. Is there anything now which resembles these former conditions? I think not. From the physiological point of view and from the viewpoint of upbringing, attraction to tobacco and alcohol are directly harmful. Why should we support smoking and laugh at anti-alcohol propaganda? It is an incorrect uncritical transfer of the methods of destruction of the bourgeois system to our own organism. It is my profound belief that groups must be created in the Union which will carry out a conscientious struggle with alcoholism and tobacco. There is no doubt in my mind about this.

The same needs to be said about sexual dissoluteness, which must be constrained. How to do this, I do not know at the moment and will not discuss now, but it is necessary for us, together with medical specialists and pedagogues, to consider and work out directives for the members of your Union.

I must still touch on some questions which go beyond the boundaries just stated. I think that we must nurture in members of the Union of Youth that which pertains to the area of any norms—party, class, Komsomol. For example, earlier it was the honor of a banner, the honor of the gentry class, etc. This must be cultivated among us. It must serve as an instrument of class pride, a sign of class adherence. You will say that all this is very strange. When in war they speak of the honor of the regiment or the honor of the banner, that is a very useful thing which binds forces and organizes them. We must have the same point of view in regard to all kinds of groups of the Komsomol, party, and class, beginning from that small cell to which we adhere, and ending with the most powerful organization to which we belong—our class, and then the Soviet state. Imagine that you are going abroad and that some bourgeois insults the Soviet Republic. It is necessary to put him down in one or another appropriate way. But he must be made to pay for it. Not with a feudal sword, since the class content is different here, although there is a formal resemblance. We must raise up a generation of youth who will defend the honor of their group, party, class and state and will allow no one to spit in their face, because it is only in the Russian proverb that it is said, "spit in a fool's face and he'll think it's heavenly dew." Komsomoltsy need not follow this. And this requires a very large effort. That nihilism which has been preached by some of our older comrades with respect to this is completely out of place.

The next point regards the intellectual education of young people.

I would like to emphasize several things which make up the heart of this matter. First, we must finally liquidate illiteracy among our working youth. This is a basic task which, unless solved, will make it very difficult to move forward. Then we must conduct communist education in two directions, in the direction of an elementary communist education of the broad mass of Komsomoltsy, and along the lines of a higher level of education among your so-called activists, that is, your directing administrative personnel. It is particularly necessary to dwell on this latter point, because judging from the reports and accounts which I received for this paper, it appears that our personnel are, on the whole, quite politically illiterate and significantly lacking in Marxist education. You zealously manage practical matters and that is very good, but on the other hand, it is necessary to combine this great pragmatism, which must be fostered in you, with some general theoretical knowledge. This theoretical knowledge cannot be brushed away, especially for those who have been called upon by the will of history to replace the older generation in the governing of the country. After all, after some time you will be governing the country, and for this you must be able to orient yourselves during possible historical upheavals. Our party, having passed through Marxist school, has been able to hold firm because its staff of personnel, its leadership, having gone through Marxist school and having a good edcuation, could predict events and easily maneuver all the sharp turns. The new generation has become confused, but for you perhaps, the future might hold in store a further series of even sharper turns. We have such a colossal range of events before us, such surprises on a world scale, that the greatest ability to correctly orient oneself is needed here. This will be done only by the good school of Marxist education. Much more attention must be given to this matter than has been up to now.

Communist youth is a reservoir which must in time place its workers in technical and other fields. It is necessary to remember that at the current time it is impossible to become attracted by a general universalism, whereby one thinks and imagines to oneself that he knows everything, when in fact he knows nothing well. It is necessary in all ways to strive in a more correct division of labor, to a conscientious study of some narrower basic areas. You must exactly and definitely say that each chooses for himself a definite area which he is studying to the end. You must be communists, and you must also receive a definite specialized qualification. You must be an engineer, a technician, a teacher of social sciences, a professor, or something else, but you must know this field thoroughly. If this does not happen, then you will have a dilettante government, one which will be reminiscent of the rulers of the nomadic period, when no one was responsible for anything, no one knew anything, and when everyone floundered around, as if this could help the conduct of affairs. Now special knowledge is necessary.

I now turn to the matter of intellectual and physical training. It is necessary to give the most profound attention to this side of the matter. All possible games and other things distinguished by the competitive principle are to be used for intellectual and physical training. You must pay particular attention to the organization of all possible games, problem solving, charades, chess and other things. Chess, however, plays a very strong role. One of our strongest chess players wrote a special book entitled *Social Sciences and the Game of Chess,* where he proves that chess gives great intellectual training. Great commanders and social activists have almost always played chess very well. Any game is to some extent a rehearsal for current actions and is a preparation, a training of the hand and mind. You must introduce the principle of competitiveness. You must conduct various contests in the quickness of problem solving, all kinds of football competitions, etc., with prizes and all such things. In all various circles—football, scientific, chess—it is necessary to preserve the principle of competition, which must be placed at the forefront. The fact is that very often the bourgeoisie shows great flexibility, while we lag behind, since, because of our centralized bureaucracy, we cannot make a turn. We must create more flexible small units, and must therefore form circles of people interested in chess; one group of chessplayers, and another one a football team, another, a third; and then arrange contests among them. Then we will have a combination of two principles, of public spiritedness and freedom of action, and not some kind of all-Russian decree. The competitive principle must in all ways be manifested in all games and these must occupy a large place among us.

Finally, I must dwell on this point. Of course it is perfectly natural that the greatest part of your educational work must be in the school and directly in the Union, but such an upbringing must pour out into a whole series of practical work by your members in various arenas of social life. And one of the most important types is direct work in the factories, the propagation of the improvement of factory life, etc. Then there is the struggle with bureaucratism, about which there has been much talk and about which you have constantly passed resolutions; in the countryside the struggle with kulak society, repulsing all organizations of our adversary, an ideological struggle involving all forms of conflicts with the ideological organizations of our enemy. In defending the interests of working youth, the acquisition here of any associational comradely habits and other organizational virtues has enormous significance. Finally, all possible technical help [must go] to the party and labor unions. We must apply ourselves to an active role in the party and unions. We must perform a series of subsidiary tasks in them, albeit of a technical character, as, for example, the dissemination and distribution of literature. This sphere of activity has enormous significance for your Union, if it is to be put in its appropriate framework.

In conclusion I would like to say that at the present time a whole series of difficult problems, very often being faced by the working class, the party and you for the first time, a whole series of negative phenomena which are connected with NEP, are producing a shuffling of our ranks, and our temporary demoralization. But now the time for that has passed. The time has passed for cries concerning the negative aspects of NEP, and these cries must disappear irrevocably, since there is now the possibility to triumph. Unquestionably there is, since we have a human cadre which we can form and reform under conditions of rejuvenating economic life, which is just beginning. At the same time our international position is being consolidated, and from the point of view of an objective analysis, there is nothing which will change this.

So long as we have dealings with young people, it is necessary that their enthusiasm, which was at the fronts of the Civil War, be entirely invested in self-preparation for an enormous future state role. This enthusiasm for knowledge revealed by young people must be supported in every way and must be the axis of all our struggle.

If we make a cadre of excellent fighters in the field of cultural struggle, then we can spread it in several years throughout the breadth of the Republic, and this new network, this new cadre, will carry with honor that banner which was carried by the older generation.

REVOLUTION AND THE CULTURAL TASKS OF THE PROLETARIAT
P. I. Lebedev-Polyansky

The question of proletarian culture is not one which has just now arisen. It was raised long ago. About ten years ago a literary group of Bolsheviks was formed abroad which advanced the thesis that to achieve greater success in political and economic struggle, the proletariat must develop its own culture, its own proletarian world attitude, which would give greater ideological independence to all forms of proletarian struggle. Analyzing the results of the 1905 revolution, comrades came to the conclusion that the propaganda and revolutionary slogans of that time were not sufficiently permeated with socialist ideology, but were of a rather democratic character. Our defeat then can be partly explained by this. In order to avoid other defeats, it was necessary to gather and unite elements of proletarian culture, thus giving greater pithiness to the political and economic struggle, which, although a component part of proletarian culture, took shape earlier than revolutionary-cultural construction itself, thanks to historical conditions.

When we advanced our program, many comrades thought of it not only skeptically, but even with hostility. They declared that it was impossible to create proletarian culture in a capitalist society, that it was possible only under socialism. We, on the contrary, held that elements of a future culture have roots in the culture of preceding generations. We have observed an analogous process in the past. After the great revolution of 1789, France entered into history under the mark of bourgeois culture. But we know full well that the elements of bourgeois culture had been laid much earlier. The French philosophers of the Enlightenment in their *Great Encyclopedia* put it down only theoretically. In the course of thirty years the ideologues of the great French revolution, Diderot, Voltaire, d'Alembert, Holbach and others, published thirty-five big volumes. Another collective work, *The System of Nature,* supplemented this gospel of the bourgeois revolutionary movement. Both these works gave answers to all the combative and burning questions of that epoch. They laid the foundations of a new science, ethics, law... in a word, all contemporary

Report and discussion at the first All-Russian Conference of Proletarian Cultural-Enlightenment Organizations, September 16, 1918, from *Protokoly pervoi vserossiiskoi konferentsii proletarskikh kul'turno-prosvetitel'nykh organizatsii, 15-20 Sent. 1918,* Moscow, 1918, pp. 17-29. Pavel Ivanovich Lebedev-Polyansky was a member of the Commissariat of Education and President of Proletkult, 1918-1920.

50

bourgeois culture, which then, as the most advanced cultural form, conducted a merciless struggle with the religious culture of a medieval society. In the same way our proletarian culture is being born in the capitalist world, but it presents sickly, pallid sprouts which we must make grow into a mighty tree.

Jean Jaures, the great parliamentary tribune, castigating bourgeois France in one of his inspired parliamentary speeches, characterized the new task of the proletariat in this way, "In my view the hour is approaching when the revolutionary socialist proletariat must master an organized doctrine of the universe and of life. The revolutionary bourgeoisie created its *Encyclopedia,* and we also need a new encyclopedia, infinitely wider and more daring, a proletarian one. It is necessary once again to review the progress of human thought. It is necessary to review the entire history of science and give its chief results to the proletariat, to that class which wishes to live a full life and to brighten the universe with a clear light, where rays of individual thought will lose themselves in the glowing dawn of social life. This living organization of the socialist encyclopedia is one of the highest tasks which the future will place on our party and on mankind."

I say that the hour has struck, and the proletariat is charged with this highest task.

Earlier they even reproached us for opportunism. Now that the proletarian revolution has taken place, this view has fundamentally changed. The question of proletarian culture has become a reality, not a dream.

In many cases in contemporary life, the Russian proletariat senses in itself bourgeois habits, moods and an insufficiency of socialist upbringing, which often interfere with fulfilling the tasks set forth by the revolution. If it wishes to be triumphant, the contemporary proletariat must educate itself to be socialist not only by conviction, but in its psychology. It must develop all creative capabilities in order to defeat petty bourgeois anarchistic elements. The latter can be fought only with the development, the creation, of a strictly class proletarian culture. If this idea seemed an empty fiction ten years ago, then now, in the course of a year, it has fully and quickly seized the attention of the working class, and there is no force which can stifle it. And this conference, the fact that we are gathered here, shows that the question is being advanced by life itself, and is not the fruit of the idle musings of comrades cut off from life.

Our proletarian culture is replacing bourgeois culture. And it is natural to assume that it will be its opposite, just as the capitalist system in its economic aspect is the opposite of the socialist. The capitalist system is anarchistic and its ideology is individualistic. The socialistic system bases itself on collective creative labor; its ideology will be strictly monistic, integral. The content of contemporary experience is so great that it is not only inaccessible to individual knowledge, but does not even fit into

51

existing forms of cognition. New forms are needed, which can freely embrace and combine the entire content of experience in its constant development. The new forms in all their grandiose complexity must be harmonious. Capitalist culture, as an anarchistic one, is not able to produce strictly monistic new forms. Only the proletariat will be able to fulfill this colossal creative work.

Bourgeois culture has gone through stages of revival, flowering and decline. Now this culture has become counter-revolutionary. And our [proletarian] culture must pass through various stages of development; this it cannot avoid. The proletarian culture will become the culture of all mankind, when class boundaries disappear in the social structure. This does not mean that it will change in its basic principles. No. It will merely pass to the highest form of an inevitable historical process. Whatever stages of development our proletarian culture passes through, the principle of collective labor must always be its foundation. This is its characteristic trait. It is in labor—by the blast furnace, to the noise of running machines and stamping tools—when formless substance is being turned into a harmonious whole, that the methods of creativity and practical logic take shape, not abstract logic, but the logic of labor, struggle and thought. In the living unity of the proletarian army, in its workday solidarity, the collectivist ideal and the socialism of feeling take shape. The second no less characteristic trait is that proletarian culture is always constructive. If the proletariat destroys the values of the past, then it does so only to the extent that it is necessary for our future, for our "tomorrow." We accept this destruction, but will always understand that our culture must be born in collective labor. The proletariat must fortify its political victory in definite cultural work. Our opponent is strong. But we know that the culture of collective labor must triumph. In the given situation it is entirely unimportant that our undertakings and efforts do not always end with success; what is important is that the working class feels an organic need to imprint its life experience and its emotions in formal systems and images, and to oppose them to the bourgeoisie, with its dying culture.

Before us is the question, how will proletarian culture be created? Up until now the broad proletarian masses have been remote not only from an understanding of bourgeois culture, but even from elementary knowledge. Therefore, in the first place, we must master and surmount our bourgeois heritage, in order to use all the social experience of preceding generations.

But since bourgeois culture is hostile to socialist culture, our attitude toward it must be a critical one, so that theories and tendencies alien to us do not seize us. We all here consider ourselves socialists, but if each of us were to analyze his own life, he would find in himself much that was bourgeois. This is our misfortune, and it is an inevitable one. Bourgeois culture has enmeshed us for many years, and it is too difficult for our generation to break the net right away with one burst. The future generation, brought up in new conditions, will avoid bourgeois fetters. But we cannot place our hopes only in the future generation. History obligates us to strengthen our political liberation ourselves. We must review the old culture, subjecting it to the test of class consciousness, and everything that passes this test, we will accept as valuable in the new building. We must approach everything from this point of view.

Let us take science. In contemporary society, the greater the division of labor, the more there arise specialists who are so profoundly detached organizationally and ideologically, that they frequently cannot even understand one another, since science is built upon various methods. And we must review other values of bourgeois culture, the values of art—music, poetry, painting, etc. This critical re-evaluation is the best means for creating a new proletarian culture. If art for the bourgeoisie was merely a diversion in life, then for us it is the means to organize life. The proletariat will better understand its ideal when it experiences its beauty and grandeur under the influence of an art form: literary, musical, in painting or in architecture. I will take an example from the distant past. A worker feels himself incapable of participating in an upcoming demonstration. Personal apprehensions keep him from doing it, but the strains of the Marseillaise penetrate his wretched hut and seize him. Giving way to the call of those strains, he joins the demonstrators and is no longer able to cut himself off from this collective. No arguments—home, wife, children, prison—can stop him. Perhaps afterwards he is sorry, but at this moment he forgets everything. Has not each of us felt the influence of music, painting or poetry? In a word, the new culture must embrace all areas of life and creativity, embrace them not superficially or piecemeal, but profoundly and entirely. This defines our task: the proletariat must gather up the elements of socialist culture, organize them into a strict system which can be applied in all spheres of existence and human thought.

True, proletarian consciousness is still young. The elements of its logic, practical and cognitive, have only been partially formulated and have not been put together into one harmonious system. The old logic, more complete and for a long time holding sway in bourgeois economics, politics, law, morals, science, philosophy and art, shakes the proletariat from the correct path of knowledge.

But who can nevertheless resolve the problem of proletarian culture? Only the proletariat. Only it, by way of independent search, by the path of revolutionary creativity. Other classes—better to say groups of society— close to the proletariat cannot resolve this problem. In separate instances they may be of temporary assistance, but only that. Whom do we have in mind? Primarily the socialist intelligentsia. It has come over to us and has a record of cultural service. But we will take from it only its special skills, putting its cultural influence under strict control. If the workers themselves are not free from bourgeois habits, even when they are at their most revolutionary, then the socialist intelligentsia has in itself a bourgeois ferment to an even greater degree. The proletariat must manifest a critical sense in its relations with assistants from other social groups.

Let the working class itself direct its greatest energies to the creation of that which it so lacks; let cultural independence be its next, and from here on, its constant slogan.

We distinguish two points in our problem—a simple educational one and a creative one. The Proletkult, not denying the first point, directs its attention chiefly to the creative side of a matter, entrusting the educational part largely to Narkompros [Commissariat of Enlightenment].

At this moment power belongs to the proletariat and the poor peasantry. State institutions, however, despite their efforts and wishes, are not able to reflect a fully proletarian worldview in their work. First of all, they are forced to a significant degree to use the bourgeois intelligentsia which, of course, introduces bourgeois ferment into their work in one degree or another. Then, the very range of activities, its breadth and immensity, requires considering the psychology of other strata of society, often revolutionary, but completely alien to the communist ideal.

The Commissariat of Enlightenment serves the entire mass of the population, the peasantry, the urban poor, etc., and not the proletariat alone, and I repeat that this interferes with the establishment of a strictly class point of view.

Proletkult, as the type of organization free in its work from petty bourgeois allies, gives to the proletariat maximum opportunities for purely class creative work. Proletkult does not compete with Narkompros and does not contradict it. On the contrary it supplements the work of the Commissariat. Proletkult exists under the Commissariat, like the laboratory of a well-equipped factory, in which strenuous, intense creative work aiming at improvement in the performance of production takes place. Proletkult and Narkompros accomplish colossal creative work; they strive for a single great aim. The former, by way of direct intercourse with the masses, consolidates the creativity of the proletariat and deposits everything of value into the treasure house of the latter, so that the latter may in one form or another make proletarian achievements the property of the entire worker-peasant mass.

The commissariat is forced to issue directives, often in hurried and imperfect form. Due to their position state institutions give the masses not only ready-made organizational forms for one or the other aspects of life, but also fill these forms with ready-made content. Proletarian culture, on the contrary, must be forged independently, from below, among the broader working masses. Only they can fully express their own world concepts. Therefore Proletkult does not give directives; in its essence it must only furnish the independent activity of the proletariat with the best form, strengthening and consolidating everything which is brought into life on its own, without ordaining this process by decrees. "Cultural independence of the proletariat," the slogan of the day, arises from life itself.

In coordinating our work with the Commissariat of Enlightenment, we have in view not the principle of subordination of a lower institution to a higher one, but rather friendly free cooperation.

In the provinces Proletkult and departments of education are often indistinguishable. We must strictly delineate these institutions as different types of organizations, created according to the principle of a definite division of labor in the struggle for future culture.

In our agonizing epoch, the majority of the workers, even in the most advanced countries, followed the bourgeoisie. Not out of fear, but out of conscience. It considered its national interests to be higher than its class interests, and made peace and alliance with the capitalists in order to annihilate enemies together—yesterday's and tomorrow's comrades. In both thought and feeling, the proletariat turned out to be unreliable and unsteadfast. Why was this so? Because they encountered a new question of unforeseen difficulty and did not possess a sufficiently deep and integral upbringing to decide it firmly and unswervingly, on their own, from the point of view of their own goals and their own ideals. The working class subordinated itself to an alien resolution, to that which was forced upon it by the entire surrounding environment, the capitalist world.

Our task is to give the class an integral upbringing, indisputably directing collective will and thought. This can be done only during the process of working out an independent spiritual culture. The proletariat lacked this, and this was its weakness. Otherwise, whatever the new and difficult situation, the old world could not have whispered its thoughts to the proletariat, could not have inspired its feelings in it, could not have corrupted the proletariat with its poison and made it into a blind instrument.

Our prospective work is enormous. There are enormous difficulties and obstacles in the path of the work to which we call our comrades. But the proletariat did not come into the world for easy tasks. We believe that its collective strength in its mighty development and self-organization will overcome everything, will achieve everything.

Long live Proletarian Culture, the great instrument of victory of world-wide socialism! (Long applause)....

Concluding Words [following discussion]

I will try to summarize the criticisms made against me. The essence of the first series of criticisms is that it is not necessary to create a special proletarian organization for the work of building proletarian culture, and that it is sufficient to be united into strong groups on a national scale. I also welcome the striving for unification, but one should never forget the tasks of one's class and especially should never confuse peasant culture with the culture of the working class. They are contradictory, as are the interests of the social groups standing behind them. We are organizing our work in such a way that the Proletkult can dictate its will to the peasant masses. We are striving with our every fibre, if it can be so expressed, for a dictatorship of the proletariat in the area of culture. They argue that with the creation of Proletkult we destroy the work of Narkompros. It is not so. First of all I will point out that under Narkompros there exists the Section of Proletarian Culture. It does not contradict the structure of the Commissariat's work, but rather supplements it, as a special type of organization, better preserving the independence of the proletarian cultural-educational organizations, better corresponding to their work. The representative of the Moscow Metal Workers' Union argued with me. But let me ask him, why does the Union of Metal Workers exist since there is a Commissariat of Labor? From his point of view, it is an absurd question. I think otherwise. Trade unions are needed, despite the fact that their work in many particular questions overlaps with the work of the Commissariat of Labor. No one will deny this. Furthermore, at the present time the VTsIK [Central Executive Committee] consists entirely of communists, but is it sufficient from this fact that the communist party should cease to exist? No. Obviously in a social historical process there are moments which force the same social groups to create several organizational cells, striving for a single goal by different routes. In the process of creating proletarian culture there are also moments when Narkompros cannot satisfy the working class. The political bloc with the peasantry interferes with this. Narkompros, like we, stands on a strictly class point of view and is accomplishing colossal creative work, but it is not completely the work about which we who are gathered here are speaking. We are summoned by history not to contradict one another, but to supplement, coordinating work in comradely fashion without any constraint on the creativity of any side.

Not long ago at an expanded session of the Executive Bureau of Moscow Proletkult the following resolution was suggested by People's Commissar for Enlightenment A. V. Lunacharsky, "Soviet power must in no way restrict the full freedom of such organizations of the proletariat (Proletkult first of all) but must, on the contrary, create for it the most beneficial circumstances, making available to it all the treasures of the past. Hence—the internal unity and full coordination of the enormous Soviet apparatus, state and local, and its cultural sections on the one hand, and independent proletarian cultural organizations, artistic, scientific, and creative, which Proletkult must be, on the other."

His point of view corresponds with ours completely, and after all, none of you would say that Comrade Lunacharsky is undermining the work of Narkompros. General cultural work is being performed by two types of organizations, the Commissariat and Proletkult. We know that the proletariat is conducting a struggle with the bourgeoisie, breaking off into political and economic organizations, despite the fact that it struggles for a single workers' cause in both organizations. The economic organization is divided in turn into trade unions and cooperatives with the latter divided into production and consumption cooperatives. The representative of the Union of Metal Workers who argued against me may be simultaneously a member of the Sovdep [Soviet of Deputies], the party, a trade union, a cooperative, and a responsible worker of the Commissariat of Labor, but does that mean that his soul is made up of separate portions conducting an irreconcilable struggle with one another? No, they are rather in harmony, and serve one cause, though divided according to various organizational units. Since Narkompros in its creative work serves the entire population, all layers of society, it meets difficulties from the peasantry and the urban poor in carrying out a strictly class point of view. The Commissariat does not have the possibility of revealing this class point of view in its full brilliance, an idea that is developed in detail in the theses, in journal articles and in today's speech. As a state institution, the Commissariat must every hour, every moment, give directives and orders to the localities, so that work does not come to a standstill, always in a hurry and sometimes allowing things which are far from tested and perfected. The Proletkult organizations are free from such difficult conditions. The results of their creative work are put into effect not by command, but by themselves, in an invisible manner, by means of an invisible social selection. If Narkompros wishes to improve its own state construction and overcome bourgeois culture more quickly, it must take care of its own laboratory, giving to the proletarian cultural-educational organizations every opportunity to work. Only this will speed up the victory of proletarian thought and proletarian art. I want to dispel the bewilderment of those comrades for whom it is still not clear what we have in mind by distinguishing between two aspects of work, the purely educational and the revolutionary-creative. The first comes down chiefly to knowledge of the cultural property of the past, from which the broad masses of the proletariat used to be removed. The second looks for new paths, to organize the heritage of the bourgeois world on new principles, to forge methods of creativity unique to the class of collective labor.

Comrades! If we first raised the banner of world social revolution and heroically are defending it on the difficult but honorable path to our ideal, then we will be brave to the end and will unfurl the Red Banner of Proletarian Culture. Let it wave over a new world born in grave torment.

Comrades! With a unanimous vote we will lay the first brick of a new and great building which will be our pride, which will stand as a monument of the daring, noble, mighty, but joyful creative rush forward to universal happiness. (Prolonged applause)

Resolutions

The First All Russian Conference of Cultural-Enlightenment Organizations, holding:

(a) That the cultural-educational movement among the proletariat must occupy an independent place along with political and economic movements;

(b) That its task is the forging of a proletarian culture which will become universal with the destruction in society of class division;

(c) That the building of this new culture must be based on social labor and comradely cooperation,—

resolves:

(1) in order to achieve this stated task, the proletariat must comprehend all the accomplishments of previous culture, and adopt from it that which carries a universal stamp;

(2) all that is accepted [from the past] must be examined critically [by the proletariat] and reworked in the crucible of its own class consciousness;

(3) proletarian culture must bear the character of revolutionary socialism, so that the proletariat can arm itself with new knowledge, organize its feelings through the medium of new art, and reform its everyday relations in a new spirit, a genuinely proletarian one, that is, a collectivist one;

(4) in building a new culture the proletariat must display a maximum of its own class energy, its own independence, while also using the help of the revolutionary-socialist intelligentsia, so far as possible;

(5) laying the foundation for a new form of the workers' movement in 'Proletkult,' defending its organizational independence, so that it might display to a full extent a strictly class proletarian creativity, the Conference maintains that state institutions, central and local, must facilitate the new movement in every way, in order to strengthen firmly the gains of the proletarian revolution, in order to defeat the bourgeoisie not only materially, but spiritually as well, and in order to more quickly erect the new structure of the coming socialist society.

[Short debate over amendments, all of which are rejected. Followed by unanimous acceptance, with five abstentions.]

II. THE NEW MAN AND THE NEW WOMAN: SEX ROLES, MARRIAGE, AND THE FAMILY

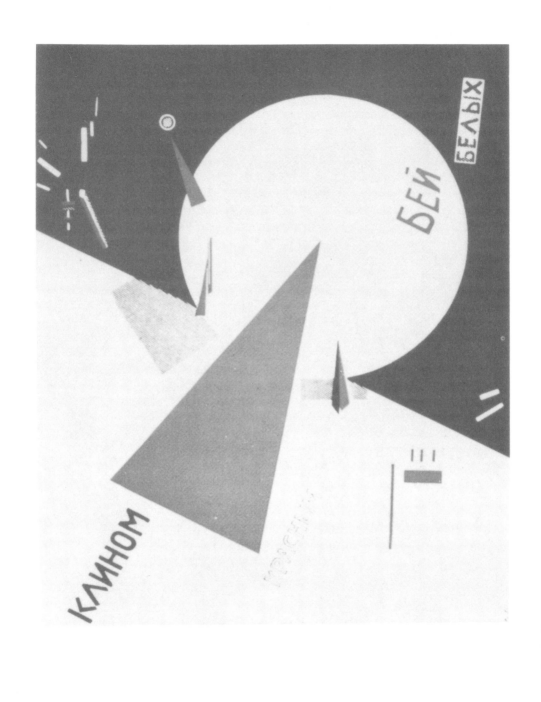

INTRODUCTION

Few issues were more distorted in the West after the Russian revolution than the Bolsheviks' attitude towards women, sex, marriage, and the family. From the *Saturday Evening Post* to the Manchester *Guardian,* Soviet Russia was portrayed as a hotbed of sexual license and moral depravity. Sex was like "a glass of water"; "free love," preached by such "libertines" as Alexandra Kollontai, was a mark of communist "commitment"; maternal instincts were "bourgeois relics of the past." "You ought to be ashamed of yourself!" a communist nurse was said to have scolded a worker's wife in one such report when the woman sobbed that her fourteen year old son had had sexual intercourse with his twelve year old sister after lectures at the "Young Communist Club." "Why worry? Both of them just followed their natural instincts."[1]

In fact, while the social dislocation of the revolutionary period engendered excess and venality in this area as well as others, there was nothing lascivious about Bolshevik policy, and certainly no official desire to encourage sexual libertarianism. "Revolution" for some meant the end of all restraints, but portraying incidents like the one just cited as "communist" was crude anti-Bolshevik propaganda. Nor was there any official effort to undermine serious commitments between men and women. Quite the contrary. The party's goal instead was to eliminate artifice from these commitments, and to infuse them with genuine, mutual feelings of responsibility and love. There also was no clear idea of how this might best be accomplished, nor any rigid ideological prescriptions. As the selections in this chapter suggest, many Bolshevik writers recognized the complex psychological and social dimensions of these issues, as well as the ways in which sex relations before 1917 in Russia conformed to other bourgeois value systems. Except for agreement on certain broad principles, the early years of Soviet rule were characterized by diversity and experiment, as Bolsheviks sought attitudes and forms appropriate to a society liberating itself from oppressive norms.

One such principle related to women's rights. Bolsheviks were not "feminists" in the usual Western sense of the term: they rejected the notion that gender, rather than class, was an appropriate way to define either exploitation or the basis of social alliance and mobilization. The grievances of women workers stemmed from their status as workers and from the accompanying exploitative values of capitalist society. Suffrage and other rights were desirable, of course, but not as an end in themselves, and not by means of feminist organizations like the Russian League for Women's Equality, which presumed all women were "sisters," regardless of social status. Such groups only blurred political consciousness among working women by weakening the power of proletarian allegiances. Their goal was the liberalization (and hence strengthening) of bourgeois social relations, rather than their overthrow. Even the most radical feminists were scorned by party activists, despite their militance, since the notion that "men cannot defend our interests" corrupted proletarian solidarity.[2]

Rather, the Bolsheviks' goal was the liberation of all women, along with men, from the prejudice, discrimination, and exploitation of capitalist society. Such liberation could only occur through revolution. Under socialism, relations between men and women, parents and children, would be structured by love rather than necessity; and the family, rather than an institution of exploitation and antagonism, would be nurturent and caring.

A good deal has been written about Marxist "theory" on the family "withering away" under socialism, some of it by reputable scholars and much of it nonsense. There is a general assumption, for example, that many early Bolsheviks wanted to "destroy" the family. The most prominent spokeswoman on the question, Alexandra Kollontai, was herself occasionally ambiguous on this question; and part of the difficulty is that only a small portion of the literature has been available in English. But the principal source of confusion lies elsewhere, in the very notion of "family."

Bolshevik writers generally wrote with two kinds of family in mind: the harried, often broken households of workers, where parents sometimes labored in factories on different shifts, and did not "even have a single hour to spend with the children"; and the rigid, patriarchal households of the bourgeoisie (partially reflected in the peasantry), where differential systems of morality prevailed, where women were kept from productive labor, and where even basic parental functions like child-rearing were often turned over to hired servants. As both Kollontai and Trotsky argue below, both *these* family structures *were* to disappear in Soviet Russia.

But in its place was to emerge a "higher union of loving and mutually trusting souls...", a family supported in the necessities of household management, as Trotsky describes, and hence capable of existing in "freedom." In reading these selections, one might best keep in mind a working class family of the inner-city, transplanted (in Russia or elsewhere) by necessity from rural to urban life (American migrants, poor blacks, Russian peasants during the war); without resources with which to provide adequately for their increasingly wayward, street-wise children; at times angry, at times resigned to slum life and deprivation. When early Bolshevik writers spoke of nurseries, kindergartens, cafeterias, and other child-support institutions, it was this form of family existence they were struggling to overcome. Similarly with the male-dominant, family "state" of the bourgeoisie, often bound more by property than love, and capable of raising its children, but not nurturing them, or inculcating cooperative, socialist values. In tsarist Russia, such a family was perpetually bound together, since the Orthodox church, like its Catholic counterpart, did not allow divorce. "Destruction" here meant liberating all family members from households which were personally oppressive and politically reactionary.

The florid (and sometimes confusing) essays of Kollontai and others should also not obscure the fact that the ideological goal here, paradoxical as it may seem to opponents of socialism (and also in terms of the Soviet Union's subsequent development), was individual self-fulfillment—the creation of conditions capable of sustaining integrated (unalienated) personalities, men as well as women. Virtually all Bolshevik writers on the subject recognized that the new Soviet man and woman had to be free from sexual prejudice and stereotyped conceptions of "appropriate" male and female roles. Inside the household or out, productive work could not be the province of either sex alone; and to be individually fulfilling, it had to be productive in the sense of contributing genuinely to the household's economy and well-being (or that of society). Here as elsewhere, Kollontai's rhetoric engendered much confusion. "Housework ceases to be necessary" meant that women would not be compelled to do unproductive household labor, not that such work could not be both an important and socially productive activity. The essential struggle was against "necessity," or household "slavery," not housework per se: communism was to "*liberate* the domestic slavery of women, so that their life can be richer, fuller, happier and freer," as Kollontai argued. That, in any case, was the vision.

Trotsky, Lenin, and others recognized, however, how difficult this ideal was to obtain. The ingrained habits of pre-revolutionary life were especially well-rooted, psychologically and socially, in family structures, and the task of attitudinal change was magnified by their constant, daily reinforcement. As Trotsky writes below in "From the Old Family to the New," achieving political power was "relatively easy"; economic equality, substantially more difficult; and "actual equality of man and woman within the family . . . infinitely more arduous. All our domestic habits must be revolutionized before that can happen." But the difficulty of the task, requiring "a great conscious effort on the part of the whole mass of the working class," only testified to its importance: "Unless there is actual equality of husband and wife in the family, . . . we cannot speak seriously of their equality in social work or even in politics." If custom found it harder to discard ceremony than the state, the persistence of traditional attitudes constituted a genuine threat to socialist integrity.[3]

Some Bolshevik women, Kollontai among them, argued quite early that special attention had to be paid to this problem through separate Bolshevik "women's sections," but most opposed this as unwarranted (and divisive) attention to gender. It was not until the summer of 1919 that Zhenotdel, the "Women's Department," was set up, and even then it was frequently derided as "Tsentro-baba" and "Bab-otdel," despite Lenin's own strong support.[4] Zhenotdel members worked particularly (but by no means exclusively) with women, trying to cope with prejudice and self-doubt, and to develop a consciousness of equality and ability. As the selection below from the journal *Delegatka* [*Woman Delegate*] reveals, however, the task required exceptional energy and commitment.

Not the least reason for this was the survival of "transitional" feelings among male party members themselves.[5] Many local party organizations insisted that Zhenotdel members do "women's tasks," i.e. unimportant ones, or dissolve altogether. Women were consistently excluded from high party positions, even while making substantial advances in industry and the professions; and even sympathizers in organizations like the Trade Unions worried that Zhenotdel implicitly continued harmful feminist positions. The essay below by L.A. and L.M. Vasilevsky shows, moreover, that as late as 1924 little real progress had been made in changing male attitudes. "A double sexual standard" continued, allowing much for men which "for women would be considered impermissible, shameful, and immoral. . . . " "Vulgar winking" and generally coarse associations still characterized popular male attitudes about sex, even to the extent that in many places, profligate sexual debauchery was paraded among men as masculine virtue.

Here, however, was another area of ideological confusion. In the main, writers on the subject agreed in Kollontai's words, that "one of the revoluton's most difficult tasks" was "to introduce beauty and humanity into sexual relations." Certainly this is a central view of Kollontai's own tortuous essay on the "Winged Eros": "The 'Unwinged Eros' [sexual relations devoid of love] contradicts the interests of the working class . . . It inevitably involves excesses . . . it impoverishes the spirit . . . [and] it usually rests on an inequality of rights in the mutual relations of the sexes, on a dependence of the woman on the man, on satiating male appetites or inconsiderateness, which undoubtedly undermines . . . a feeling of association. The presence of the 'Winged Eros' [love] has an entirely opposite effect . . . [While here there is] the same attraction of one sex to the other which exists for Unwinged Eros, the difference is that in a person experiencing love for another person, there are aroused, and there appear simultaneously, those qualities of the spirit which are necessary for builders of the new culture: directness, sympathy, a wish to help others. . . . "

The problem was that inhibitions about sex—Kollontai's "Unwinged Eros"—could also be labelled "bourgeois," even "Victorian," and frequently were. Vinogradskaya's scathing critique of Kollontai, below, turns in part on the fact that Kollontai seemed to encourage sexual license as a means of assaulting bourgeois values. Could a woman be politically radical, and not, at the same time, have sexual relations with every male who desired them? The answer from Lenin and others was emphatically "yes!", but Kollontai's own writings often seemed to imply the opposite. In part, as readers may judge for themselves from her "Winged Eros" essay, this may have been due to genuine confusion on Kollontai's part, or at least some muddled writing. It may also be due to her use of sex in her novels, like *Love of Three Generations,* to expose double standards and depict woman's independence.

In any event, sexual excesses were indeed a serious problem during the civil war years, along with growing numbers of homeless and illegitimate children. The Bolsheviks took immediate steps after coming to power in 1917 to free men and women from tsarist strictures on marriage and divorce, and in October 1918, enacted a comprehensive, progressive family law (although certainly not a particularly radical one by contemporary standards).[6] The legal power of the church over marriage and divorce was abolished, and particular duties and obligations of spouses to their children and each other were spelled out. Divorces could be obtained "without fault," but only through court decision; no community or property was secured by marriage, but 10,000 rubles value was assumed to belong to a surviving spouse in the event of death; married persons were entitled to choose whether they would adopt the husband's or wife's surname, or use their joint surnames; "maintenance" of an amount determined by court would be paid by one spouse to another in the event of divorce; until children were 13, parents were obligated to take care of them, provide for their education and training for a "useful activity." In November 1920, abortions were legalized; and new rules on inheritance were passed in 1922. But as in the case of sexual relations, a more radical ethic often developed in practice than was formally allowed by decree. Also, the law itself in this area was confusing, and subject, as several selections below indicate, to various interpretations. Issues of child support, property rights, and particularly the casualness of some family ties consequently became quite contentious, and began increasingly to concern party leaders.

Some reasons for this become clear from the letters to *Pravda* and *Izvestiya* included below. The lack of stability in family life was far more a consequence of war and revolution than it was of Bolshevik policy, Western press reports to the contrary notwithstanding, and with the end of the civil war, the party's goal above all was economic recovery. This prompted efforts to discourage frequent and disruptive changes in family relations, and closer attention in the courts to issues of child care and parental responsibility. By the mid-1920s, court rulings were becoming increasingly conservative, although still, as illustrated in this chapter, showing special attention to social circumstances and questions of proletarian morality.

Two additional factors were probably much more important in the party's growng "Thermidorian reaction" in this area, however, suggested particularly by Vinogradskaya's essay and the Vasilevskys' article. One was popular reaction, particularly among male peasants, to the party's support for women's independence, and a residual male defensiveness about appropriate "masculine roles," particularly concerning sexual freedom.[7] The other was a related unwillingness on the part of party figures to give these issues the energy and attention they required. Other problems had higher priorities; as Vinogradskaya insisted, the problem of love did not have "one-tenth the significance in our lives that comrade Kollontai wishes to attach to it . . . " Still, the explosion of traditional myths and prejudices concerning the "appropriate" roles for men and women in society, the freeing of church restraints in this regard, and particularly the liberation of women in many national minority areas from conditions approaching forced female servitude, remained one of the revolution's most remarkable cultural achievements.

THE FAMILY AND THE COMMUNIST STATE
A. Kollontai

1. The Family and Women's Hired Labor

Will the family be preserved under the communist state? Will it be the same as it is now? This question troubles the hearts of many working class women and it concerns men, their comrades, as well. Working women have been asking themselves this question especially often since life started to change before our eyes. The old ways and customs are disappearing, and the entire existence of the proletarian family is taking a different shape, a new, unaccustomed form, and as some think, an odd one. Here confusion is redoubled by the fact that separation has become easier in Soviet Russia. By a decree of the People's Commissars on December 18, 1917, separation ceased to be a luxury available only to the rich. Now a working class woman does not have to spend months or even years striving for a separate residence permit from her husband, who has harassed his wife with drinking, beating, and crudity. Now separation by mutual consent can be obtained in a week or two, no more. But it is this ease with which separation can be obtained and which is being applauded by those women who have gone through a lot in their families, which frightens other women, especially those who have become accustomed to regarding their husbands as the breadwinner and as their only support in life, and who do not understand that *a woman should learn to look for support somewhere else, to look for it and find it not from men, but from the collective, from the state.*

There is no reason to hide the truth: the old traditional family, in which the man was the head and the breadwinner and the wife existed only in terms of her husband, having no will of her own, nor money, nor time of her own—this family is changing before our eyes. But there is no need to be afraid of this. It is only our lack of knowledge, our ignorance which makes

Speech delivered to the First All-Russian Congress of Women, 1918, published later in the year as a separate pamphlet by "Kommunist." Translated from the pamphlet *Sem'ia i kommunisticheskoe gosudarstvo*, Moscow–Leningrad–N. Novgorod, 1918. A prominent member of the Bolshevik "Workers' Opposition" group during the Civil War, writer, lecturer, and Soviet Russia's Ambassador to Norway, Sweden and Mexico after 1923, Kollontai was the party's best known spokeswoman on questions of sex, sex roles, and women. See Barbara E. Clements, *Bolshevik Feminist: A Life of Alexandra Kollontai*, Bloomington, Ind., 1979; and Beatrice Farnsworth, *Aleksandra Kollontai: Socialism, Feminism, and the Bolshevik Revolution*, Stanford, 1980.

us think that all those customary things never change. "As it was, so it will be!" Nothing could be more wrong than that saying. If you read about how people used to live, it becomes clear that everything changes, that there are no morals and manners, no state structure, no customs, which have remained unchanged. And the family, at various points in the existence of mankind, has changed its form many times. It has been altogether different from what we are accustomed to seeing. Once people thought that the single right kind of family was the *matrilineal* family; that is, headed by the mother, around whom lived and worked the children, grandchildren and great grandchildren. There was [also] a *patriarchal* family, in which the head of the family was the father-master, and with whom lived, under his paternal eye, his children and grandchildren, subordinating themselves to his will and his law. This kind of family can still be found now among peasants in the villages. There the morals and laws of family life are different from those of a city worker's family. Many of the customs there have no place in the family of the urban proletariat. The form of the family and its customs change and differ from people to people. There are peoples—the Turks, Arabs and Persians—where it is customary and legal for a man to have several wives. There have been, and still are, tribes which, on the other hand, allow a single woman to have several husbands. We are accustomed to having men demand that women be chaste from girlhood until marriage, but there have been people among whom women have boasted of the number of their lovers, wearing on their arms and legs bracelets whose number represents the number of men they have had. Many of the customs which would surprise us or which we would call immoral are considered lawful among other peoples and tribes, and our customs and laws seem "sinful" to them. Therefore there is no basis for taking fright about their being changes at the moment in the family, about the dying-off of the old and unnecessary, and because before our eyes, relationships between men and women are taking a new form. One has only to look into it sensibly: What in the family is outmoded and which laws and customs in the relationship between men and women workers, and men and women peasants, are the most appropriate to the whole tenor of life of our new laboring Soviet Russia? What is applicable will survive, and that which is left from the old, the past, the outlived, from the cursed time of servitude under landowners and proprietary capitalists, well, let it die and disappear with the proprietors themselves, the enemies of the proletariat, the enemies of the poor...

The family to which the proletariat of the city and villages has become accustomed is also a part of that which we have outlived. That kind of family—closed, strong, recognizing that the marriage which the priest had blessed was indissoluble forever—was once necessary to all family members. Without that family, who would have fed, dressed, raised the children; who would have taught them wisdom and reason? To be an orphan in the past was to be bitterly unfortunate. In the family to which we are accustomed, the man earned money; he fed the wife and children. The wife took care of the house and to the best of her ability raised the children. But since the last century, in all countries where capital rules, where factories, mills and other capitalist enterprises have sprung up, worked by hired labor, the traditional family is being destroyed. Its customs and standards are changing, changing with the general conditions of life around it. Above all, great changes in family standards were introduced by the general acceptance of female labor. In the past, the breadwinner was the man alone. But in the last fifty or sixty years in Russia (and in other countries, a little earlier) capitalism forced the woman also to seek work outside the family, outside the home. The wages of the male provider were not sufficient for the family, so wives had to go to work; women too had to knock on the factory's office door. Every year the number of women of the working class who work outside the home, in factories or as daily workers, at the counter or in an office, in domestic service, in a laundry or in an eating-place, had grown. According to a count made before the beginning of World War I, there were sixty million self-supporting, wage-earning women in the states of Europe and America. During the war, this number rose sharply. Almost half these women are married. What kind of a family life is that, when the wife and mother works for maybe eight, but with travel and everything else, ten hours! The family is less looked after; the children grow up, not under their mother's eyes, but more on the street, left to themselves and all kinds of dangerous occurrences. The wife, mother, worker runs out of strength to cope with three things at once, to complete her work at the factory, equal with her husband at the press or in the office, and then to have time to take care of housework and to concern herself with children. Capitalism lays an unbearable burden on a woman's shoulders. It has turned her into a hired laborer without making housework or motherhood any easier. And women's shoulders bow under the triple back-breaking weight, from her breast a half-muffled groan bursts forth and the tears do not dry in her eyes. "A woman's fate" ("Babya Dolya") has never been sweet, but women have never lived with such difficulty, so hopelessly as do the millions of women working under the yoke of capitalism, under the flowering of factory and mill production...

The faster the hired labor of women grows, the faster the former family is being destroyed. What kind of family life is it, if husband and wife work on different shifts! What kind of family life is it if the wife has no time even to prepare dinner! What kind of parents are they who, because of heavy twenty-four hour work demands do not have an hour to spend with the children! Before the mother and housewife worked at home on housework and the children were with her, under her vigilant eye. Now, at the sound of the whistle, they rush to the shop, and at the whistle hurry home, to turn around and take care of the house, and then, without even

69

having enough sleep—back to work. It is not life, but hard labor for every married working woman. In such conditions, the family is destroyed, falls apart, everything that had held the family together disappears from it bit by bit. *The family ceases to be necessary for the family members and for the state.* The old kind of family becomes nothing but a burden.

But what held together the old tightly bound family? First of all, the fact that the husband and father was the breadwinner. Secondly, the general necessity of housekeeping for all members of the family. Thirdly, the raising of the children by the parents. What is now left of the old family? We have already said that the husband has ceased to be the only family breadwinner. The woman worker earns as much as he does. She has learned to earn her own keep, support children and even, not infrequently her husband. What is left is housework and child-raising and care for small children. Let's look closer and see if these functions are also being taken away from the family.

2. Housekeeping Ceases to Be Necessary

There was a time when the whole life of poor women in the village and in cities was spent in the family. Women knew nothing outside the home and very few of them cared to know what was happening there. There was so much work in one's own family! And it was work that was varied, needed, required not only for the immediate family, but for the state. A woman did not only cook for the family, clean and pick up the house, darn and fix linen—that is, she did not do only the work that every woman worker or poor peasant woman does today, but she managed a number of other things. She spun wool and flax, wove cloth and broadcloth, knitted stockings, tatted lace, fixed salted food and preserves for winter, smoke-cured and salted meat, and as well as her resources would allow, prepared kvass, poured and melted down candles—you could not list all the things women used to do! That is how our mothers and grandmothers lived. And now there are remote villages and hamlets, hidden far from the railroad or from our navigable rivers, where life goes on as before, where women-housewives are burdened with all the work which women working class families in big cities and populous big factory centers have not done for a long time.

In our grandmothers' time, all this domestic work was necessary, useful; the well-being of the family depended upon it. The more industriously the housewife worked, the better the peasant's or workman's life was, the greater the order and sufficiency in the family. The whole state economy benefited from the housewife's work. The hands of women did not just prepare soup and boiled potatoes, which were eaten right away, that is, they were for the family's immediate use, but they also made cloth, yarn, butter and so on, things which could be sold, that is wares, valuables.

In truth though, the work of our grandmothers and great-grand-mothers was not valued in money. But every man in a family, every peasant or artisan, choosing a wife, tried to select one who would have "golden hands" in household and family work. Men knew that "without household work" by his wife, a family would not exist. And from the point of view of the state, from the point of view of the people's interests, it turned out that the faster and more industriously a woman and her family members prepared products (cloth, leather, wool) which were necessary for her family and brought the surplus to the market for sale, the more the entire economy and the whole state benefited.

But capitalism changed the old life. Under capitalism, tasks which had previously been done in the family, by and large by housewives' hands, were made in mass quantities by factories and workshops. What housewife now pours tallow candles, spins wool, weaves cloth, when all these products are for sale? There was a time every young woman learned to knit stockings. But would it cross a working woman's mind to knit them now? Where would she find the time? Time is money and it should not be wasted unproductively, uselessly and without profit. And now it is more profitable for the housewife-worker to buy ready-made stockings than waste her time knitting them. It is a rare working woman who salts cucumbers for the winter or prepares other food products, when all those products can be bought for money at any grocer's shop. Perhaps ready-made products are worse; perhaps cheap factory goods are of lower quality then those made at home by the housewife; the worker has not time or strength to spend on housework. She is, above all, labor hired outside the home. Thus, little by little, all of the old practices, without which our grandmothers could not imagine a family, are being eliminated from household management. That which the family made is now prepared by the work of men and women laborers in special workshops, factories and mills.

Only consumption, not production, is left to the family. Housework now consists of four kinds of work: first, cleaning house (washing floors, dusting, stoking the stove, trimming lamps, and so on); second, concocting and cooking dinners and lunches; third—washing; fourth—darning and fixing linens and the clothes of family members.

The work is not easy; it is exhausting, time- and energy-consuming for a woman, especially if one remembers that she is working at the same time at some other enterprise. But all of this is not the work that our grandmothers did. How is this work different? Above all, in that these four sides of housework as it now exists are not necessary to the state, nor to the economy. This work does not contribute any additional value, nothing useful to the national wealth.

A housewife-worker can work morning to night in cleaning her wretched dwelling. She can wash and iron linens daily. She can darn and mend clothing in the most thorough way. She can prepare any kind of dish from her frugal supplies, but in the evening no trace of her work will remain, her workmanship will have produced nothing which has value on the market. And if she lives a thousand years, she will have to start her housework from the beginning every day. The shelves will again gather dust. Her husband will again come home from work hungry. The children will again get their clothing dirty. Housework becomes less useful, less productive with every passing day.

Housework is dying out. It is giving way to social management. Instead of the wife-worker cleaning her apartment, there can and will be special workers, men and women, under the Communist state, who will go around the rooms and clean up in the morning. The wealthy have long since taken this boring and tiresome work off their wives' shoulders. Why should a working woman have to suffer? In Soviet Russia, the lives of all working women will be supplied with these comforts, the same light, hygiene and beauty which used to be accessible only to the rich. Instead of bothering with cooking, of wasting one's last free hours in the kitchen preparing suppers and dinners, *in the Communist society, public cafeterias and central kitchens will be widely established.* This was the trend even under capitalism. In the last half century, restaurants and coffeehouses have grown up in all the big cities with unusual speed, like mushrooms after an autumn rain. But the difference is, that under the capitalist order, restaurants were used by people with money, and under communism, cafeterias and central kitchens will be generally accessible. In the same way, the necessity for a working woman to slave over the washtub or to blind herself over darning will become obsolete. *Central laundries,* where the worker can take the family's linen and receive cleaned and ironed linens, will take this burden off the shoulders of women. *Special workshops for darning clothing* will allow the working woman to spend the evening hours over a good book, or going to concerts, meetings, gatherings, instead of sitting for hours over patching. All four kinds of housework, by which the family economy is still supported, are doomed to die out with the approaching success of the communist order. It is not necessary for working women to cry over the death of this kind of work. Communism will liberate woman from domestic slavery, so that her life can be richer, fuller, happier and freer.

3. The Upbringing of Children—A Matter for the State

But what will be left of the family if there is no housework? One more family tie—the children. Even here, in this matter, a comradely workers' state will overcome the family. Society is taking upon itself little by little all concerns which previously were parental. Even under capitalism the teaching of children had ceased to be the work of the family. Children were taught in school. When children reached school age, parents accepted that the work of the child's intellectual development would now be taken from them. But quite a few other tasks were left to the family: to feed the children, to provide clothes and shoes for them, to raise them as honest and efficient workers, who would be able to feed themselves and their parents in their old age, rather than leaving them without support. Still, only rarely was the worker's family able to fulfill its parental duties. Small wages hardly ever allowed for feeding the children sufficiently, and the lack of leisure, of free time, did not allow either parent to contribute to the raising of a younger generation with the attention which was necessary. It was believed that the family raised children. But was that the case? Proletarian children are raised on the street. Proletarian children already do not know what family life is, as our mothers and fathers still knew it.

Besides, parents' low pay, want and the hunger of the family often lead to the sons of the proletariat already becoming self-supporting workers at age ten. If a boy or girl is earning his or her own wage, parental words and admonitions are no longer law. The former obedience disappears; parental power weakens. Just as housework is disappearing, less and less is left of these obligations which only parents can fulfill in the family with relation to children. These obligations, that is, the support and rearing of children, are slowly being transferred from the shoulders of parents to the shoulders of society. For a proletarian family under capitalism, children were often, too often, a heavy and insupportable burden.

Communist society without doubt will hurry to meet parents' needs and to relieve their difficult burden. Already in Soviet Russia we have Commissariats of Peoples' Education and Social Welfare which are doing much to lighten the difficult task of the family in raising and supporting children and a family. Homes for infants, creches, nurseries, kindergartens, children's colonies and homes, hospitals and sanitoria for curing and healing sick children, as well as children's cafeterias, school lunches, the distribution of free books to children, the outfitting of schoolchildren with warm clothing, boots—doesn't this show that caring for children is moving beyond the boundaries of the family, is being taken away from parents and transferred to the collective, to society?

Parental care for children in the family, like housework, previously fell into three categories: first, the care of infants; second, their upbringing; and third, their education. Teaching children in schools, then in gymnasia and universities, had already become a matter for the state under capitalism. The demands and conditions of working class life strongly pressed capitalist society to establish a number of institutions for raising children: playgrounds, kindergartens, and so on. The more conscious workers were, the better organized under this government, the more child care was taken off the shoulders of parents by society. But bourgeois society was afraid of

73

going too far to meet the working class's needs so as not to contribute to the disintegration of the family. Capitalists understand perfectly well that the former family, with the slavery of women and the responsibility of the husband for the family's feeding and well-being is the best way of halting a striving for freedom, for weakening the revolutionary spirit of working men and women. Worries over family bow workers down to the ground, force them to compromise with capital. What would fathers and mothers not do if their children are hungry? If in the capitalist order the raising of children could not be at all the concern of the state, of society, if that got in the way of proprietors and the bourgeois class, in the communist state, on the contrary, the raising of children is the basis of new laws and customs of life. The narrow, closed family, with quarrelling parents who are accustomed to think only of the advantages of blood relations, cannot raise the new man; only child-rearing institutions can, such as playgrounds, kindergartens, and nurseries where children will spend most of the day and where wise educators will make them conscious communists, recognizing one sacred slogan: solidarity, comradeship, mutuality, and devotion to the collective.

What will be left to the family with regard to children, what are parental duties, if teaching, rearing, and even a large part of material concerns are taken from parents? Only care for infants while they are still at the mother's breast, while they are wandering, unsteadily, hanging on her skirt? Even here, the communist state hurries to the aid of the mother-worker. There should not be any solitary, discarded, girl-mothers, abandoned wives with infants in their arms. The working class government has the aim of supporting every wedded or unwedded mother while she is feeding an infant, to build maternity homes everywhere, in cities and villages, to have creches and nurseries at every business, to allow women the possibility of combining useful work for the state with the obligations of motherhood.

Mother-workers, do not be frightened: communist society is not going to take children away from their parents, to tear infants from their mothers' breasts, nor forcibly destroy the family. Nothing of the sort! Communist society sets itself an entirely different task. It sees that the older, previous form of family is being pulled down, that all the work, all the ties which held it together are disappearing. Household work is dying out. Proletarian parents cannot concern themselves with children, are unable to support or raise them. Both children and parents suffer from these conditions. Therefore, communist society hurries to meet male and female workers and says to them: You are young. You have fallen in love with one another. Everyone has the right to happiness. Don't let your lives frighten you. Don't run away from happiness, don't be afraid of marriage as workers became afraid of marriage under capitalism, when they saw that it would be bondage for them. Nor should you, young and healthy, be afraid of giving

74

working society new citizen-children. A working society needs new working strength and it welcomes the arrival of every infant to the world. Don't be afraid of what his or her lot will be. Neglect, hunger, and cold do not await them, as they did under capitalism. In a communist society, every infant will be taken into account, and they and their mothers will be supplied with rations and concern on the part of the government. Society will feed the infant, educate and raise it, and not tear it away from those parents who want to participate in raising their own children. Society will shoulder the material burden of raising children, while the joy of fatherhood and motherhood will be left for those who have the capacity to understand and feel those joys. Is this a forcible disruption of the family? Is this the forcible removal of a child from its mother?

There is nothing to hide: the old family is becoming obsolete. But not because socialist society is destroying it by force, but because it is outmoded and the new conditions of life are doing away with it.

The family is ceasing to be a necessity. It is not necessary to the state, because housework is not profitable for the state. It needlessly attracts workers away from other more useful and productive work. It is not necessary to the members of the family themselves because the other task of the family—raising children—is gradually being taken over by society. Instead of the previous family, a new form of relationship between men and women is developing, *a comradely and loving union of two free, independent, self-supporting equal members of a communist society.* There is no more domestic slavery for women! There is no inequality in the family! A woman now has no fear of being left without support and help with children on her hands if her husband leaves. A woman in communist society is no longer dependent upon her husband, but on her own working strength. Not her husband, but her own working hands feed her. Neither is there fear for the children's future. The working state assumes responsibility for them. All material and monetary worries which spoil and cripple family life are disappearing from marriage. Marriage is being changed into that higher union of loving and mutually trusting souls, which promises greater happiness and greater satisfaction for every conscious worker, male and female, who has pondered about life. A *free,* but due to its comradely spirit, a solid, close *union of man and woman, instead of the slavery of the old family—this is what communist society promises workers.* And with changing conditions of work, with the growth of material security of women workers, and with the changing of the earlier, indissoluble, hypocritical church marriage (which sometimes seems strong but is actually thoroughly rotten) into a free, comradely union, that other disgusting, dark, debasing human evil and scourge of hungry working women—prostitution—will also disappear.

The existence of property and commodity economy gave birth to prostitution. With the abolition of both there will be no further place for

75

the trade in women's bodies.

So let women of the working class stop grieving that the family is doomed to destruction. On the contrary, let them greet with rejoicing the dawn of a new society, in which the chains of domestic slavery will be taken off every woman, in which the cross of motherhood will be lightened for every woman, when the end will come of that most terrible curse hanging over women, the scourge of prostitution.

The working woman, becoming a social fighter for the great cause of the freedom of workers, must learn to understand that old divisions need not exist. These are my children, and all my maternal concern, all my love, is for them. And these are your children, the neighbor's, and I have no concern with them. Let them be hungrier than mine, colder than mine. I have no concern for another's children! Now the worker-mother who is aware must learn not to make a distinction between yours and mine, but to remember that there are only *our* children, children of working, communist Russia.

The new working class state has need of a new form of relationship between the sexes. Instead of the narrow love of a mother for her child alone, a mother's love must grow to include all the children of the great working family. Instead of indissoluble marriage-slavery, a comradely union of two loving and equal members of a working society is created. Instead of the locked, egotistical family box, there will be a big, universal working family, in which those who work, men and women, will be brothers and comrades above all. That is the form which relationships between men and women will take in a communist society. And that form will specifically guarantee to humanity the flowering of those joys of free love, fanned by feelings of equality and camaraderie, which were unknown to the mercenary, materialistic society of capitalist times.

Make way for healthy, blossoming children, for a strong, life-loving younger generation, free and unrestrained in its spiritual and emotional experiences! Such is the slogan of communist society, which sweeps away the enslaving forms of the family of a bourgeois capitalist past. Let the old family become obsolete and let workers and peasants, men and women, in the name of true equality, freedom and comradely love in a new marriage, begin with faith and enthusiasm the work of rebuilding society on a new, more realistic, more just, and brighter communist base. The red banner of socialist revolution, unfolding in other countries of the world following Russia's path, tells us that the paradise on earth for which humanity has longed for ages is not far distant.

FROM THE OLD FAMILY TO THE NEW
L. Trotsky

The inner relations and happenings within the family are by their very nature the most difficult to investigate, the least subject to statistics. It is not easy, therefore, to say how far family ties are more easily and frequently broken nowadays (in actual life, not merely on paper) than formerly. To a great extent we must be content to judge by eye. The difference, moreover, between prerevolutionary times and the present day is that formerly all the troubles and dramatic conflicts in working class families used to pass unnoticed by the workers themselves; whereas now a large upper part of the workers occupy responsible posts, their life is much more in the limelight, and every domestic tragedy in their life becomes a subject of much comment and sometimes of idle gossip.

Subject to this serious reservation, there is no denying, however, that family relations, those of the proletarian class included, are shattered. This was stated as a firmly established fact at the conference of Moscow party propagandists, and no one contested it. They were only differently impressed by it—all in their own way. Some viewed it with great misgivings, others with reserve, and still others seemed perplexed. It was, anyhow, clear to all that some great process was going on, very chaotically assuming alternatively morbid or revolting, ridiculous or tragic forms, and which had not yet had time to disclose its hidden possibilities of inaugurating a new and higher order of family life.

Some information about the disintegration of the family has crept into the press, but just occasionally, and in very vague, general terms. In an article on the subject, I have read that the disintegration of the family in the working class was represented as a case of "bourgeois influence on the proletariat."

It is not so simple as this. The root of the question lies deeper and is more complicated. The influence of the bourgeois past and the bourgeois present is there, but the main process consists in a painful evolution of the proletarian family itself, an evolution leading up to a crisis, and we are witnessing now the first chaotic stages of the process.

The deeply destructive influence of the war on the family is well known. To begin with, war dissolves the family automatically, separating

Article in *Pravda*, July 13, 1923, reprinted by permission from *Problems of Everyday Life* by Leon Trotsky, Monad Press, New York. Copyright 1973 by the Anchor Foundation, Inc.

77

people for a long time or bringing people together by chance. This influence of the war was continued and strengthened by the revolution. The years of the war shattered all that had stood only by the inertia of historic tradition. They shattered the power of tsardom, class privileges, the old traditional family. The revolution began by building up the new state and has achieved thereby its simplest and most urgent aim.

The economic part of its problem proved much more complicated. The war shook the old economic order; the revolution overthrew it. Now we are constructing a new economic state—doing it as yet mostly from the old elements, reorganizing them in new ways. In the domain of economics we have but recently emerged from the destructive period and begun to ascend. Our progress is still very slow, and the achievement of new socialistic forms of economic life are still very distant. But we are definitely out of the period of destruction and ruin. The lowest point was reached in the years 1920-21.

The first destructive period is still far from being over in the life of the family. The disintegrating process is still in full swing. We must bear that in mind. Family and domestic life are still passing, so to speak, their 1920-21 period and have not reached the 1923 standard. Domestic life is more conservative than economic, and one of the reasons is that it is still less conscious than the latter. In politics and economics the working class acts as a whole and pushes on to the front rank its vanguard, the Communist Party, accomplishing through its medium the historic aims of the proletariat. In domestic life the working class is split into cells constituted by families. The change of political regime, the change even of the economic order of the state—the passing of the factories and mills into the hands of the workers—all this has certainly had some influence on family conditions, but only indirectly and externally, and without touching on the forms of domestic traditions inherited from the past.

A radical reform of the family and, more generally, of the whole order of domestic life requires a great conscious effort on the part of the whole mass of the working class, and presumes the existence in the class itself of a powerful molecular force of inner desire for culture and progress. A deep-going plough is needed to turn up heavy clods of soil. To institute the political equality of men and women in the Soviet state was one problem and the simplest. A much more difficult one was the next—that of instituting the industrial equality of men and women workers in the factories, the mills, and the trade unions, and of doing it in such a way that the men should not put the women to disadvantage. But to achieve the actual equality of man and woman within the family is an infinitely more arduous problem. All our domestic habits must be revolutionized before that can happen. And yet it is quite obvious that unless there is actual equality of husband and wife in the family, in a normal sense as well as in the conditions of life, we cannot speak seriously of their equality in social

78

work or even in politics. As long as woman is chained to her housework, the care of the family, the cooking and sewing, all her chances of participation in social and political life are cut down in the extreme.

The easiest problem was that of assuming power. Yet just that problem alone absorbed all our forces in the early period of the revolution. It demanded endless sacrifices. The civil war necessitated measures of the utmost severity. Philistine vulgarians cried out about the barbarization of morality, about the proletariat becoming bloody and depraved, and so on. What was actually happening was that the proletariat, using the means of revolutionary violence forced into its hands, started to fight for a new culture, for genuine human values.

In the first four or five years we have passed economically through a period of terrific breakdown. The productivity of labor collapsed, and the products were of an appallingly low quality. Enemies saw, or chose to see, in such a situation a sign of the rottenness of the Soviet regime. In reality, however, it was but the inevitable stage of the destruction of the old economic forms and of the first unaided attempts at the creation of new ones.

In regard to family relations and forms of individual life in general, there must also be an inevitable period of disintegration of things as they were, of the traditions, inherited from the past, which had not passed under the control of thought. But in this domain of domestic life the period of criticism and destruction begins later, lasts very long, and assumes morbid and painful forms, which, however, are complex and not always perceptible to superficial observation. These progressive landmarks of critical change in state conditions, in economics and life in general, ought to be very clearly defined to prevent our getting alarmed by the phenomena we observed. We must learn to judge them in their right light, to understand their proper place in the development of the working class, and consciously to direct the new conditions towards socialist forms of life.

The warning is a necessary one, as we already hear voices expressing alarm. At the conference of the Moscow party propagandists some comrades spoke with great and natural anxiety of the ease with which old family ties are broken for the sake of new ones as fleeting as the old. The victims in all cases are the mother and children. On the other hand, who in our midst has not heard in private conversations complaints, not to say lamentations, about the "collapse" or morality among Soviet youth, in particular among Young Communists? Not everything in these complaints is exaggeration—there is also truth in them. We certainly must and will fight the dark sides of this truth—this being a fight for higher culture and the ascent of human personality. But in order to begin our work, to tackle the ABC of the problem without reactionary moralizing or sentimental downheartedness, we must first make sure of the facts and begin to see clearly what is actually happening.

Gigantic events, as we said above, have descended on the family in its old shape, the war and the revolution. And following them came creeping slowly the underground mole—critical thought, the conscious study and evaluation of family relations and the forms of life. It was the mechanical force of great events combined with the critical force of the awakened mind that generated the destructive period in family relations that we are witnessing now. The Russian worker must now, after the conquest of power, make his first conscious steps towards culture in many departments of his life. Under the impulse of great collisions, his personality shakes off for the first time all traditional forms of life, all domestic habits, church practices and relationships.

No wonder that, in the beginning, the protest of the individual, his revolt against the traditional past, is assuming anarchic, or to put it more crudely, dissolute forms. We have witnessed it in politics, in military affairs, in economics; here anarchic individualism took on every form of extremism, partisanship, public-meeting rhetoric. And no wonder also that this process reacts in the most intimate and hence most painful way on family relationships. There the awakened personality, wanting to re-organize in a new way, removed from the old beaten tracks, resorts to "dissipation," "wickedness," and all the sins denounced in the Moscow conference.

The husband, torn away from his usual surroundings by mobilization, changed into a revolutionary citizen at the civic front. A momentous change. His outlook is wider, his spiritual aspirations higher and of a more complicated order. He is a different man. And then he returns to find everything there practically unchanged. The old harmony and under-standing with the people at home in family relationship is gone. No new understanding arises. The mutual wondering changes into mutual dis-content, then into ill will. The family is broken up.

The husband is a communist. He lives an active life, is engaged in social work, his mind grows, his personal life is absorbed by his work. But his wife is also a communist. She wants to join in social work, attend public meetings, work in the soviet or the union. Home life becomes practically nonexistent before they are aware of it, or the missing of home atmosphere results in continual collisions. Husband and wife disagree. The family is broken up.

The husband is a communist, the wife is nonparty. The husband is absorbed by his work; the wife, as before, only looks after her home. Relations are "peaceful," based, in fact, on customary estrangement. But the husband's committee—the communist "cell"—decrees that he should take away the icons hanging in his house. He is quite willing to obey, finding it but natural. For his wife it is a catastrophe. Just such a small occurrence exposes the abyss that separates the minds of husband and wife. Relations are spoiled. The family is broken up.

An old family. Ten to fifteen years of common life. The husband is a good worker, devoted to his family; the wife lives also for her home, giving it all her energy. But just by chance she comes in touch with a communist women's organization. A new world opens before her eyes. Her energy finds a new and wider object. The family is neglected. The husband is irritated. The wife is hurt in her newly awakened civic consciousness. The family is broken up.

Examples of such domestic tragedies, all leading to one end—the breaking up of the family—could be multiplied endlessly. We have indicated the most typical cases. In all our examples the tragedy is due to a collision between communist and nonparty elements. But the breaking up of the family, that is to say, of the old-type family, is not confined to just the top of the class as the one most exposed to the influence of new conditions. The disintegrating movement in family relationships penetrates deeper. The communist vanguard merely passes sooner and more violently through what is inevitable for the class as a whole. The censorious attitude towards old conditions, the new claims upon the family, extend far beyond the border line between the communist and the working class as a whole.

The institution of civil marriage was already a heavy blow to the traditional consecrated family which lived a great deal for appearances. The less personal attachment there was in the old marriage ties, the greater was the binding power of the external forces, social traditions, and more particularly religious rites. The blow to the power of the church was also a blow to the family. Rites, deprived of binding significance and of state recognition, still remain in use through inertia, serving as one of the props to the tottering family. But when there is no inner bond within the family, when nothing but inertia keeps the family itself from complete collapse, then every push from outside is likely to shatter it to pieces, while, at the same time, it is a blow at the adherence to church rites. And pushes from the outside are infinitely more likely to come now than ever before. That is the reason why the family totters and fails to recover and then tumbles again. Life sits in judgment on its conditions and does it by the cruel and painful condemnation of the family. History fells the old wood—and the chips fly in the wind.

But is life evolving any elements of a new type of family? Undoubtedly. We must only conceive clearly the nature of these elements and the process of their formation. As in other cases, we must separate the physical conditions from the psychological, the general from the individual. Psychologically the evolution of the new family, of new human relationships in general, for us means the advancement in culture of the working class, the development of the individual, a raising of the standard of his requirements and inner discipline. From this aspect, the revolution in itself has meant, of course, a big step forward, and the worst phenomena of the disintegrating family signify merely an expression, painful in form, of

81

the awakening of the class and of the individual within the class. All our work relating to culture, the work we are doing and the work we ought to be doing, becomes, from this viewpoint, a preparation for new relationships and a new family. Without a raising of the standard of the culture of the individual working man and woman, there cannot be a new, higher type of family, for in this domain we can only, of course, speak of inner discipline and not of external compulsion. The force then of the inner discipline of the individual in the family is conditioned by the tenor of the inner life, the scope and value of the ties that unite husband and wife.

The physical preparations for the conditions of the new life and the new family, again, cannot fundamentally be separated from the general work of socialist construction. The workers' state must become wealthier in order that it may be possible seriously to tackle the public education of children and the releasing of the family from the burden of the kitchen and the laundry. Socialization of family housekeeping and public education of children are unthinkable without a marked improvement in our economics as a whole. We need more socialist economic forms. Only under such conditions can we free the family from the functions and cares that now oppress and disintegrate it. Washing must be done by a public laundry, catering by a public restaurant, sewing by a public workshop. Children must be educated by good public teachers who have a real vocation for the work. Then the bond between husband and wife would be freed from everything external and accidental, and the one would cease to absorb the life of the other. Genuine equality would at last be established. The bond will depend on mutual attachment. And on that account particularly, it will acquire inner stability, not the same, of course, for everyone, but compulsory for no one.

Thus, the way to the new family is twofold: *(a)* the raising of the standard of culture and education of the working class and the individuals composing the class; *(b)* an improvement in the material conditions of the class organized by the state. The two processes are intimately connected with one another.

The above statements do not, of course, imply that at a given moment in material betterment the family of the future will instantly step into its rights. No. A certain advance towards the new family is possible even now. It is true that the state cannot as yet undertake either the education of children or the establishment of public kitchens that would be an improvement on the family kitchen, or the establishment of public laundries where the clothes would not be torn or stolen. But this does not mean that the more enterprising and progressive families cannot group themselves even now into collective housekeeping units. Experiments of this kind must, of course, be made carefully; the technical equipment of the collective unit must answer to the interests and requirements of the group itself, and should give manifest advantages to every one of its members, even though they be modest at first.

"This task," Comrade Semashko recently wrote of the necessity of reconstructing our family life,

> is best performed practically; decrees and moralizing alone will have little effect. But an example, an illustration of a new form, will do more than a thousand excellent pamphlets. This practical propaganda is best conducted on the method surgeons in their practice call transplantation. When a big surface is bare of skin either as the result of wound or burn, and there is no hope that the skin will grow sufficiently to cover it, pieces of skin are cut off from healthy places of the body and attached in islets on the bare surface; these islets adhere and grow until the whole surface is covered with skin.
>
> The same thing happens in practical propaganda. When one factory or works adopts communist forms, other factories will follow. [N. Semashko, "The Dead Holds on to the Living," *Izvestiya,* no. 81, April 14, 1923]

The experience of such collective family housekeeping units representing the first, still very incomplete approximations to a communist way of life, should be carefully studied and given attentive thought. The combination of private initiative with support by the state power—above all, by the local soviets and economic bodies—should have priority. The building of new houses—and, after all, we are going to build houses!—must be regulated by the requirements of the family group communities. The first apparent and indisputable success in this direction, however slight and limited in extent, will inevitably arouse a desire in more widespread groups to organize their life on similar lines. For a thought-out scheme, initiated from above, the time is not yet ripe, either from the point of view of the material resources of the state or from that of the preparation of the proletariat itself. We can escape the deadlock at present only by the creation of model communities. The ground beneath our feet must be strengthened step by step; there must be no rushing too far ahead or lapsing into bureaucratic fanciful experiments. At a given moment, the state will be able, with the help of local soviets, cooperative units, and so on, to socialize the work done, to widen and deepen it. In this way the human family, in the words of Engels, will "jump from the realm of necessity to the realm of freedom."

MAKE WAY FOR THE WINGED EROS
A. Kollontai

You ask me, my young comrade, what place does proletarian ideology give to love? It disturbs you that working class youth "is now more occupied with love and other such questions" than with the large tasks which are before the working people's republic. If that is the case (and from afar it is difficult for me to judge this), then let us look for the explanation of this phenomenon, and then it will be easier to find an answer to the first question: what place does love occupy in the ideology of the working class?

There is no doubt that Soviet Russia has entered a new phase of the civil war. The revolutionary front has moved into the sphere of struggle between two ideologies, two cultures: bourgeois and proletarian. All the more obvious is the incompatibility of these two ideologies, and all the sharper is the opposition of these two fundamentally different cultures.

Together with a victory of communist principles and ideals in the area of politics and economics, there inevitably must be a revolution in world views, in feelings, in the spirit of laboring mankind. New relations to life, to society, to work, to art, to "the rules of life" (that is, to morality) are already being observed. Relations between the sexes are a component part of the rules of life. Revolution on the spiritual front is accomplishing a great advance in the thinking of mankind, prompted by the five year existence of the labor republic.

But the fiercer the struggle of two ideologies, the greater the number of spheres it embraces, the more inevitable will be the collision of mankind with more and more new "mysteries of life," problems for which a satisfactory answer can only be given by the ideology of the working class. Related to these problems is the question already raised by you, that of the relations between the sexes—a mystery as old as human society itself. At various stages of its historical development, mankind has approached this differently. The "enigma" remains, the clues change. These clues depend on the epoch, on the class, on "the spirit of the times" (on culture).

Not long ago, in the years of acute civil war and struggle with devastation, this enigma was of little concern to anyone in Russia. Other feelings, other more real passions and emotions possessed humanity.

One of Kollontai's "Letters to the Toiling Youth," from the journal *Molodaia Gvardiia,* No. 3, 1923, pp. 111-24. See the discussion by Kendall Bailes, "Alexandra Kollontai et la Nouvelle Morale," *Cahiers du monde russe et soviétique,* VI:4 (Oct.-Dec. 1965), pp. 472-96.

Before the threatening face of the great insurgent-rebel, gentle-winged eros ("the god of love") had to disappear timidly from the surface of life. There was no time for love's "joys and anguishes," no surplus of emotional energy. Such is the law of the preservation of the social-emotional energy of mankind. This energy, in sum, always directs itself toward the major, most immediate goal of the historical moment. The master of the situation for a time was the uncomplicated, natural call of nature—the biological instinct of reproduction, the attraction of two sexual individuals. Man and woman easily, much easier than formerly, much more simply than formerly, came together and separated. They came together without painful, heartfelt emotions and separated without tears and pain.

> "Love was without joy.
> Separation will have no sorrow."

Prostitution, of course, disappeared, and similarly there increased a free contact of the sexes (without mutual obligations), whose driving force was the bare instinct of reproduction (unadorned by feelings of love). This fact frightened some people. But in those years the relations between the sexes could really not have been organized differently. Either marriage would continue to be held in the firm, tested, feeling of community, of friendship of many years duration, strengthened still further by the seriousness of the moment, or the marriage contact would arise in passing, in the midst of a pursuit of the cause, for the satisfaction of purely biological need, from which both sides hurried to untie themselves, so that it would not interfere with the fundamental, the major thing: the work for the revolution.

The naked instinct of reproduction is easily aroused and it quickly passes, since it is just mutual sexual attraction without emotional ties. "Unwinged Eros" absorbs emotional energies less than does the "winged Eros," love, which is woven from the finest net of all possible heartfelt-spiritual emotions. Unwinged Eros does not cause sleepless nights, does not soften the will, does not confuse cold reasoning of the mind. For the class of fighters at a moment when the bell of revolution was being incessantly rung over working mankind, it was not permissible to fall under the power of the winged Eros. In those days it was inexpedient to dissipate the emotional energies of members of the fighting collective on secondary emotional experiences not directly serving the revolution.

Now, when the revolution in Russia has gained the upper hand and has been strengthened, when the atmosphere of revolutionary combat has ceased absorbing man entirely and without respite, gentle-winged Eros, temporarily slighted on the thornbush of neglect, once again is beginning to claim its rights. It frowns on the bold unwinged Eros—the instinct of reproduction unadorned by the charms of love. Unwinged Eros ceases to

85

satisfy emotional demands. Surplus spiritual energy accumulates, which contemporary people, even representatives of the working class, still cannot apply to the spiritual life of the collective. This surplus energy of the soul looks for application in love experiences. The many-stringed lyre of the variegated god of love drowns out the single-stringed voice of the unwinged Eros... Man and woman now do not simply "come together," do not merely strike up a transitory tie for quenching sex instincts, as was most often done during the years of the revolution, but are beginning again to experience "romances," and are becoming aware of all the torments of love, all the inspiration of the happiness of mutual love.

What is this? Reaction? The symptom of a commencing decline in revolutionary creativity? Nothing of the kind. It is time to get away from the hypocrisy of bourgeois thinking. It is time to admit openly that love is not only a powerful factor of nature, a biological force, but also a social factor. Love in its essence is a profoundly social emotion. In all the stages of human development, love in its various forms and types has been a necessary component part in the spiritual culture of society. Even the bourgeoisie, while declaring love "a private matter," really managed to direct love, by moral norms, along a course which served its class interests.

The ideology of the working class should take into account, to an even greater degree, the significance of love emotions as factors which might be directed (as any other psycho-social phenomenon) for the benefit of the collective. That love is not at all a "private" phenomenon, a matter only of two loving "hearts," and that in love there is a connecting principle valuable to the collective, is clear from the fact that at all stages of its historical development, mankind has established norms, defining under what conditions and when love is "legal" (that is, answers the interests of a given collective), and when it is "sinful," criminal (that is, contrary to the aims of a given society)....

The new labor communist society is being built on the principle of comradeship, of solidarity. But what is solidarity? It is not only the awareness of a community of interests, but further a sincere emotional tie established among members of the working collective. A social structure built on solidarity and cooperation, however, demands that the given society possess a highly developed "potential of love," that is a capacity of people to experience mutual sympathy. Without the presence of these sensations, there cannot be solidarity. That is why proletarian ideology strives to nurture and strengthen in each member of the working class the feeling of sympathy for the sufferings and needs of one's class compatriots, a sensitive understanding of the needs of the other, a profound, heartfelt consciousness of his or her tie with the other members of the collective. But all these sympathetic feelings—sensitivity, compassion, responsiveness— flow from one common source, the capacity to love; to love not in the narrow sexual, but rather in the broad meaning of the word.

Love is a heartfelt emotion of a binding and consequently an organizing character. The bourgeoisie marvelously understood and took into account the fact that love is a great connecting force. Therefore, striving to solidify the family, bourgeois ideology turned "conjugal love" into a moral virtue. To be a "good family man" in the eyes of the bourgeoisie was a great and valued quality.

The proletariat cannot help but consider the psycho-social role which the feeling of love in the broad sense of the word and in the sphere of relations between the sexes, can and must play, not in the area of solidifying family-marital relations, but in the sphere of the development of collectivist solidarity.

What is the ideal of love of the working class? What feelings, what experiences will proletarian ideology build into the foundation of the relations between the sexes?

Each epoch has its own ideal of love; each class strives in its own interests to insert its own content into the moral conception of love. Each level of culture, bearing the ever richer spiritual and emotional experiences of mankind, paints the gentle tones of the wings of Eros with its own special color. The content making up the concept of love altered with successive levels of development of the economy and social life. The shades of emotions which were component parts of the feeling of love either were strengthened, or conversely, died off.

From an uncomplicated biological instinct—the striving for re-production, inherent in all forms of animals from the highest to the lowest, divided into representatives of the opposite sexes—love has, with the passage of its thousands of years of existence, accumulated newer and newer spiritual-emotional experiences.* From a biological phenomenon, love became a psycho-social factor.

Under the effect of economic and social forces, the biological instinct of reproduction, which determined relations between the sexes at early stages in the development of mankind, underwent a regeneration in two diametrically opposed directions. On one hand, the healthy sex instinct, the attraction of the two sexes for the aim of reproduction, turned into unhealthy lust under the pressure of abnormal socio-economic relations, particularly under the hegemony of capitalism. The sex act became a self-sustaining aim, a way of achieving one more "extra pleasure," in lust, aggravated by excesses, perversions and harmful urging of the flesh. A man then does not come together with a woman because a healthy sexual attraction draws him to the given woman, but in fact the reverse; the man looks for a woman without feeling any sexual need, in order that, thanks to

---

* Another natural-biological source of love is the maternal instinct, concern for offspring on the part of the woman. Both instincts intermingling with one another, created a natural base for the development, with the help of social community, of complex feelings of love. [A.K.].

87

the nearness of this woman, sexual attraction will be aroused and in this way he will be given pleasure by the very fact of the sex act. Prostitution is built on this. If nearness to the woman does not evoke the expected arousal, then people satiated by sexual excesses have recourse to perversions of every type.

This is a digression of the biological instinct, underlying intersexual attraction, in the direction of unhealthy lust, which takes instinct away from its origin.

On the other hand, the bodily attraction of the two sexes during the thousands of years of mankind's social life and the changing of cultures has brought forth whole strata of spiritual-emotional feelings. Love in its present day form is a very complex condition of the soul, which has long since been divorced from its primary source of the biological instinct of reproduction and is not infrequently in sharp contradiction to it. Love is a conglomerate, a complex combination of friendship, passion, maternal affection, amorousness, harmony of the spirit, pity, admiration, habit and many other shades of feelings and emotions. It is all the more difficult with such a complexity of the shades of love itself to establish a direct connection between the voice of nature, "unwinged Eros" (the bodily attraction of sex) and "winged Eros" (attraction of the body intermeshed with spiritual-heartfelt emotion). Love-friendship, in which there is not an atom of physical attraction, spiritual love for a cause, for an idea, impersonal love for the collective—all these are phenomena which bear witness to how divorced the feeling of love has become from its biological base, and the extent to which it has become "spiritualized."

But this is not all. There often arises among the various manifestations of the feeling of love a glaring contradiction, and a struggle begins. Love for the "loved object" (not simply for the object, but precisely for the "loved") finds no room for love of the chosen one of the heart.* Love for the collective struggles with the feeling of love for husband, wife, children. Love-friendship simultaneously contradicts love-passion. In one instance of love, spiritual harmony predominates, in another, love is based on "harmony of the body."

Love became many-sided and many-chorded. That which the present day person experiences in the sphere of love emotions (feelings), which cultural phases over thousands of years have nourished and emphasized as various nuances of love, absolutely does not find expression in the too general and therefore inexact word—love.**

* This is not a rare conflict, especially among women in the contemporary transitional period. [A.K.]

** New mankind will have to find new words to express those multiformed nuances of emotions, since those used now only in coarse form render such states as love, passion, amorousness, friendship. All the numerous half-tones, the entire complex pattern of the soul, composed of the meshing of these various feelings, are absolutely not conveyed by these stiff concepts and obscure definitions. [A.K.]

The many-sidedness of love, under the hegemony of bourgeois ideology and bourgeois-capitalist life, created a series of severe and insoluble emotional dramas. Already from the end of the nineteenth century, the many-sidedness of love was made a favorite theme of writer-psychologists. "Love for two" even "love for three" occupied and confused thoughtful representatives of bourgeois culture with its mysteriousness. Already in the 1860s our Russian thinker-publicist A. Herzen (Iskander) tried to reveal this complexity of the soul, this bifurcation of feeling in his novel *Who Is Guilty?* And Chernyshevsky approached the resolution of this problem in his social narrative *What Is To Be Done?* The greatest writers of Scandinavia—(Gamsun, Ibsen, Bjernsen, Geierstam) have also touched on this duality of feeling, this splintering of love. The French fiction writers of the last century returned to it more than once; Roman Rolland, who is close to communism in spirit, writes about it, and Maeterlinck, who is far from us. Such poetic geniuses as Goethe and Byron, such bold pioneers in the area of the inter-relations of the sexes as Georges Sand, tried in living practice to resolve this complex problem, this "mystery of love." Herzen, the author of *Who Is Guilty?* as well as many other great thinkers, poets and social activists, knew it in his own experience. And now the shoulders of many "not so great" people are burdened by the weight of "this mystery of the duality of love," and these people are searching in vain for the key to its resolution within the boundaries of bourgeois thought. But meanwhile, the key is in the hands of the proletariat. Only the ideology and life of the new laboring humanity can unravel this complex problem of emotion.

We are here speaking of the duality of love, of the complexities of "winged Eros," but one must not confuse such duality with sexual relations without Eros, between one man and many women or one woman and many men. Polygamy, in which emotion plays no part, can entail unpleasant harmful consequences (premature exhaustion of the organism, an increase in chances for venereal diseases in contemporary conditions, etc.), but such ties, no matter how intricate they might be, do not create "emotional dramas." The "drama," the conflicts, begin when there is love in its many-faceted nuances and manifestations. The woman loves one man "with the heights of her soul," with her thoughts, strivings, and wishes, in harmony with his. Another strongly attracts her by the force of physical affinity. In one woman, a man tests the feeling of thoughtful affection, of concerned pity, in another he finds support and understanding for the best strivings of his "ego." To which of the two must he devote the fullness of Eros? And why must he tear and maim his soul, if only the presence of both one and the other spiritual tie gives him a completeness of being?

Under the bourgeois system, such a bifurcation of spirit and emotion carries with it inevitable sufferings. Over thousands of years, the culture based on the institution of property nourished in people the conviction that the feeling of love also must have the principle of property as its base. Bourgeois ideology taught, rammed into the heads of people, that love, especially when reciprocal, allows for the mastery of the heart of the loved person entirely and indivisibly. Such an ideal, such an exclusiveness of love, flowed naturally from the established form of conjugal pair marriage and from the bourgeois ideal of the "all-embracing love" of two spouses. But can such an ideal answer the interests of the working class? Is it not, on the contrary, important and desirable from the point of view of proletarian ideology, that the feelings of people become richer, many-chorded? Is not the many-chorded quality of the spirit and many-sidedness of the soul that very factor which facilitates the growth and nourishment of a complex, intermeshed net of spiritual-emotional ties, by which the social-labor collective is bound? The more these threads are extended from spirit to spirit, from heart to heart, from mind to mind, then the more firmly will be inculcated the spirit of solidarity and the more easily the ideal of the working class, association and unity, will be realized.

Exclusiveness of love, like "all-embracing" love, cannot be the ideal of love conditioning the relations between the sexes from the point of view of proletarian ideology. On the contrary, the proletariat, taking into account the many-sidedness and many-chorded nature of "winged Eros," is not thrown into indescribable horror and moral indignation by this discovery, like the hypocritical morality of the bourgeoisie. On the contrary, the proletariat rushes to direct this phenomenon (the result of complex social causes) into a course which will answer its class aims in the moment of struggle and in the moment of the construction of a communist society.

The many-sidedness of love is not in and of itself contrary to the interest of the proletariat. On the contrary, it makes for the triumph of that ideal of love in mutual relations between the sexes which is already being formed and crystallized in the midst of the working class, namely, of love-comradeship.

Ancestral mankind imagined love to be in the form of familial attachment (love of sisters and brothers, love for parents). Ancient pagan culture put love-friendship higher than all the rest. The feudal world raised as an ideal the "spiritual" love of the knight, a love separate from marriage and not connected with satisfying lust. The ideal of love in bourgeois morality was the love of a lawfully married, conjugal pair.

The ideal of love of the working class, flowing from working cooperation and spiritual-volitional solidarity of members of the working class, men and women, naturally differs in form and content, from the conception of love in other cultural epochs. But what is "love-comradeship"? Does it mean that the severe ideology of the working class, forged in the fighting atmosphere of struggle for a workers' dictatorship, is planning to expunge ruthlessly from the mutual community of the sexes that gentle-winged, fragile Eros? Nothing of the kind. The ideology of the working class is not only not destroying "winged Eros," but is clearing the way toward a recognition of the value of love as a psycho-social force.

The hypocritical morality of bourgeois culture ruthlessly pulled the feathers from the variegated, multi-colored wings of Eros, obligating Eros to visit only the "legally-married pair." Outside of the conjugal relationship, bourgeois ideology granted a place only to a plucked unwinged Eros, to a shortlived sexual attraction of the sexes, in the form of purchased (prostitution) or stolen caresses (adultery-fornication).

On the contrary, the morality of the working class, in so far as it has crystallized, resolutely discards the superficial form which the loving community of the sexes takes. For the purposes of the working class, it makes absolutely no difference whether love takes the form of a long-term and documented union or is expressed in the form of a transitory tie. The ideology of the working class puts no formal boundaries on love. But in return the ideology of the working class is already thoughtfully regarding the content of love, the nuances of feelings and emotions binding the two sexes. And in that sense the ideology of the working class will much more strictly and ruthlessly persecute "unwinged Eros" (carnality, the one-sided satisfaction of lust through prostitution, the conversion of the "sex act" into a self-satisfying aim taken from the category of "easy pleasures"), than did bourgeois morality. "Unwinged Eros" contradicts the interests of the working class. First it inevitably carries with it excesses, and consequently bodily dissipation, which lowers the supply of laboring energy in humankind. Secondly, it impoverishes the spirit, blocking the development and strengthening of spiritual ties and sympathetic emotions. Thirdly, it usually is based on an inequality of rights in the mutual relations of the sexes, on a dependence of the woman on the man, on male egocentrism or inconsiderateness, which undoubtedly undermines the development of a feeling of association. The presence of "winged Eros" has an entirely opposite effect.

It stands to reason that at the basis of "winged Eros" there lies the attraction of one sex to the other which exists for "unwinged Eros," with the difference being that in the person experiencing love for another person, there are aroused and there appear simultaneously those qualities of the spirit which are necessary for builders of the new culture: directness, sympathy, a wish to help others. Bourgeois ideology demanded that these qualities of the human being be manifested only toward the chosen of the heart, to one single person. Proletarian ideology values chiefly that these given qualities be aroused and nurtured in humanity and be manifested not only in community with the one chosen of the heart, but in community with all the members of the collective.

The proletariat also does not care which shades and facets predominate in "winged Eros," the affectionate tones of amorousness, the hot colors of passion or a community and harmony of the soul. Only one thing is important, that those warm spiritual elements which serve to develop and strengthen the feeling of association accompany all these shades of love.

Recognition of mutual rights and the ability to consider the personality of the other, even in love, a firm mutual support, direct participation and attentive responsiveness to another's needs, with a community of interests and strivings—such is the ideal of love-association which is being forged by proletarian ideology, in place of the moribund ideal of "all-consuming" and "all-exclusive" conjugal love of bourgeois culture.

Love-comradeship is an ideal which the proletariat needs in the responsible and difficult period of the struggle for dictatorship and the consolidation of dictatorship. But there is no doubt that in the accomplished Communist society, love, "winged Eros," will be transformed into something completely unfamiliar to us. By that time "sympathetic ties" among all members of the new society will grow and strengthen, "love potentiality" will rise, and love-solidarity will be the same driving force which competition and self-love were in the bourgeois system. Collectivism of the soul and will shall conquer individualistic self-sufficiency. "The coldness of spiritual isolation," from which people under bourgeois culture often searched for salvation in love and marriage, will disappear. Multiformed threads will grow, intertwining people with sincere and spiritual cohesion. People's feelings will become collective ones, and inequality between the sexes, as well as the dependence of woman on man, will disappear without a trace, lost in the memory of past centuries.

In this new society, communist in soul and emotions, against a background of joyful unity and comradely community of all members of the working, creative collective, Eros will occupy an honored place, as an emotion magnifying human happiness. What will this new reformed Eros be? The boldest fantasy is unable to capture its form. But one thing is clear. The more firmly bound the new humanity by strong chains of solidarity, the higher will be its spiritual and emotional ties in all spheres of life, creativity, and community, and the less place there will remain for love in the contemporary meaning of the word. Contemporary love is always at fault in that it preoccupies the thoughts and feelings of "loving hearts," but at the same time isolates and separates the loving pair from the collective. Such a separation of the "loving couple" and moral isolation from the collective, in which the interests, aims, and strivings of all the members are interwoven in a thick net, will become not only superfluous, but psychologically unrealizable. In this new world, the recognized, normal and desirable form of communion of the sexes probably will rest on a healthy, free, natural attraction (without perversions and excesses), on a "transformed Eros."

But until then we find ourselves at the crossroads of two cultures. And in this transitional period, accompanied by the fiery combat of two worlds

92

on all fronts, including the ideological front, the proletariat is interested in that which by all measures will facilitate the most rapid accumulation of reserves of "sympathetic feelings." In this period the moral ideal conditioning the communion of the sexes is not the naked instinct of sex, but rather the many-sided loving-friendly emotions of both man and woman. These emotions, to answer the newly-formed demands of the new proletarian morality, must base themselves on three fundamental principles:

(1) equality in mutual relations (without male egocentrism and slavish dissolution of her own personality in love by the woman.

(2) mutual recognition of the rights of the other, without pretentions of indivisibly possessing the heart and spirit of the other (a feeling of property cultivated by bourgeois culture).

(3) comradely sensitivity, an ability to heed and understand the work of the spirit of a close and beloved person (bourgeois culture demanded this sensitivity in love on the part of the woman).

But proclaiming the rights of "winged Eros" (of love), the ideology of the working class also subordinates the love of members of the laboring collective toward one another to a more powerful feeling—love and duty to the collective. However great the love connecting two sexes, however many tender and spiritual ties bind them together, such bonds with the entire collective must be still stronger and more numerous and more organic. Bourgeois morality demanded everything for the beloved person. The morality of the proletariat prescribes—everything for the collective.

But I hear your question. Let it be so. Let loving communion, on the soil of a strengthened spirit of comradeship, become the ideal of the working class. But does not this ideal, this "moral criterion" of love again impose a heavy hand on romantic feelings? What if it crumples, cripples the gentle wings of "easily frightened Eros"? Having freed love from the fetters of bourgeois morality, are we not binding it with new chains?

Yes, you are right. The ideology of the proletariat, discarding bourgeois "morality" in the spheres of romantic-marital relations, nevertheless inevitably works out its own class morality, its own new rules of communion between the sexes, which more closely meet the demands of the working class, nurture the feelings of the members of the class in a given direction, and by so doing put certain chains on emotion. Insofar as the matter concerns love, cultivated by bourgeois culture, the proletariat must undoubtedly pluck many feathers from the wings of the Eros of bourgeois origin. But to complain that the laboring class is putting its stamp on the relations between the sexes in order to bring the emotion love into alignment with its tasks, means not to have the ability to look into the future. It is clear that in place of the former feathers in the wings of Eros, the ideology of the ascending class will succeed in cultivating new feathers of an heretofore unseen beauty, strength and brightness. Do not forget that love inevitably changes form and transforms itself together with change in the cultural-economic base of humanity.

If in loving relations blind, demanding, all-embracing passion weakens; if the feeling of possession and the egoistical desire to forever fasten the beloved around oneself is washed away; if the self-satiety of the man and criminal renunciation of her own "I" on the part of the woman disappears: then there will develop other valued aspects of love. Respect for the personality of the other and the ability to consider others' rights will grow stronger. A mutual sincere sympathy will develop. The striving to express love not only in kisses and embraces, but in togetherness of action, in unity of will, in joint creation, will grow.

The task of proletarian ideology is not to banish Eros from the social community, but only to rearm its quiver with the arrows of a new structure, to nurture the feeling of love between the sexes in the spirit of the greatest force, comradely solidarity.

THE SEX LIFE OF MAN
L. A. and L. M. Vasilevsky

It has long been known that a healthy spirit can only be housed in a healthy body, and the new world can be created only by a thoroughly healthy, strong and cheerful generation. And only a generation which orders its sexual life on a rational and healthy basis can be healthy. The condition of the sexual system of man is decidedly reflected in its most profound form in all aspects of our existence, not only in physical health, but in our moods, our capacity for work, our relations with people, our social activity, our creativity.

Meanwhile, our entire sexual life, the mutual relations between the sexes, is extraordinarily deformed. Our marriage, which still to a significant degree is determined by the economic dependence of the woman, is abnormal. The abundance of girls, remaining for material reasons outside of the sexual union and its pleasures, is abnormal. The gloomy phenomenon of the sale by women of their bodies, the impropriety of sexual relations, their impersonality, unworthy of humans, is disgraceful. The greatest harm to the physical and spiritual well-being of society is the unheard of spread of venereal disease, the terrible rise in abortions and the overall rejection of motherhood. The birth of a child for an enormous number of mothers and for the conjugal pair in general is turning from a blessing and source of happiness into a source of hard deprivation, almost a curse. Finally, there is the appalling and abnormal attitude of people to questions of sex. Either they hypocritically are too ashamed to speak about it, as if in this cradle of mankind there is something dirty and shameful, or they speak with a foul grin, with a wink and cynicism.

Even now a double sexual standard of morality for men and for women still prevails. Men are allowed—not only by law, but by custom, by generally recognized habits—much that would be considered impermissible for women, shameful and immoral, it being the case that such a "male" evaluation is maintained not only by men, but to a significant degree by women. Maintained in their centuries old, stagnant power are vile proverbs such as "no hearsay can soil a good guy's reputation," that a man in the sexual sense must "sow his wild oats," but for a woman nothing

From A.M. Kalmanson, ed., *Polovoi vopros*, Moscow-Leningrad, 1924, pp. 39-43.
L.A. and L.M. Vasilevsky were both physicians and writers on sex issues.

is winked at, and they condemn her for a petty, chance sin in the area of sex.

It does not follow that the above should be understood in the sense that it would be a normal situation for women to become equal with men in sexual dissoluteness and cynicism. On the contrary, the ideal would be a restrained and worthy sexual life for both sexes. And once again this does not mean that mankind must turn away from sexual pleasures. Love, equal with hunger, is the greatest motive force of life, and existence, deprived of the pleasures of mutual love, does not know the fullness of life's sensations and does not give satisfaction and happiness. In personal love there flowers all that is elevated and bright in our natures and the hiding places where the noblest and most valued sides of our "I" are lodged, are revealed.

As regards the creation of a new generation and the desire to continue one's existence in children, with all the great importance of this element of love, with all its enormous significance in the history of mankind, personal love, the direct sexual feeling, is not limited to this and is not reduced to this. One and the other are lawful and fine; both to continue oneself, to express oneself in a child, and simply to take pleasure in the mutual nearness, to tie one's life with the life of a close person. But it is necessary that bodily closeness go hand-in-hand with spiritual closeness, or at least, with mutual sympathy, with some commonality of interests.

To introduce beauty and humanity into the sexual relations of people is one of the most difficult tasks which, among others, stand before the revolution. For this, quite apart from everything else, two conditions are indispensable. First we must change at its root the view of the masses toward the themes touched on here. Instead of vulgar winking or hypocritical silence, a serious and honest view of people must be attained in the entire area of sexual relations, one corresponding to the importance of the task. Second, we must arm youth from their early years with an intelligible familiarity with problems of sex, with the mysteries of birth, with correct and sensible opinions in this regard. The second condition must obviously precede the first. Our sexual life can be made healthy only when our younger generation is raised with new, more worthy views on the role and desirable character of sexual life. From this the importance of a sensibly organized and expeditiously executed sex education is clear.

Much unhappiness in our sexual life could be avoided if our children received in this regard a better preparation for what they could expect in their future sex lives. At the present time this matter finds itself in truly awful conditions. The young boy or girl first becomes familiar with sex from murky and filthy sources, which frequently make their idea of love filthy for all their lives, which inculcate in them a twisted and often savage notion of it. Their source of information is often either the cynicism and foul language of their elders or the boastful and no less filthy communication of more mature and "experienced" friends, or the foul street pamphlet, film, etc. As a result the child enters life with a disfigured, twisted understanding, that everything touched on here is "shameful" and indecent to talk about, and that one can only make various conjectures about it.

The situation of female youth is especially sad. With doubled diligence, they take her away from "delicate" themes, in order to preserve her "chastity," so that even marrying and preparing herself to become a mother, she still imagines the essence of sexual relations dimly, connecting it with danger, duty and fear. Among workers, the intimate closeness of all members of the family, the habitation density, the necessity to enter life too early (earlier industrial and other kinds of labor), usually in the years of childhood, acquaint the youth with this side of life, but here familiarity is achieved at great cost, and it is difficult to evaluate the moral harm which is inflicted on young consciousness by the coarseness and nakedness of this familiarity.

Parents, who could most easily and naturally take upon themselves such a preparation of the young for their future sexual lives, either intentionally divert children from questions on these themes, with the aim of not "corrupting" them, and even directly refuse to answer them, seeing here a dangerous signal of early profligacy, or they do not know how to approach this dangerous theme, how to talk about these things to the child, and at what age to undertake it. This theme is in fact very crucial and complex, and if undertaken clumsily or prematurely, it can, instead of bringing benefit, inflict serious harm on the child, and be a source of severe spiritual wound. As a result, sex education in the family is either completely lacking or is undertaken blindly and incorrectly. And as for sex education in school, that requires even greater care in approach. Familiarizing children in school presumes not only a rational division of children into groups by age, development, and personal characteristics, but also great sensitivity and tact on the part of the educator.

While referring to the school, it is impossible not to note the great prophylactic significance of co-education. With all the shortcomings of the labor school now being established in Soviet Russia, one of the most valuable merits is precisely this co-education from the earliest years. Thanks to this, children of both sexes begin very early to get used to the society of children of the opposite sex, and learn to see in them real comrades, close and understandable. By the time sexual feeling begins to arise, there is none of that estrangement and mysterious and disturbing secrecy among children of different sexes, which earlier had been fed school children due to that artificial disassociation. In this way that simplicity, that clarity of relations between the sexes is prepared, the lack of which is painfully told in early amorousness, in unhealthy instincts, in the extreme role of sexual feelings for the entire subsequent life.

Only the co-education of children will weaken the excessively great significance which love plays in the life of contemporary man. It is impermissible that in the new world the entire life of a person should depend on whether the creature beloved by him responds in kind or rejects him. It is unworthy of a truly free man to become a slave of his personal ,attachment, if the lack of success in love is capable of turning his life's plans upside down, of filling his soul with despair and of shoving his hand toward a vial of poison, or dooming him to wicked displays of jealousy and vengeance worthy of a savage.

The sphere of love must occupy an appropriate place in the life of man, a strong and significant place, but by no means the determining and predominant one.

THE LAW, LIFE, AND EVERYDAY LIVING
Letters to *Pravda* and *Izvestiya*

From the Judicial Chronicle: On the Rights of Parents To Bring up Their Children (*Izvestiya,* Oct. 29, 1925)

A quarrel sprang up between Mr. P. and his former wife, Ms. Ch. about the upbringing of their eight year old son.

The details of this unusual quarrel are as follows:

About two years ago, after living for twelve years with Ch., P. separated from her and married a young girl and stayed in Moscow to live, while Ch., for whom the separation was a severe blow, settled with the son at her parent's home in Kashir and devoted herself wholeheartedly to bringing him up. This went on for about a year and a half. In February of the current year, Mr. P. brought suit against his former wife in order to have his son turned over to him for educating. The People's Court of the First District of Kashir issued the following judgement:

"Turn over the son for educating to the father. The mother Ch. is instructed to come into Moscow to an apartment with which the said P. has to provide her. Said P. is also bound to pay Ms. Ch. one hundred rubles a month in support for her and the son, who must live in Moscow with his mother. In the case that Ch. refuses to go to Moscow, the law allows P. to take the son with him into Moscow, while not denying Ch. the right to see the son in Moscow."

At the instigation of a complaint by Ms. Ch., this decision was annulled by the Appeals Section of the Moscow Guberniya Court, and the matter was given for review to the Moscow Guberniya Court.

In the meantime, P., apparently on the basis of the People's Court decision, illegally took the son away to Moscow and settled him in at his place.

There is an interesting document in the case: the act of inquiry, carried out at the proposal of the Court (Moscow Guberniya) by the MONO inspector Comrade Nikolsky, which testifies that the son lived well at his mother's, surrounded by loving relatives, who did not leave him unattended for a moment. Comrade Nikolsky characterizes Ms. Ch.

From *Brak i Sem'ia,* Moscow-Leningrad, 1926.

as an unquestionably loving mother, wholly given over to the interest of the child. Now the child lives with his father. The young wife of the latter and the housekeeper treat him (the son) with the greatest attention.

Comrade Nikolsky came to the conclusion that "only persistent presence near the child of a person who loves him and is given over to his interests can repair and calm his excited nervous system."

Adding up the sum of this investigation, Comrade Nikolsky finds it difficult, nevertheless, to answer the question of why and on what basis the boy was deprived of maternal concern by the father and taken away from the mother . . . At the moment the position is the following, according to the investigative dossier: "The mother, correctly believing that the father is overly occupied with his new family life and with important government and scientific work, is constantly trying to reclaim her son. She is ready to move with the son wherever the father suggests, and to raise him under the father's direction, from whom she had not thought of nor desired separating the son."

The Moscow Guberniya Court decided that the decision about the removal of the child from his mother had been taken by the father without any other reason than his love for the boy. Moving on to the question of with whom the son should live, the Court found it expedient to lodge the son with the mother and requested that he definitely remain with Ms. Ch., conferring upon P. the right to see his son for unlimited time (i.e., no limitations imposed by Ch.), and likewise the right to supervise his son's upbringing.

The higher court, where the matter was brought by P.'s complaint, made a principled determination, putting the interests of the child in the first place, in the name of which parental rights themselves exist. "Thus, while deciding these kinds of questions the Court, leaving aside not only the child's will but the parents' feelings, has to choose as the child's conditions of life those which are most favorable to him. The appeal's reference to the fact that the Court did not take into account the child's desire to stay with his father is not sound, since the expression of the child's will, resulting in some legal relationship, can have juridical meaning only when the child reaches majority (with the exception of the contractual hiring of children from sixteen to eighteen years old, according to statute 157 of the Law Code on acts of citizens' conditions). The expression of his desires on the part of a child in minority does not mean that he clearly understands his interest, in accordance with which the Moscow Guberniya Court made an absolutely correct decision taking into account all the concrete circumstances of the case." In view of these considerations, the higher court decided that the complaint entered by P. should not be acted upon.

On Property Rights of the Spouse (Izvestiya, Dec. 6, 1925)

Does property acquired during marriage become the mutual property of the spouses?

This question has long since been answered affirmatively in Soviet society. At the last session of VTsIK, the corresponding Ninth Article of the Project of Law Code on Marriage and Family, categorically establishing the mutuality of all possessions acquired by spouses during marriage, found no objections even from among those peasant-deputies, who were afraid that some of the positions of the Narkomyustov [People's Commisariat of Justice, *ed.*] project would deprive them of their rights and would offer more property to women than to men in daily peasant life.

But acceptance of the Code project was postponed (because of the necessity for discussing it in local areas) and to this day what is in effect is the categorical, unambiguous Article 105 of the outmoded Code of Civil Laws: "Marriage does not create community of property between the spouses." Judges, it is true, considering claims for the division of spouses' property, try in every case to find a compromise solution, which would soften the severity of Article 105, but in the end, these attempts are shattered by the letter of the law.

Emelyanova lived with Zelentsov for a whole forty-seven years. In the duration of the long cohabitation, the spouses acquired some belongings, built a house, acquired cattle and so on. There were no children. It happened that, in old age, Zelentsov went with another woman and separated from the old woman. Emelyanova presented a demand for alimony to Zelentsov, since she was unable to work, and the court bound Zelentsov to pay her a living allowance of one third of his salary (fifty-three rubles a month). After some time Emelyanova presented Zelentsov with another demand about the division of property acquired during the period of their marriage.

The Moscow Guberniya Court found that the property in Zelentsov's possession and the house were indeed acquired by the mutual labor of both spouses. But, taking into account that Zelentsov at the moment had a wife and child and was paying the petitioner a monthly allowance, it found it "fair" to recognize her right to one quarter of the property, except the house and the domestic animals, and specified that Emelyanova should take out a couch, an armchair, a mirror closet, samovar, a carpet, etc., from the total property. In addition, the court gave the petitioner the lifetime right to possess one room in their "common" house.

Emelyanova was dissatisfied with this decision and appealed it to the higher court, petitioning that all the property (including the house and livestock), having been acquired by the mutual labor of the spouses during forty-seven years of living together, should be divided between her and her former husband equally.

The higher court found the decision of the Moscow Guberniya Court incorrect, primarily in that marriage does not create dual ownership by the spouses (Statute 105) and that the right of mutual possessions can be acquired only by the agreement of both sides.

Then the higher court indicated the following errors committed by the court of the first instance: the Guberniya Court did not find out whether the plaintiff possessed the belongings together with her husband, what her exact share was, and whether this share was enough to provide her with the minimum support, stipulated by Article 107 of the Code of Civil Laws. It was not discovered, either, why the plaintiff had to get a certain share of belongings in addition to lifetime alimony from her former husband.

"Elucidation of these questions," as the higher court states, "would affect the decision about allotting the plaintiff a certain share of belongings. If this share is sufficient for supporting the plaintiff, the defendant should be given the right to submit a petition to the People's Court for the reduction or even for complete cessation of monetary payments to the plaintiff, in view of the changed material situation of the parties."

Therefore, the higher court resolved to cancel the decision of the Moscow Guberniya Court and to bring the case to trial once again.

The future will show how the Moscow Guberniya Court will emerge from the situation thus created, and how it will make use of the instructions handed down to it from the higher court.

The Pestrikov Case (*Izvestiya,* Jan. 19, 1926)

In 1913 after twenty-four years of working life together the Pestrikovs acquired a small house in Irkutsk, which was registered in the name of I. G. Pestrikov. In February of the following year Pestrikov died and his wife, Zinaida Pestrikova, instituted proceedings before the Irkutsk Guberniya Court about the recognition of her right of personal ownership of one half of the house.

In view of the fact that the house was insured in 1924 for 17,921 rubles (the right of inheritance terminates at 10,000 rubles) the Irkutsk Guberniya Financial Department appeared as opponent, trying to demonstrate Pestrikova's lack of right to present the suit.

The court was filled with a whole series of witnesses, who had known the Pestrikov family for many years, who unanimously demonstrated that Pestrikova worked equally with her husband and that all property was obtained by them by their common means. One of the witnesses, by the way, showed that the late Pestrikov had said more than once that all their belongings and the house composed their (his and his wife's) common property. Besides, the guberniya engineer valued the house at a total of only 4,686 rubles. As a result of all these facts, the Guberniya Court recognized Pestrikova as the owner of one half of the house, since she was the sole heir of her husband, having established her right as well to the second half of the property as that acquired for hard-earned money. Therefore, the Guberniya Court also established that Pestrikova had to pay an inheritance duty on only half of the property.

The Guberniya Financial Department appealed this decision and the Higher Court approached the matter in principle thus:

In accordance with regulations about the tax from inheritance, only officially acknowledged debts of the heir are excluded from the cost of inherited property. On the other hand, according to the current code of civil laws (Statute 105) mutual ownership of spouse's property does not result from marriage, and the courts can, according to the principle of work, recognize such mutuality of property exclusively in the interests of the defense of the rights of one of the spouses if a disagreement between them about that property occurs, as, for example, at separation. There is no legal right, however, to apply this practice of the courts in the case of a demand for the inheritance of a deceased spouse. Taking into account that the plaintiff has no right to file the current suit and that the question (in real terms) of the inherited property belongs to the jurisdiction of the Guberniya Finance Section (and in the case of their refusal, to the People's Court), the Higher Court determined to overturn the decision of the Guberniya Court and to close the case.

The Suit of an Unregistered Wife About the Division of Property (*Izvestiya*, Jan. 9, 1926)

Ms. Makarova lived for eight years in an unregistered marriage with Mr. Egorov. In June of 1923, using both their resources they opened a business in the trading of old iron, in which Makarova was engaged on an equal basis with Egorov. In September they separated and Egorov dismissed Makarova from the business, not sharing anything with her from their mutual property.

Makarova filed a suit against Egorov for the division of the store of iron and two houses built by Egorov during the time they lived together, one in Moscow, in Marina Grove, and one in a village in Tver guberniya.

Holding that the iron trade was opened on the mutual resources of Egorov and the plaintiff and that the profits of that trade were used to build the house in Marina Grove, the Moscow Guberniya Court ordered Egorov to allow half the cost of the iron found in the warehouse and half the cost of the house in Marina Grove, a total of 1,340 rubles for the use of Makarova.

Egorov appealed this decision to the Higher Court, showing that the Guberniya Court had not taken into account the liabilities of the property and had not subtracted from the sum judged Makarova's share of the debts in taxes incurred on that property. Furthermore, Egorov attempted in his appeal to view the suit filed against him as a claim based on an agreement of simple comradeship rather than a suit for the division of common property.

The Higher Court did not find Egorov's appeal worthy of consideration since the question of the property being burdened with debts and arrears had not even been brought up by Egorov in the court in the first instance. As to the suit itself, the court recognized it as a suit for the division of common property. In view of this, the Higher Court, having recognized the decision of the Moscow Guberniya Court to be completely correct and properly motivated, approved it unchanged, leaving Egorov's higher appeal unacted upon.

In the Special Higher Control Board for Land Disputes: Dowry (*Izvestiya*, Jan. 1, 1926)

After Ekaterina Shamarina's young husband did not return to her from the Red Army and all the old people of Palkino decided that he was one of the "missing, unknown", her countryman Feofilin asked her hand in marriage. In order to "forestall trouble", on the day after the betrothal she moved to the cottage of her betrothed and for a dowry took from her sister-in-law Anna Shamarina, a meadow, which was called "Stream and Across the Bog."

The original dowry was secured for Ekaterina by the verbal agreement of the Palkino community against the will of Anna Shamarina and the latter, however difficult it may have been for her to go against the will of the *mir,* filed a suit against Ekaterina for arbitrariness, with the Shuisk Volost Land Committee [VLC].

The VLC decided to give the meadow to its legal owner, Anna.

Dissatisfied with this resolution of the matter, Ekaterina complained about the decision of the VLC to the Vologda Uezd Land Committee [ULC]. According to the decision of the latter, "Stream and Across the Bog" again fell to her.

Then Anna appealed to the Vologda Guberniya Land Committee [GLC] about the decision of the ULC. The GLC left the decision of the Shuisk VLC in force.

At this point, Ekaterina received a written verdict from the Palkino commune. In this verdict, "in the name of all sixty-four house-holders, equal and empowered," deriving from the fact that "Anna Shamarina, due to her poor management, has a good deal of excess hay-mowing to do," decided "to give the meadow 'Stream and Across the Bog' into the use of Ekaterina Shamarina."

With this decision in her hands, Ekaterina came to defend her dowry at the OKVK [Higher Control Board]. "I have few meadows and the commune recognizes me as the owner of this meadow; and what is the obstacle at the guberniya level? You figure it out; that is what you are here for!" Feofilina reported to the special board.

The board decided that before her marriage to Feofilin, Ekaterina had not divided the property with Anna Shamarina, so in view of Statute 66 of the Land Code, she lost her right by her marriage to the land and property comprising Anna's household. Her appeal was not answered.

Exchange of Wives and Children (*Izvestiya*, Dec. 15, 1925)

Citizens Gulin and Sheltyrev of the village of Kozhukhov (in Moscow guberniya) separated from their wives and agreed between themselves that each of them would "take as a wife the wife who had separated from the other, with the children" (and with their allotments of land), and that they would commit themselves to "view the children as their own, to raise them and be concerned with them." The wives likewise signed the agreement and promised, for themselves and for the children "not to touch the property of the separated husbands and not to lay claims in this matter."

As a result of this original agreement, Sheltyreva with four children went to Gulin, and Gulina went with a son to Sheltyrev.

After a month and a half Sheltyreva separated from Gulin and filed a suit against her former husband (Sheltyrev) about the division of property and the People's Court of the Fifth Section of the Rogozhsk-Simonovsk district (in Moscow) ruled to apportion to the plaintiff five-sixths of the property and to Sheltyrev, one-sixth, and to evict him from the house.

The matter was brought before the High Court at the protest of the Procurator of the Republic, but the Civil Appeals Board confirmed the decision of the People's Court on the following basis: It is demonstrated in the decision of the appeals court, that before the elimination of the quarrel between the Sheltyrev spouses about their property relationship, Sheltyrev's new wife had not attained any rights in his household. The court therefore divided the property into 6 shares eliminating from this division Sheltyrev's new wife, Gulina, and her child.... Sheltyreva's entrance into the Gulin household cannot be considered as accomplished as she only stayed there for a total of one and a half months and it was not reflected in the registration of the changed composition of households in the by-household lists of the village soviet (Act 72 of the Land Code). Likewise, it is impossible to "make official" the "marriage" of Sheltyreva with Gulin simply because it is based on a clearly negligible agreement about the exchange of wives...

Still, the matter did not end with this.

In accordance with the special opinion of one of the members of the

Civil Appeals Board, the matter was transferred for clarification to the plenum of the Higher Court, and the latter discovered the following injustices in the decision of the People's Court and in the remarks of the Appeals Board:

The People's Court completely neglected to clarify conditions which had essential significance for the matter. For example, had the new marriage between Sheltyrevs and Gulins been registered, had the plaintiff received anything from the possessions of Gulin after her having left him? In whose control, in practice, do the land allotments which previously belonged to Sheltyrev and Gulin, now lie? And so on. The Appeals Board's consideration that Gulina, entering into marriage with Sheltyrev, did not acquire any rights in his household, since she was not registered by the village soviet as a member of his household, violates Statutes 62 and 97 of the Law Code on Civic Acts and the Statute 66 of the Land Code, from which the meaning can be clearly perceived that persons entering into the composition of a household as a result of marriage acquire the rights of a member of the household from the moment of actual entry into marriage and into the household, and not from the moment of the registration with the village soviet. Furthermore, the length of time for acquiring the right of membership in a household and the right to demand division has not yet been established and consequently this right is acquired immediately after entry into the household (Statute 66, Land Code). It does matter how long a person who wants to separate himself from some household lives within it, as well as his real participation in the household's working processes and in the acquisition of divisible property; other economic considerations are of great importance here also.

The plenum of the Higher Court therefore resolved that the decision of the Civil Appeals Board and the decision of the People's Court should be altered and that the matter should be transferred to the Moscow Guberniya Court for assignment to a new examination in a different People's Court.

Alimony

1. Izvestiya, Dec. 27, 1925

The affair took place in the village of Upper Cheldak, Omsk province. A peasant, Afanasy Komarov, was ordered by the court to pay Citizeness Telnova for the support of a child at the rate of seven rubles a month. Komarov could not resign himself to the prospect of monthly payments, and after consulting his relatives, the old people Pavel and Anna Komarov, he decided with their help to "steal" the child. He promised them the mill, and the deal was concluded. On June 21, when there were guests at Telnova's, including the Komarovs, who were often there, Anna carried the

106

cradle with the child out into the passageway, and then immediately returned to the cottage and talked everyone into setting off for her place, promising to offer them something to eat and drink. After a half hour, Telnova's neighbor informed those gathered there that the child, left alone, had unexpectedly died. The child was indeed dead, and Anna and Pavel Komarov most wholeheartedly condoled with the grief-stricken mother. Anna took care of the child's little corpse, washed it, wrapped it in linen. Pavel saw to the coffin and the child was buried that same day. But witnesses were found, who knew about Afanasy's promise concerning the mill. The baby's pacifier which the child had used before his death was found, left in the cradle. The corpse was exhumed and expertise determined that the child was despatched with a quick-acting poison.

The Omsk Guberniya Court, recognizing all of the accused as guilty of the premeditated murder of the child, sentenced all three to deprivation of freedom in strict isolation for eight years each. Taking into account the peasant backgrounds and the first conviction of the Komarovs, and likewise the advanced ages of Pavel and Anna Komarov (55 and 54 years), the court lowered their punishments according to Statute 28 of the Penal Code to five years for Afanasy Komarov and for Pavel and Anna up to three years.

The Komarovs appealed the sentence, basically emphasizing their ignorance. The Higher Court found the sentence of the court of the first instance correct, and confirmed it without change, dropping the appeal without taking action.

2. *Izvestiya,* Feb. 9, 1926

A member of R.L.K.S.M. [Young Communist League, ed.] a twenty year old middle-peasant, Timothy Saprykin, was to pay Solomonida Storozheva five rubles and forty kopecks a month for the support of the eight month old child Anisya. Before the trial of the alimony suit at the People's Court by Storozheva, and after the satisfaction of that suit, Saprykin threatened to beat Storozheva if she tried to collect the alimony which she had been awarded. Storozheva took these threats seriously and was willing to settle with him for thirty rubles, but on the night of August 24, Saprykin got into the barn where Storozheva slept with the child and smothered them both . . . He stopped the child's mouth with a rag and put it in the cradle face downward and he carried Storozheva's corpse into a shed that stood next door and hung her with a rope by the neck from a beam.

In court Saprykin denied his part in the killing of the child and Storozheva, but witnesses' testimony established his mother's and brothers' numerous attempts to bribe witnesses, and the Kursk Guberniya Court, declaring him guilty under Statute 142 of the Criminal Code, sentenced him to eight years' deprivation of freedom in strict isolation and three years' disenfranchisement after the completion of the punishment.

The Higher Court where the matter was taken by Saprykin's appeal, found the court of the first instance had sentenced correctly, and reaffirmed it unchanged.

3. *Pravda,* Jan. 15, 1925

It is not the first alimony suit that this young sweet-looking peasant girl, Anna Semenova, has filed against the son of her employer, twenty year old Gradusov. Five years ago, they sent for her, being her distant relatives, to come in from the village to do work in the house and in 1922 she took up with Aleksei and became pregnant by him. The first time she consented to an abortion. The second time, she did not agree to this. Then Aleksei decided to cause a miscarriage "by his own means." When she was seven months pregnant, he exposed Anna to very severe torture, beating her with his fists and feet in the stomach, head and face in front of the yardkeeper and his own mother, who was admiring that savage reprisal out of the window. He was brought to court and sentenced to a year's deprivation of freedom in strict isolation. Having worked off the punishment, Aleksei, as if nothing had happened, proposed to renew his ties with Anna:

"After all, there is nothing to care for. The child died; I did not offend your feelings with alimony, everything has passed."

After Gradusov further promised Semenova "not to pay attention to his parents and to register the marriage" she subdued her grudge against the father and murderer of her first child and once again became his wife, in practice.

"He was impossible to understand," mused witnesses in court. "The Gradusovs are followers of the old ways. Near them, Aleksei kept up appearances, and when he had passed the gates, went arm in arm with Anna to the theater, to the cinema..."

Whether he was keeping up appearances or simply exploiting Anna's defenselessness like a master, as soon as Semenova demanded from him an allowance for childbirth, as the father of her second child which was to be born, he refused to recognize his paternity.

"I sat for her in prison for a year, and now not only that... I am not even speaking to her any more!"

The judge begins from the old matter:

"Let bygones be bygones, Gradusov, but tell us, was the first child yours?"

"Well, I won't hide this."

"But that time you denied it in court. How can we believe you now?" Gradusov felt that he had let the cat out of the bag.

"Well, my mother locks me up at night." He invented new proofs of his "lack of involvement" in the matter. "If I go to the bathroom, I have to wake up my mother; she has the key. How could this be me?!"

This declaration evoked laughter from listeners and witnesses.

"Oh, yes, indeed! Nothing of the sort! He has been brought in for hooliganism so many times... He knows no restraint even if you chain him up..."

The court determined to consider him the father of Semenova's child and required from him a payment to Semenova before she gave birth of one hundred rubles and from the time of the child's birth a support allowance of thirty rubles a month.

4. *Izvestiya*, Dec. 12, 1925

The young peasant man Lavrov (the story took place in the settlement of Kuteinikov, in the Don Region) was returning from a visit with his fellow villager, Mirushchenko. Going past his house, he suggested to her that she come in to rest. They went in. They talked about love. Lavrov, promising to marry her, proposed that she give herself to him. Mirushchenko categorically refused this proposal and when Lavrov took her by the hand, tore herself away and ran toward the gate. Lavrov caught up with her, threw her on the ground and raped her... Mirushchenko told no one about this... She was afraid of the laughter of the other girls in the village...

Lavrov met Mirushchenko; their tie continued, and the whole village knew that "Lavrov is going with Mirushchenko." But then Mirushchenko discovered that she was pregnant and turned to Lavrov for advice. He calmed her down, repeated his promise to marry her, and then... decided to take measures, so that in the future he would be able to deny the child.. to get out of alimony. His plan was one of worldly simplicity: to throw Mirushchenko together with other young men, and to spread the word that she was promiscuous. Taking advantage of Mirushchenko's downtroddenness and backwardness, having arranged things with Golubov and Degtyarev beforehand, he invited Mirushchenko to go with him to visit some friends. Golubov and Degtyarev turned out to be the only ones there. All three threw Mirushchenko on the bed and raped her in turn... Even then Mirushchenko did not tell anyone about what had happened, since Lavrov threatened that he would not marry her if she were not obedient. It seemed to Lavrov, nonetheless, that two witnesses to Mirushchenko's "looseness" were not enough and he talked Garkushenko, Kiss and the same Golubov and Degtyarev to go to Golubova's (Golubov's sister) house, where he promised to bring Mirushchenko. But Mirushchenko was on guard and only through cleverness and by force was he able to get her to Golubova's. He set off to take a walk with her and walking past the doors of the Golubov home, shoved her forcibly into the house, slammed the door behind him, took out a lash with a buckle prepared beforehand and ordered her to lie down on the floor. Lavrov raped her first and then the others...

Ladvinsky and Glushchenko, young men of that village, somehow found out about the events at the Golubovs, forced their way in, stopped these outrages, and took the barely-alive Mirushchenko home. ...

The trial of this matter took place in the North Caucasus Regional Court.

The defendants (all between eighteen and twenty years old) did not plead guilty.

"Everything that happened was with Mirushchenko's permission... Lavrov did not incite us and none of us knew that she was pregnant."

Mirushchenko's terrible tale in court was interrupted by her hysterical outbursts.

"Lavrov," she said among other things, "ordered me to listen to him, threatening not to marry me otherwise.. Everything was fine between us until I became pregnant; he feared alimony.. He beat me three times that day, when I didn't want to go for a walk that day when it all happened at the Golubovs... They didn't let me scream, stopping my mouth with my skirt."

Ladvinsky and Glushchenko corroborated that Mirushchenko was lying on the floor naked, her head tied up in a skirt...

She was shaking all over and was unconscious. She could not have "willingly" agreed to have relations with them.

Olga Golubova showed that Lavrov had led Mirushchenko to lie down on the floor, and that when she, Golubova, had begun to tell them to go away, and wanted to go and tell her father, Lavrov had not let her, and had stood with the lash next to the door...

The court found all five guilty according to part one of Statute 169 of the Penal Code and sentenced Lavrov to deprivation of freedom for five years, with diminution of the punishment by one third due to his not having attained legal majority, and for the remainder, three years apiece, and taking into account that Garkushenko, Kiss, Golubov, and Degtyarev were all acting under Lavrov's influence, the court lowered their sentences to one and a half years.

The Higher Court, to which the matter was transferred upon complaint from the defendants, could see no cause for appeal and affirmed the sentence of the court of the first instance without change.

5. *Does the Father Pay Alimony For the Son?*

Izvestiya, Jan. 22, 1926

Citizen Rappaport filed a suit for alimony against her husband, A. Rappaport and the latter's father R. Rappaport, for the support of a child. Indicating in the filing of her suit that her husband, who lived at that time in

Arzamas, was in practice the co-manager of a trading establishment, the formal owner of which was her husband's father, she asked the Moscow Guberniya Court to award her a monthly payment of one hundred and fifty rubles for the support of the child, taken as an alimony from both her husband and his father.

In court it was indeed established that the Rappaports, Ruvim and Aleksandr, were viewed in Arzamas as very "solid" traders in leather, with their own home, and that the trading establishment, like the rest of the property, was in the name of Ruvim Rappaport. The Moscow Guberniya Court, being guided by Statutes 172, 173, and 174 of the Code of Civil Law and taking into account the property status of the respondents, established the joint responsibility of A. and R. Rappaport for supporting the child (until its majority) with fifty rubles a month, beginning August 1, 1925.

The Higher Court reviewed the matter in an appeal procedure and found that the Moscow Guberniya Court had not been guided by the clearly expressed meaning of Statute 173 of the Civil Code, since, according to this article, alimony should be recovered in the order of degree of kinship and only in the case of the demonstration of the impossibility of its being received from a closer relative. The demand for alimony from two individuals of different levels of relationship at once was unquestionably illegal. As far as the motivation of the Guberniya Court that the respondents led a mutual establishment and household, this condition only gave the Guberniya Court a basis for inquiring into the question of Aleksandr Rappaport's share in the father's property, and depending upon that share, and consequently, his (A's) material condition, to establish the size of the alimony. In its resolution the Higher Court, among other things, showed that insofar as property relations of members of a family in the city are regulated on the basis of private civil law or labor law, there is no legal basis for the extension to them of that practice which exists in relationship to the peasant household for the exaction of alimony, where the relationship between members of the household is regulated by special provision of the Law Code, and as to the exaction of alimony from the property of the whole household, by a Special Circular of the People's Commissariat of Justice.

Therefore, the Higher Court decided to change the decision of the Moscow Guberniya Court and to refer the matter for re-examination.

THE "WINGED EROS" OF COMRADE KOLLONTAI
P. Vinogradskaya

In her article entitled "Make Way for the Winged Eros" (and these are letters to the working youth! P.V.), Comrade Kollontai begins thus:

"You ask me, my young comrade, what place does proletarian ideology give to love? It disturbs you that working class youth 'is now more occupied with love and other such questions' than with the large tasks which are before the working people's republic. If that is the case (and from afar it is difficult for me to judge this), then let us look for the explanation of this phenomenon, and then it will be easier to find an answer to the first question: 'What place does love occupy in the ideology of the working class?'" . . .

In her previous letter on morality, Comrade Kollontai restated the questions of her correspondent in her own words, so that there were some reasons for thinking that there was generally nothing to quote. But in this article the question of the "young comrade" is enclosed in quotation marks, so that it might be seen as a real letter. If this letter belongs to a living person from Soviet Russia, then we may, I believe, with the full agreement of the overwhelming majority of genuinely proletarian student youth, declare that it is a slander on youth. Perhaps there are individuals among the youth, possibly including the party youth, for whom sexual questions have eclipsed all else, having shoved all remaining issues into the background, including the problem of the proletarian revolution, which has only just barely begun and has only been brought to victory in one country. But it would be a base untruth to declare that such a mood is characteristic of "all laboring youth" or a majority of them. If Comrade Kollontai needs to represent that she is writing on her beloved "erotic themes" not out of her own inclination, but because she was provoked by youth itself, then she could manage this without quotes from letters misinterpreting the situation in Russia. In this she is probably not lacking in imagination.

However, Comrade Kollontai, instead of checking how things stand in reality, straight away declares, "Let us look for explanations."

A good exercise, to look for explanations for that which does not exist! A question might involuntarily appear to the reader: How about

From the journal *Molodaia Gvardiia*, No. 3, May 1923, pp. 111–24. Polina Vinogradskaya was a member of Zhenotdel, the Bolshevik party's Women's Section, and on the editorial board of *Kommunistka* [*Communist Woman*].

looking for the explanation of why Comrade Kollontai longs so to give this "explanation" and whether all is well with her Marxism and communism? Why, after all, does Comrade Kollontai so stubbornly wish to be the Verbitskaya in our communist journalism and overemphasize the sex problem high and low? Does an old experienced Communist really have nothing more to write about? Have we really already in all areas of life such prosperity that there only remains how to spread the wings of Eros? Or is it that only those questions which the socialist intellectual philistine is able to put come to her ears and consciousness, while what the present day worker from among the masses (not from among hysterical women and weak-nerved philistines) thinks and feels is unknown to her?

Comrade Kollontai made the reservation that "from afar," in Norway, it is not apparent to her how much questions of love are of vital importance among the young. This did not stop her, however, from adopting a version to the effect that the young are head and ears immersed in love, in the search for "happiness."

How do things really stand with us in questions of love and sex among the young and among male and female workers?

Has anything changed from the time of the civil war? Undoubtedly, changes, shifts, upheavals have taken place here as they have in the entire situation of life in the period of temporary calm after the civil war, or better said, in the period of change in the form of struggle with the bourgeoisie under NEP. The revolution unleashed all the energies, both physical and intellectual, of each individual in the laboring classes, and gave a great scope to their realization. However, it itself did not allow "freedoms" to be realized in the building of new forms of life until the struggle was finished. In the period of sharp class struggle, with its slogans and requirements of "war until complete victory," all the will and all the attention of the masses have been concentrated on questions of direct struggle with the enemy. But within, the above-stated process of dissolving old forms was already fully maturing. All sexual life with its problems was therefore put to the side and only now can these questions of secondary importance begin to play a more notable role (if the German revolution does not remove it, once again, from the agenda). A *more* notable role—it must be expressed in that way so as not to make the mistake of exaggeration, that is all.

It is unarguable that questions of love are beginning to interest the student youth more than in the past. The questionnaire on sexual life filled out by students of Sverdlov University contains interesting material in this regard. But there is an enormous distance between this interest and an enthusiasm for sexual questions carried fully to the point of obliterating the business of studying and the fundamental tasks of proletarian struggle. On the contrary, we know that the student youth gives the greater part of its energies to study, despite the difficult material conditions in which our

113

proletarian student youth and communist student body find themselves, and if there is an interest in sexual problems, then there is a twofold interest in materialism and a threefold interest in economics, etc. The journal of Sverdlov University, in which the above mentioned article was placed, can serve as evidence of this. This journal, obviously proceeding from the needs of student youth and their necessities, devotes almost all its pages to scholarly questions and leaves only the most insignificant portion to questions of sex.

In working life, both questions of sex and problems of the new family are being advanced in much greater measure than earlier. But it would be a gross injustice to state that we have on hand a predominance of Sanin's decadent sentiments and interests. A case is known to us in which a communist, an old member of the party, shot a non-party person out of jealousy. Further, not that long ago in Moscow two students of the War Academy fought a duel over a woman. This fact in and of itself deserves attention. It must be calculated among the other changes in the situation of the public mood. But it would be a slander to say of the whole staff of the Red Army that rabid dueling in general has begun to prevail among them. . . .

On the other hand, there is no doubt that old ties in the sphere of the family and sexual relations are in the process of breaking up and are experiencing continual change everywhere, caused by the new economy and the psyche of the people, which is in some respects even outrunning the economy. But this dissolution proceeds extremely slowly. The transition from War Communism to NEP has more delayed (temporarily at least) than sped up this process. If the proletarian students and youth protest rather stormily in general against old petty bourgeois precepts in the area of sexual relations, going even as far as forms of disordered sexual relations and trying even to ground this on principle, then it is, generally speaking, only a small part of the class body of the proletariat and is far from characteristic of the whole. But all this speaks of rather careless attitudes toward questions of sex life and of an inattentive, uncomradely attitude toward women, since, in *the present situation,* women alone have to deal with the fruits of this love. But I repeat that this is far from meaning that sexual questions attract the earnest attention of the young and deflect them from the main thing. More often the reverse is spoken of, the rule of "wingless Eros," whose adornment with peacock feathers Comrade Kollontai pronounces to be the first order of business of Marxism and proletarian ideology.

It is necessary to have further in view the fact that thanks to coeducation of the young, thanks to their joint participation in all forms of sports and finally, thanks to the general smoothing away of artificially erected partitions between men and women in all our public life, thanks to the general spirit of more comradely (but still far from sufficiently

114

comradely) attitudes toward women—among us both love and the female body are no longer that forbidden fruit, that paradise apple, the subjects of all kinds of sighs and repressed dreams, which they were in the past. When Renaissance painters on their canvasses sang hymns to the magnificent female body, violating the etiquette of Christian asceticism and the precept of "struggle with the flesh"; when such motifs resounded in the liberationist bourgeois literature of the following centuries, all this was natural, comprehensible, necessary and progressive. But now, after all, are different times, different morals, different songs. Forbidden fruits became accessible to all long ago. Relations between the sexes are completely different—they are far more rational. In such a situation, the Georges Sand pathos of Comrade Kollontai, her overemphasis of the problems of love, her ostentatious stilted revolutionariness in this area, produce a funny and lamentable impression.

The problem of love does not have one-tenth of the significance in our lives that Comrade Kollontai wishes to attach to it in her articles, where she is pointlessly wasting her pathos and enthusiasm. It is in truth the breaking of a butterfly on the wheel.

On the other hand, what is really important and connected with the problem of sex other than eroticism, for example, are questions of the family, the question of children, of posterity in general, questions which trouble the workers, especially the women, more than anything. These questions Comrade Kollontai passes in silence. But about this below. . . .

What a style, indeed, we are dealing with a masterpiece! So, Comrade Kollontai thinks that the situation in Russia is now such that it is already time to become occupied with "winged Eros" and calls for putting one's sexual relations in new order. How, we will investigate concretely further. Though out of habit she says above that the pause "is temporary and relative," by her conclusions and practical suggestions it appears that the change is a fundamental one. Such an evaluation of the general situation is a most harmful illusion, the inadmissibility of which is so clearly supported now by the events in Germany. And it is necessary to say that the mistake of Comrade Kollontai is far from only her own individual mistake. In the environment of NEP for some three years of truce, a large number of our comrades have become consolidated in the psychology of "peaceful renovation." Somehow it is put out of view and forgotten that the proletarian revolution triumphed only in one sector, a sector far from as important as the economic or cultural. All of us out of habit repeat that the main battles are ahead, that the dangers threatening us are enormous. Nevertheless in practice, many act as if socialism is already in the bag, if not completely, then by half. It would not be therefore superfluous to remind everybody, in particular the propagandists of the new epoch in the sphere of love, of the fine words of Comrade Trotsky in this regard, although spoken on a different occasion: "We as before are soldiers on the march.

We are taking a day's rest. We must wash our shirts, trim and brush our hair, and as our first duty, clean and grease our rifles. All the present administrative-cultural work is nothing more than putting ourselves in some order between two battles and marches. The main battles are ahead and perhaps, not very far ahead . . ."

If we were to ask Comrade Kollontai whether she agrees with these lines, she might take offense at the question. One should think so. She is, after all, such a "leftist"! But at the same time, by all appearances, she lacks the logic to think out what her current intensified statements about a new period in the area of Eros mean politically. She lacks a Marxist and Communist intuition to understand that irrespective of the substance of her ideas, her very over-stressing and overemphasis of this problem is a coarse political mistake. It is also a mistake from the point of view of the real conditions in which our male and female workers and communists must still live and work, which must not be forgotten.* What, in fact, is recommended? Over what is one supposed to rack one's brains? We have want, poverty, low wages. The elementary requirements of the working masses are far from satisfied. More than half the country is illiterate. Young students often live in terrible quarters and material conditions; they lack food, clothing; there are not enough textbooks. Thousands of young people suffer from tuberculosis and nervous disorders because of mental strain and malnutrition. Many years of work are needed before socialist accumulation can begin as it should, so that we can build houses for, dress, and bring up hundreds of thousands of orphans, etc. But the thoughts of Comrade Kollontai are on something else. "Gentle-winged Eros," just imagine, is once again claiming its rights; "the surplus energy of the soul is looking for release in spiritual experiences;" "the many-stringed lyre of the multi-winged idol of love," etc., etc.

It can be said with assurance that to all these lamentations of Comrade Kollontai our conscientious youth (not the gymnasia students or the sons of NEPmen) will answer, not on a "many-stringed lyre," but will blow into a monotonous instrument, which is called a "whistle." And, moreover, we may be accused, for all I know, of ploughing the sand when we use a pen instead of this more appropriate simple device. However, if we continue serious analysis of the writings of our respected Ambassador to Norway, then, since Comrade Kollontai still enjoys some respect in definite circles of working women and the young, her admirers will demand of us arguments to the point.

---

* It is sufficient to point out that it is not always the case that the husband, ceasing to love his wife and abandoning his family, considers it his duty to support the children materially. "The abandoned" wife, until the state can, on a mass scale, take care of raising the children, is forced to turn to the court for defense. Nowadays we have many such legal actions. Where is winged Eros here? [P.V.]

116

By the way, it seems to me that if the latest writings of Comrade Kollontai were translated into German and read by German working women and communists, then they would consider us, having published these things in communist organs for women and young people, either crazy, or . . . beginning to degenerate quickly. One need only recall what the tormented, exhausted German proletariat is faced with to realize what a great lack of tact such literature has on the international scale, coming from the pen of one of the recent leaders of the international Communist movement of working women.

Moreover, Comrade Kollontai sees in future society, too, that which she wishes to see, and despite the fact that she (and this has already developed into a habit among us) repeats over and over again that one must not make prophecies about the future, soothing her Marxist conscience with this phrase, she still cannot restrain herself from curiosity, from peering into the future and widely expanding on it. She writes: "In this new society, collectivist in spirit and emotions, against a background of joyful unity and the comradely community of all the members of the working, creative collective, Eros will occupy an honored place as an emotion magnifying human happiness . . . In this new world, the recognized, normal and desirable form of communion of the sexes probably will rest on a healthy, free, natural (without perversions and excesses) mutual attraction of the sexes, on a 'transformed Eros'."

Thus Comrade Kollontai is prepared, in the interests of propagandizing her own view of Eros, not only to distort all history, but to reshape the entire future according to her taste. In communist society, it turns out, relations between the sexes will necessarily be organized "in Kollontai's way." True, "every man to his taste", thus the proverb goes, but as to any attempts to foist one's current and private tastes on future society, we must protest against them at all costs. In this respect Comrade Preobrazhensky is completely correct when he writes in his brochure: "Concretely, is it possible, from the point of view of proletarian interests, to raise and answer the question as to which forms of relations of the sexes are more compatible, if not with today's social relations and social interests, then with the relations of socialist society: monogamy, temporary ties or so-called disordered sexual contact? Up until now, defenders of one or another viewpoint on this question have tended more to substantiate with all sorts of arguments their personal tastes and habits in this sphere, rather than to give a sociologically correct and class-based answer. He who liked better the somewhat philistine personal family life of Marx, and by his inclinations preferred monogamy, tried to make the monogamous form of marriage into a dogma and norm, advancing medical and social arguments. Those who are inclined to the opposite try to pass "transient marriages" and "sexual communism" as the natural form of marriage in future society. Realization of this type of contact between the sexes is

117

sometimes looked at with pride, as a "protest in action" against the present petty bourgeois family morality.

In reality all such statements of the question come down to the fact that people recommend for communist society their personal tastes and pass off their personal sympathies as "objective necessity." * . . .

What does Comrade Kollontai recommend to male and female workers, male and female communists, and to our youth?

Her entire article is composed of continuous moral philosophizing in the field of sexual relations. And the history of the Middle Ages is critically examined just for the sake of this morality. She recommends the following:

"The many-sidedness of love is not in and of itself contrary to the interests of the proletariat. On the contrary, it makes for the triumph of that ideal of love in mutual relations between the sexes which is already being formed and crystallized in the midst of the working class. Namely, of love-comradeship."

By the many-sidedness of love is meant here the cohabitation of one man with several women and the reverse. We are far from thinking of arguing against such a "many-sidedness" in love. But it is necessary to say one thing. The need to live together with many others is first of all a matter of temperament, a product of the purely subjective characteristics and tastes of the individual. But the possibility of a wide realization of such personal tastes depends first of all on the economy, on how far ahead the construction of socialism has marched, on how great the surplus product of society is, in a word, it depends on how the collective has accomplished the leap from the Rule of Necessity to the Rule of Freedom.

It is fully possible that in the future society, where the successes of production will make it possible to fully develop all sides of the human personality, each person will have enough freedom in life and in action to allow that forms of mutual relations between the sexes be determined almost completely by people's personal inclinations, by their temperaments, etc. However, one must believe that in all likelihood there too will

---

* But if Comrade Kollontai is wrong in principle when she raises the question of "many-faceted" love (that is, simultaneous cohabitation with many), since such problems lie outside the domain of party regulations, equally wrong, though for the opposite reason, is a moral precept of Comrade Sorin, when he sets communists right: "never live with three wives at a time." (*Pravda*, No. 237, Oct. 19, 1922, "Copy-book maxims").

In addition to all the other hard duties of Control Commissions, Comrade Sorin thrusts on them a new one, to trace and count the number of wives each communist has in excess of one's full due, a sole "legal" wife (or, in case of women communists, a sole "legal" husband). But Comrade Sorin betrays thus his old-fashioned concept of marriage as an economic family union, the structure of which presupposes threefold material expenses on the part of the husband for his three wives (as it is with Moslems). However, nowadays living with many women or men does not necessarily imply material consequences, so, in such a case, this kind of cohabitational formation would not affect the collective and would lie outside the domain of moral regulations. [P.V.]

118

be regulating principles in terms of which forms of interaction are best from the point of view of medicine and eugenics.

But moving on to the situation of our everyday existence, to our reality, we must say that all questions of the rationalization of sexual relations turn first of all (under our conditions of poverty, unemployment, especially among women, lack of social education) on the questions of the family, of children. On this question our author is diligently silent, limiting herself to the area of purely psychological discussions of love and invariably dragging in "proletarian interests," "proletarian ideology," etc. To be silent about this is to be silent about what is most important, about what is most burning, about what most profoundly troubles the woman worker, any woman and also, it stands to reason, all men. . . . The masses do not at all share the view that absolute love exists only for love itself, and that a man and woman must look at one another as objects of pleasure. Is love really, taken in a social and biological connection, some sort of art for art's sake? Is it really not the prelude to reproduction, to the bearing of children? It is not superfluous here to indicate the fact that at the jubilee party organized by the Section of Women Workers of the Central Committee in honor of the three year existence of the journal *Kommunistka,* several workers in their speeches protested against the fact that in the journal articles like those of Comrade Kollontai were published. In this regard one of them pointed out that the article of "Sister" Comrade Kollontai was so alien in spirit to the women workers that they generally did not understand it. Thus the jubilee in honor of *Kommunistka* unexpectedly ended with a criticism of the position of Comrade Kollontai in the sphere of Eros. One woman worker of the Women's Section in the Donbass was also absolutely correct in noting: "Before us are not questions of love. Before us stands the question of children. That is the issue. And what is the position of the children? More than half a million homeless children, finding themselves dependent on the State and maintained in poverty stricken, shocking, often nightmarish conditions. Tens of thousands of children of workers having nowhere to be placed because of a lack of enough nurseries, children's homes and kindergartens. The question of social upbringing is the central question of the family and the problem of sex doesn't bother us today." But all these questions, so profoundly troubling working women, questions for which they are awaiting an answer most of all, Comrade Kollontai bypasses with stubborn silence. She is occupied exclusively with the psychology of love, with the subjective emotions of lovers, that is, she is not thinking about the fact that if our workers become utterly engrossed on a large scale in "variegated Eros" and rolled in the luxury of "many-sided love," that for a rather large number of them it would mean an increase in the family, the addition of new children, at a time when they do not know what to do with those they already have. . . .

119

We live in a century of great social upheavals, in comparison with which even the unprecedented earthquake in Japan seems minor and insignificant. Decades of revolution and socialist wars will require an enormous intensification of proletarian strength. They will require people tempered in their own sphere no less than the steel with which they will settle accounts with the old world. Our Party has succeeded in bringing up such people. But neither our Party nor the generation of revolutionary populists preceding it educated the youth following them on problems of love. They had too much to worry about. And now our youth will respond with bewilderment at best to the attempts of Comrade Kollontai to educate the younger generation of the revolution in questions of love, which captivated in their own time the parasite Pechorins and Onegins, as they sat on the backs of the serfs.

MY LIFE (THE STORY OF MARIA FEDOTOVNA FILIPENKO)
M. F. Filipenko

I was in domestic service until 1913. In 1914 I got married and started to work at a factory, because my husband was a fireman and there wasn't enough to support the family. And our daughter, a year and a half old, was left alone in a locked room. Then my husband went away for course in firefighting; a second son was born and I supported them.

During the 1917 Revolution, I did not understand anything and when we came out of the gates against tsarism, we met Cossacks. I became frightened, but they lowered their rifles and joined us. But I was still afraid. I arrived at the courtyard and there were soldiers there. I was crying from fright. They asked—was it possible that I was sorry for the tsar? What was I supposed to say? I had heard that he was the terrestial king and I didn't know anything more about it. I wasn't sorry for him, but afraid. Afraid what would happen next, how the children would live.

Then we went to bury the dead. Comrade Batyshev led us. He worked with us at the tool-making shop (now he's a member of the Raikom [District Committee—Ed.] of Krasnaya Presna) and he led us then, although not all of us believed him, and even called him a bandit. He probably remembers now and laughs.

Well, we went to the funerals. They put me in the choir and we sang verses: "exhausted with heavy slavery." That song entered into my soul. And I started to distinguish the truth. But I still lived my own life and talked my husband out of public life. I thought that he would carouse at the meetings. And I wouldn't let him join the party. And I argued to the teeth with the workers. I was that ignorant. And the people who lived around us weren't good. The tenants, especially the women, called me 'factory worker' and 'desperado' and I argued with them. Because I had found a family at the factory. I'm a "shpitomka" [orphan, ed.]. I don't have any relatives and I have been alone all my life. I was a domestic servant, and the lady of the house prodded me in the teeth with a plate [maltreated me, ed.], but when I went to the factory the workers treated me kindly and taught me how to work on machines.

You couldn't find out a thing from the foreman; he wouldn't say a kind word; he swore. Then he was replaced when the Soviets came to power.

I began to sympathize with our power, but was still afraid of everything. I was invited to bring the children to the nursery, and I was as

From the journal *Delegatka*, No. 2-3, 1924, pp. 19-20.

afraid as if they were going to take them from me forever. I left the children in a locked room. I tied the girl to a table by the leg, so that she would not hurt the younger child.

I was finally talked into bringing them to the nursery. I brought them, I was in a flood of tears, kissing the children, as if saying goodbye forever. I went to get them in the evening. They were given to me. I checked under their clothing. Had they broken anything or were they covered with bruises. I saw that nothing was the matter. The child was full; shortly he began to grow better looking; he gained weight, became clean and rosy. And then I believed that the nursery was our salvation. I became conscious. And then, because of that, the women workers chose me as a delegate.

I went to the Soviet for the first time, but I was afraid to go in. I just stood near the door and then went home. But I was ashamed to tell them at the factory. "They wouldn't let me in," I said. Then our organizer raised a stink. He got everybody excited, "They wouldn't let a woman delegate into the Soviet." Then I admitted that I hadn't told the truth, that I'd just been afraid to go alone. Then the organizer took me himself. First there was a speech by Comrade Loginov about the dangers of religion. And I was so excited, came home, took down all the ikons, wanted to thrown them away. My husband and I quarreled—he's religious, but I later reformed him. When I was ignorant I hung like a weight on his legs, preventing him from joining the Party. But when I understood myself I stopped trying to restrain him. Quite the opposite, I pushed him toward public life. That's how important it is for a man, his wife to be conscientious.

So I began to work as a delegate. It's been two years and I've joined the party. After me, my husband was enrolled in the party, and we work together as comrades.

Now as a delegate, I help in the Presnensky Zhenotdel to meet our needs.

In the Section of the Department of Health Care of the Soviet, a dispensary (which distributes to the sick) has been opened and a new cafeteria, and we are opening a night sanatorium there. A sick worker can come straight from the factory and rest in pleasant surroundings. He'll receive good food and any treatment that he requires. In other words, work and be treated. Before they sent him off to a sanatorium and he got better, and then he would come back and the recovery was undone. With us the worker can undergo further treatment in the night sanatorium until he is completely well.

At the dispensary we give out to sick workers (who are being cured at home) whatever they need; medicine to some, linen and shoes to others, even beds, if they sleep on the floor.

We're fighting tuberculosis this way.

I am also connected, through my work as a delegate, with various hospitals, maternity homes, children's homes.

122

I track down where there is disorder, I help to eliminate them. [*sic*]

My life is no longer without purpose and I call on you comrade workers and peasants (both female) to join in public work.

III. SOCIALISM AND SOCIAL WELFARE

ИЗВЕСТИЯ

ГОД ИЗДАНИЯ 13-й

СОВЕТСКОМУ

ЖАЮЩИЕ ОРГАНИЗАЦИИ ПОЛНОСТЬЮ ОЦЕНИЛИ
Е СОЦИАЛИСТИЧЕСКОЙ РЕКОНСТРУКЦИИ СЕЛЬСКОГО

INTRODUCTION

The area of health and welfare may not generally be thought of in conjunction with cultural revolution or change, but in fact, such questions as "For whom should social services be provided?" or "What is the relationship between health care and one's personal finances" touch basic issues of cultural norms and values. Tsarist society had a long history of public medicine through the zemstvos, and self-sacrificing "third element" zemstvo physicians were, for a time, one of the few groups of social activists generally respected at all social levels. There was also a large number of middle level health care workers: mid-wives, feldshers, even psychiatric attendants. Health care as a whole, however, remained woefully inadequate. Skilled physicians served Russia's social elite, and provided superb facilities for those who could pay, but twenty-five years after the introduction of zemstvo medicine, there were less than 2000 doctors to serve a peasant and worker population of more than 100,000,000. Rural Russia had available only some 43,000 hospital beds. These figures increased between 1890 and 1914, but on the eve of the first World War, Russia still had fewer than 50,000 hospital beds in the countryside, and less than 20,000 physicians, most of whom practiced in the cities.[1] Equally important, provincial zemstvo boards had dismissed doctors wholesale after the 1905 revolution, regarding them as "subversives". In the struggle between maintaining public welfare and repressing political dissidence, reactionaries won with ease.

Bolsheviks came to power determined to reverse the social priorities of pre-revolutionary health care. One of the new government's early acts was to establish full-fledged commissariats for health and welfare, and to initiate a comprehensive public health and welfare program, revolutionary in conception and orientation. Unlike their adversaries in the civil war, the Bolsheviks not only appreciated the need for popular health care facilities in their own right, but recognized the relationship between social maintenance, the control of disease, and the consolidation of political power. "Either socialism will defeat the louse," Lenin declared in 1919, "or the louse will defeat socialism."[2]

As the essays below by the first Commissar of Health, Dr. N. A. Semashko, indicate, the new regime also hoped to provide free, comprehensive medical care for all ordinary citizens, even at the expense of weakening elite medical institutions. Health was considered a "matter of right"; and the promotion of health, an important tool in social and economic construction. Unlike "bourgeois" systems, structured essentially on treating the sick, the new regime hoped to orient its program as much or more towards disease prevention. Resources which might have been pledged to developing specialized new equipment were diverted to mass programs in hygene and prophylactic public health instruction. Whereas 95% of Russian health rubles had been spent before 1917 on treatment, and only 5% on disease prevention, the new commissariat had by 1920 substantially reversed these figures, alloting somewhat more than half of the available funds to prevention.

Such an approach allowed the Bolsheviks to make maximum use of scant resources. Without the time and means to build new treatment facilities, the best the regime could do in this area was to confiscate private hospitals and sanitaria, opening their doors to anyone, regardless of ability to pay. This often meant reducing private rooms to wards, and it "ruined" hospital facilities in the eyes of private patients who had never previously been inside a "clinic". A number of doctors also felt medical services were being "destroyed", and fled Russia for the comforts of London or Paris. But for the sick and injured who had never previously seen a hospital bed, the new regime was convincingly and admirably "revolutionary".

A good example of the importance of preventive medicine can be seen in Semashko's article on the "Protection of Mother and Child". Infant mortality was a major scourge of pre-revolutionary Russia, with figures two and three times as high as Western Europe; similarly with medical problems of new mothers. With relatively meager resources, rates of disease and death associated with childbirth could be (and were) readily reduced, particularly if adequate maternity leave was provided, wages and jobs guaranteed, and instruction offered in even elementary areas of hygiene and baby care.

The fact that such instruction could be provided by "middle level" medical personnel, rather than physicians, also prompted the new regime to put its resources into medical education here, rather than try at first to build a new corps of highly trained doctors. Specialized training, leading to specialized, sophisticated treatment, had to be less high a priority than raising the minimal level of care available to all. As a consequence, while the number of doctors increased very slowly after 1917 (in part, however, because many simply left the country, and had to be replaced), the number of nurses, medical "technicians", feldshers, and the like increased quite dramatically. Health delivery systems remained haphazard and inadequate at first, as Semashko himself indicates, and much was done by improvisation. But the new regime's commitment to popular welfare was firmly established.

Even the creation of independent commissariats of health and welfare was a revolutionary innovation. (By contrast, the United States did not create a Department of Health until 1953, and then grouped its functions with those of Education and Welfare.) Bolsheviks hoped in both areas to establish centralized control over delivery systems, and hence to enforce the institution of radical changes, particularly in light of expected resistance from pre-revolutionary medical personnel whose services were very much needed. Centralization also allowed for tight government control over funds and other resources, particularly important in Vinokurov's Commissariat of Welfare, which took on responsibility for social insurance programs, accident and health insurance, old-age pension, and unemployment compensation for those unable to work. It was recognized, of course, that draining business coffers to provide social maintenance might have consequences in terms of economic development, and that in any case, confiscation and other "improvisational" measures were hardly solutions to serious problems of funding and support. But for the time being at least, such stop-gap procedures underscored the importance to the party of social welfare issues, however imperfect the system was in practice.

In sum, the cultural revolution in the area of health and welfare meant replacing the notion of "privilege" with the concept of "right", and developing mass services oriented towards prevention, rather than treatment services for a social elite. For many torn with infection and disease, these new objectives were appreciated as among the cultural revolution's most laudable goals.

THE TASKS OF PUBLIC HEALTH IN SOVIET RUSSIA
N. Semashko

In the area of public health, Soviet medicine must first of all set before itself those basic democratic aims which the former so-called public (that is, municipal and zemstvo) medicine did not achieve. These goals are: free and widely accessible medical help, together with an increase in quality, and the elimination of unsanitary and harmful living and working conditions for workers.

The old (zemstvo and municipal) medicine did much of the value in the direction of democratization of medicine and sanitation. But there was much that it could not do, even if it wished to. To move the urban poor from musty dungeons to spacious rooms in well-built houses, to really struggle with social disease, to create normal conditions of work for the worker—all this is unattainable if we are to regard private property as something holy and inviolable. The old health system hesitated before it as before an insurmountable barrier; Soviet power—Communist power—has broken this barrier. And with Soviet health services the possibility has been opened for carrying out real health gains, not merely lip-service to policy, particularly in housing, in the interest of the poor. The perspective of real democratization of medical practice has come into being with Soviet medicine.

But all these reforms require colossal monetary expenditures. For example, for the implementation in Moscow alone of only one reform for rendering free medical care at home required several million rubles. The raising of the quality of medical care, the general accessibility of special help*—all this would simply be a back-breaking burden on local and general state finances.

Medical practice up to recent times was organized on the principle of departmentalization. Departmental partitions truncated the unified living body of medical organization. As a result, municipal and zemstvo institutions and organizations had their own special existence, while governmental ones (that is, those of the Ministry of the Interior) acted on

---

Statement of the Commissar of Health published in the compendium *Oktiabr'skii perevorot i diktatura proletariata,* Moscow, 1919. See also the author's *Health Protection in the USSR,* London, 1934, and the discussion by Mark G. Field, *Doctor and Patient in Soviet Russia,* Cambridge, Mass., 1957.

*The introduction of free dental care alone cost the Moscow Soviet several million rubles. [N.S.]

their own; military ones acted independently also from one another; charitable ones (the so-called departments of the Empress Maria) acted autonomously from all the others, etc., ad infinitum. It is clear that such a situation could lead only to the most complete lack of coordination of aims, the most harmful discord in actions, and to a completely unnecessary dispersal of energies and means.

Out of this there arose another organizational task for Soviet medicine: the consolidation of all medicine, its organization both in the capitals and in the localities according to one general plan, and the elimination of any distinctions in formal dress and of any privileges in medical work. After a series of preparatory steps, the reform of unification was finally accomplished by a decree of the Council of People's Commissars on the creation of a Commissariat of Health, on July 11 [1918].

Besides the organization of all medical matters, this unification made it financially possible to put into effect most major hospital and sanitation reforms in the interest of the poor. Supplies of resources and institutions were colossal. There were many during peacetime. They grew during the period of the war. They were left criminally unutilized (if not plundered), because during the time of Romanov and Kerensky, uniformed department bureaucrats kept them from general consumption.

When Soviet medicine in Moscow received the opportunity of absorbing the "departmental" institutions (of Empress Maria etc.), a startling picture was revealed. These hospitals represent colossal riches, they are marvelously equipped, but they were either not used at all, or not used in a way necessary for the interests of the city population. As a result, the mere reorganization of these hospitals according to one urban plan offered an opportunity for raising medical care in Moscow right away, of opening branches which the Moscow population only dreamed about, and all this not only without supplemental expenditures, but even with a reduction of former unproductive expenditures.

The same in the area of sanitation. The history of each epidemic wailed against uncoordinated activities of the former departments. And if, for example, the struggle with the current cholera epidemic were to be waged according to the rules of departmental discord, then exhausted, war ravaged and starving Russia could cruelly be made to pay for the advancing epidemic. But only the concentration of the entire struggle in the hands of the Commissariat of Health has maintained the possibility of conducting business with such an economy of energy and means and with such intensity, that even correspondents of foreign bourgeois newspapers have had to recognize that this time Soviet Russia has defeated cholera with hitherto unseen success.

For an explanation of this success, and also for a characterization of the entire medical organization from top to bottom, it is necessary to keep in mind that this entire organization is constructed on a proletarian basis.

131

The Soviets of Workers' and Peasants' Deputies in the localities elect their own medical-sanitation departments, which guide all medical and sanitation activity. Physicians as such are no more than specialists, assisting with their knowledge, putting the organization of health care properly into order with their advice. It stands to reason that it is the duty of the Soviets to give to these specialists the opportunity to carry out their activities widely and without obstacles. And in all practical undertakings, in the discussion of their plans, and in their implementation proletarian organizations take the most active and direct part—factory committees, trade unions, workers' cooperatives, etc.

It is also necessary to note the growth of medical insurance, which is increasing with each month. The circle of insured has expanded to all forms of hired labor. Organizations of medical insurance are even beginning to penetrate into the working elements of the peasantry. Therefore, medical insurance is quantitatively expanding to the greater circle of the Soviet Republic's population. Qualitatively, it is being organized as a model of proletarian medicine, being at the same time of high quality and scientifically organized. In the future it will lead to the nationalization of medicine, which is the culmination of medical and sanitation reform based on proletarian principles.

THE TASKS OF SOCIAL WELFARE IN SOVIET RUSSIA
A. Vinokurov

At the present moment, while we are terminating the old war with Germany, while we are being pulled into a new war with Anglo-French imperialism, and are carrying on Civil War, while the breaking of capitalistic relations is taking place, life has made the tasks of social welfare into matters of the first importance.

The war with Germany has left behind millions of invalids and deserted families. No accurate count has yet been made of how many lives that imperialist slaughterhouse cost us. Judging by available data it is an enormous number. For example, according to the data of the All-Russian Zemstvo Union, of four and one-half million soldiers who passed through their hospital facilities, only forty-eight percent checked out in good health. More than half are either invalids or in need of further care. In addition, up to three million prisoners are in captivity in Germany and Austria, among whom no less than half are ill and maimed.

In addition to invalids, the war resulted in no less than a million deserted families, left for the most part without means of subsistence. The Civil War, war with the Czechs, the White armies, with the Anglo-French as well as Japanese and Americans at their backs, are producing new cadres of wounded, sick, dead, and more abandoned families.

The war brings about the destruction of the industrial life of the country, curtails production, disgorges masses of workers and creates new populations who are in need of social services.

Even peaceful work in mills and factories, in trade, industry, and transport results in hundreds of thousands who have become sick, incapacitated and invalid, and are in need of social support.

The sickness and death rates of the working class are many times greater than those of well-to-do segments of the population and they create huge armies of invalids and families of widows and orphans, deprived of their breadwinners and without the possibility of supporting themselves through their own efforts.

If one adds to this the intensification of illness and death rates due to a worsening diet, to an insufficient food supply as a result of war with the

Statement of the Commissar of Public Welfare published in the compendium *Oktiabr'skii perevorot i diktatura proletariata*, Moscow, 1919. See also the discussion by Bernice Madison, *Social Welfare in the Soviet Union*, Stanford, 1968.

White Guard, Czechs, etc., then it becomes clear what an enormous task confronts the Worker-Peasant Government at this time with respect to social welfare.

What inheritance did the Russian Soviet Federated Socialist Republic receive from the tsarist and compromise [Provisional Government, ed.] regimes, and what did the latter regimes do for the social support of workers and victims of imperialist war?

The tsarist and compromise regimes left the law of 1912 on pensions for those maimed in war as an inheritance to Soviet Russia. They threw to war invalids a beggarly pension of thirty to two-hundred and sixteen rubles a year and to the families of soldiers, rations of an average of no more than ten rubles per family member a month.

In one of its first acts, the Worker-Peasant Government raised the pension of war-maimed to 1125 rubles a year for complete invalids. In addition, it introduced class-based rations for soldiers' families, depriving kulak elements, with the released sums used to raise the rations of the city and village poor.

Putting aside for some time full support according to a minimum living wage for invalids of previous wars, until the introduction in the near future of a general law on social welfare, the Worker-Peasant Government has introduced for the soldiers of the Red Army, who are carrying on the war for the socialist fatherland, and for their families, support in sums ranging from 450 to 3000 rubles, the exact sum depending upon the degree of loss of the ability to work, and 1500 to 2250 rubles for their families, depending upon the number of children. In addition it has increased the distribution of supply rations to families of soldiers currently serving and has augmented the children's ration to equal the amount of an adult's.

In addition to support for war invalids through pensions, the Worker-Peasant Government is spending large sums (ninety-four million rubles are being requested for the second half of 1918) on further treatment, production of artificial limbs, training war invalids and care of chronic invalids.

The events through which we are living—the war with the Czechs, the White Guard, and with Anglo-French imperialism—are creating large cadres of victims of counter-revolution. In areas occupied by Czechs, by Anglo-French troops, by Krasnov's supporters and other bands, White Guard rebellions are accompanied by the flight of working classes of the population and by the destruction of their economy and by the execution of Soviet workers, who leave behind deserted families.

The Worker-Peasant Government has allocated one-hundred million rubles into a fund for aid to victims of counter-revolution, and has promulgated a decree concerning the formation of central and local committees to render this assistance.

At the moment, a central committee, attached to the People's

Commissariat of Social Welfare, has already been formed, with representatives of the following commissariats: Social Welfare, Interior, Labor, the Supreme Soviet of Agriculture, Health Care, Finance, and others. Administrators for the organization of aid on the local level have been sent on missions to the southern front, to the Volga front (in Simbirsk, Saratov, Kazan), and to the northern Caucasus and to the Urals.

The Soviet Republic has, from the beginning, worked to realize for the social welfare of the working class full social insurance on the principles of: (1) the extension of insurance to all workers without exception and for any kind of loss of the ability to work due to illness, injury, invalidism, age, maternity and unemployment; (2) support, according to a minimum living wage, for those who lose the ability to work; (3) charging businesses and establishments with insurance premiums independently of workers' wages; (4) placing the direction of all insurance matters into the hands of workers, and removing employers from this process. The tsarist and compromise governments did very little for the working class in this respect. The insurance laws of 1912 applied only to workers in major factory and mill industry and left aside the support of workers in small industries, of the commercial and agricultural proletariat, of workers in transport and domestic industry, and so on. Support applied only to illness and injury. Costs were largely borne (three-fifths) by the workers, and allowances were miniscule, from one half to two-thirds of the wage.

Kerensky's 1917 compromise government did not alter things much. The number of insured workers was broadened to include workers in smaller industries. Commercial, agricultural, transport and domestic workers, servants, even public service workers, were left aside as before. The maximum payments remained the same two-thirds; half the cost fell upon the workers.

The Worker-Peasant Government issued decrees in November and December [1917] authorizing the initiation of full social welfare. A decree was issued regarding support in cases of illness and unemployment, which extended to all hired workers without exception, and placed the cost entirely upon businesses and firms, raised the payments to the level of full wages, and turned over the management of these matters to the workers, removing it from the employers.

Along with this, the Worker-Peasant Government began working out a general insurance law, a project which has already been accomplished and which will be submitted in the immediate future for consideration to the All-Russian Insured Workers' Congress and for ratification by the Soviet of People's Commissars and the All-Russian Central Executive Committee.

This general social welfare law will undoubtedly initiate a new era in the area of social welfare for working people, surpassing all available benefits in that respect in the most advanced countries of the world, and will constitute the gateway to socialism.

It will make all kinds of insurance a reality, affecting all those who live by their own labor, paying everyone who has lost the ability to work, according to a minimum living wage, and giving abandoned workers' families, which are incapable of working, the pension necessary for their survival after the wage earner's death. Finally, it will place the burden of payments upon enterprises and businesses, freeing the worker from such payments. Every kind of insurance payments will be combined to form a general insurance treasury, with divisions of the various types. All of Soviet Russia will be covered with city and neighborhood social welfare offices, where anyone who earns his own living can receive, in case of the loss of ability to work, necessary treatment, stipends, and in the case of chronic invalidism, a pension, and where abandoned families will find the necessary support. This will demand an enormous expenditure (up to twenty-five percent of earned income) but this will not prevent the Worker-Peasant Government from taking this necessary step on the road to socialism.

One of the major tasks of social welfare is that of supporting orphaned and homeless children. The bourgeois order has left the Soviet Republic with a legacy of "foundling hospitals" for abandoned children and the so-called "foster homes business", sending children from orphanages to peasants in the villages for "raising", where the children have died like flies and the death rate among the children has been one-hundred percent. These were in the full sense of the word "starvers of children", "angel factories". The old order left behind it dirty asylums for the children of poverty, with aged male orderlies as educators in charge, and rich institutes for children of the well-to-do and privileged classes, where children were raised in the spirit of autocracy, orthodoxy and idleness.

The Worker-Peasant Government had to initiate a radical break, and had to clear away these institutions for children, reorganizing them on the basis of communist social welfare.

With this aim in mind, the old foundling hospitals and foster home system had to be abandoned, and in their places new "homes" for mothers and children, nurseries and caretakers in the villages set up, so that mothers who, for one reason or another, are unable to raise their children, do not break their ties with them, do not abandon them, but openly bring them in to be raised, and maintain their ties with their children on a regular basis. This kind of "home for mothers and children," "nurseries" and the like are becoming public homes for raising children of breast-feeding and infant ages. The children are receiving appropriate food, care and upbringing, under the supervision of specially instructed nurses, doctors, and educators.

The Worker-Peasant Government has "homes for mothers and children" organized in this exemplary way in Moscow; they are beginning

136

to appear all over the provinces. Thus a blow will be struck against the bourgeois order of things, which dispatched to the other world, because of abnormal familial relations, hundreds of thousands of babies, and thus the lives of more than a hundred thousand children will be saved.

The Worker-Peasant Government had to make a similar break in the upbringing of older children with respect to orphanages, institutes, and so on.

The children had to be made more sanitary, they had to be dressed, the old orderlies had to be replaced with a new contingent of workers, and the principle of labor had to be introduced. The institutes had to be emptied of children of well-to-do and privileged parents and their doors opened to the children of the village and city poor.

The main principle upon which the Worker-Peasant Government bases social welfare is that of necessary government aid on a rational basis to those who are unable to work and who are needy, aid free from any taint of charity or beggarly presents, calculated so that anyone becoming needy can, if possible, get back on his feet and return to a life of work. If that is not possible due to his invalidism, then appropriate care is offered to him.

Guided by this principle, the Commissariat of Social Welfare offers aid only to those who are unable to work and who do not have other forms of support. Guided by this principle, the Commissariat of Social Welfare has begun an interminable war against parasitism and idleness in all its forms. It is introducing the principle of labor in all institutions for the support of children, teaching them from the first days of their lives to work and to be independent. It opens the doors of childrens' homes for social support only to the children of the urban and village poor, evicting from them well-to-do and privileged elements, who stuck to these places under the tsarist and conciliatory regimes. It opens the doors of "homes" for those who have lost the ability to work and for those who have no means of survival, to invalids, to widows, to the old, driving out of these "homes" those who can work, training invalids for work and thus returning them to a working life, subsidizing work communes for invalids and giving them the possibility of continuing to work and not to be a burden on the state. It deprives of their pensions the henchmen of the old regime, who are capable of work and who have other means of support.

Rebuilding social welfare on these principles, as described, dispensing with charity, the Worker-Peasant Government implements communist social welfare, by which it means that anyone who is an invalid or in need, anyone who is unable to work, be that person a child or adult, can count on not dying of hunger and on receiving rational aid from the government. Thus the Soviet Republic indeed supports all who are in need in this respect, dismissing parasitism from society and educating its citizens in work and socialist habits.

In order to accomplish this immense work, it is necessary to involve

137

workers' organizations in it, professional workers, insurance workers, and so on. In this connection, the merger of all agencies managing social services is absolutely necessary: the Department of Social Insurance in the Commissariat of Labor, various pension departments in different commissariats, pension and savings units and other offices, into one independent agency in the Commissariat of Social Insurance and Welfare. Only by uniting all matters relating to social welfare into one organization, only by giving that agency independence and self-sufficiency, will the Worker-Peasant Government have enough strength to accomplish the immense tasks which communist social service places before it.

WORK OF THE PEOPLE'S COMMISSARIAT OF HEALTH
N. Semashko

Great difficulty has attended the carrying out of the work of the People's Commissariat of Health. Epidemics, the general disorganization left by the imperialistic war, which was much increased by the civil war, and food difficulties, were among the serious impediments met with in the work of the institutions concerned with public health. One epidemic followed close upon the heels of the other, requiring the entire attention of the medical staff, and, as a result, even the most essential reforms and improvements were capable only of partial accomplishments, if they did not have to be postponed altogether.

The year 1918 was marked by a cholera epidemic. The People's Commissariat of Health undertook the most energetic measures to stop this epidemic and, in spite of very difficult working conditions, the outcome was a success: only 35,619 cases of cholera were recorded in 1918, while the previous cholera epidemic, in 1908, had more than 200,000 such cases. In the autumn of 1918, the "Spanish Influenza" swept over the country; more than 700,000 cases were recorded. In addition to the practical measures, the People's Commissariat of Health also undertook a far-reaching scientific study of this as yet little known disease; scientific staffs were organized and instructed to gather all possible information concerning the nature and the types of the disease; meetings were held and much material was collected. Now a special commission, including many experts, is digesting this material and preparing it for publication.

After the Spanish influenza came the typhus. This epidemic began in the autumn of 1918 and reached its climax in the spring of 1919. During the eight months ending with July, 1919, the total number of cases of typhus registered was 1,299,263, of which between eight and ten per cent ended fatally. The cities, whose food situation was particularly grave, were most affected.

In July and August the typhus subsided, only a few cases still being recorded. In October, and more particularly in November and December, the typhus again began to increase. Its revival occurred about the time of the advance of our army in Siberia, and was due to the fact that all the districts that were being evacuated by the Whites were full of typhus. As a matter of fact, it was the friendly relations between our soldiers and the

---

From *Soviet Russia*, Sept. 18, 1920.

local population and the war prisoners that aided in spreading this epidemic in the army. Serious efforts had to be put forth to prevent it from reaching the rest of the country. When the epidemic subsided in the East, and our army was advancing in the South, the disease began to infiltrate from the South; other epidemics encountered by the advancing army were: intermittent fever, very serious typhoid fever and cholera epidemics. We did not succeed in putting down these South Russian epidemics until late in March, 1920. Other sections of the country had already been cleared of it by the beginning of the same month. No epidemic appearances of typhoid fever were still to be observed in May.

There was no cholera in the summer of 1919, only a few sporadic cases being recorded.

The People's Commissariat of Health also paid special attention to smallpox infection; from November 1, 1918, to July, 1919, there were 81,851 such cases registered. The most energetic measures were taken by the People's Commissariat of Health to oppose this epidemic. Former governments had never dared attempt to take such measures; by decree of the Soviet of People's Commissars of April 16, 1919, obligatory vaccination was provided for in Russia. Large credits were allotted and vaccine distributed with the purpose of exterminating this epidemic. Smallpox is now nonexistent.

Details of the Soviet Medical System

Owing to the extremely hard conditions of work, already suggested above, the People's Commissariat of Health could never have carried out its duties if the Revolution, which so completely altered the course of Russian national life, had not also made considerable changes in this field of activity.

The great alteration in question was the complete reorganization of public service. All medical services were united into a single institution which now exists as an independent department, or the People's Commissariat of Health.

Already before the war the European medical press was discussing the possibility of such a department. In 1913, a well-known French medical writer, Mirman, in one of the articles contributed by him to "Hygiene" asked what would be the source of information to answer a French deputy who might ask what measures the French Government undertook in order to fight phthisis, and arrived at the conclusion that four ministers would have to answer the question, the Ministers of Labor, Agriculture, Interior, and Public Instruction, possibly, in addition, the Ministers of War and of the Navy. Of course, the sanitary efforts of the hygienic service among various institutions produce clashes and endless expenditures of labor and funds. "The organization of a Department of Public Health," writes

Mirman, "would bring order into this chaos." The honor of having established the first Commissariat of Public Health belongs to Soviet Russia. Furthermore, such unification was a necessity brought about by the situation, and made possible the task of carrying out a health service at all, by coordinating the work of the military and civil medical services, avoiding duplication, utilizing in the most economic manner the limited medical staff (reduced by the mobilization and by the epidemics) and the very small supply of medications (which could not be increased owing to the blockade).

We see, therefore, that the creation of the People's Commissariat of Health is important not only from the standpoint of principle, but also from the practical point of view.

There is an additional factor which much facilitated the work of public health. It is the watchword set up by the People's Commissariat of Health, which has been strictly followed from the very outset: "the workers themselves must take care of their health."

Everyone understands that in Russia all branches of government, including therefore the Commissariat of Health, are in the hands of representatives of the workers and peasants: "the Soviets of Workers', Peasants' and Red Soldiers' Delegates." But the watchword of the Commissariat of Health means more than this. It means particularly that a great deal of assistance is received in the daily work of the Commissariat from the people themselves. In explanation, let us mention the Workers' Committees to Combat Epidemics, established in 1918 by the Soviet of People's Commissars. These committees functioned not only in the cities, but also in the larger villages, assisting the local sections of the People's Commissariat of Health. During typhus epidemics, the duties of such committees consisted in inspecting the baths, the supply of soap, cleanliness of lodgings, especially of public institutions (stations, jails, boarding houses, etc.), and in spreading among the population correct information and advice on hygiene. Such committees are appointed in all the important districts of large cities; the elected have representatives in the factories. The assistance of women (workers and peasants) is particularly desired, for, being housekeepers, it is easy for them to teach the population habits of cleanliness. We may say without exaggeration that the epidemics of typhus and cholera were stopped chiefly by the assistance of the workers' and peasants' committees. But this is not all. Not a single important problem has been carried out without the assistance of the workers. The question of systematic measures to combat social diseases, such as phthisis and venereal diseases, was discussed with the representatives of trade unions, Women's Organizations, Young People's Unions, etc. The organization of sanitary protection for workers was carried out by special inspectors, elected from among the workers themselves: inspectors of dwellings were organized in the same way. Not only from the standpoint of organization,

141

but also from the standpoint of its practical value, this system was of great importance. It is a fact that the People's Commissariat of Health can only overcome the numerous difficulties met with in this impoverished and devastated country by assuring itself of the support and assistance of the population.

The third peculiarity of the Soviet medical organization is this: it is now operating on an entirely different social basis. Formerly, necessary sanitary measures for the benefit of the poorer classes always met with obstacles. For instance, sanitary protection of labor in factories always interferes with the profit of the capitalists. Motherhood and childhood could not be fully protected, even though such protection may be provided for, owing to the merciless necessity of increasing the production of the plant. Private property rights also interfered with the improvements of housing conditions, etc. In Soviet Russia, sanitary reforms do not know such obstacles.

The above circumstances played a very important part in combatting the so-called social diseases. The name "social disease" was derived from the social conditions in a capitalistic state, as even the bourgeois medical service recognizes the fact that diseases, such as phthisis and venereal diseases, are an outcome of these conditions.

The betterment of the economic conditions of the working class, the abolition of the system of exploitation, the establishment of protection of labor, motherhood and childhood—all these measures formed a strong foundation for success in combatting social diseases, this evil of humanity.

Purely curative measures, however, are only one of the links in the long chain of measures for combatting tuberculosis and venereal diseases. A great deal of work has been done in this field: in the year 1919 we had 17 summer sanatoriums with 876 beds; 54 permanent sanatoriums with 4,750 beds; 5 infirmaries for the tuberculous, with 310 beds; 5 children's sanatoriums with 280 beds and 9 dispensaries.

This summer (1920) beds are installed much more rapidly, as large private estates are used for this purpose, and there is, therefore, sufficient reason to believe that at the end of this year the number of beds will have increased fifty per cent.

For combatting syphilis alone, 3,363 special beds and 29 ambulances were available in the period from January 1, 1919, to May 1, 1920, in addition to 11 laboratories performing the Waserman test.

In addition, the work of instruction in hygiene has been directed very methodically along the line of combatting these social diseases, thus making the fight particularly against infantile tuberculosis and syphilis effective. Also, the protection of motherhood and infancy has attracted particular attention on the part of the Soviet Government. At present, the following institutions are available in Soviet Russia:

142

	Homes for Babes in Arms	Institutions for Children 1-3 years old	Day-Nurseries	Consulta-tions	Milk Kitchens	Homes for Mothers' Children
Total for Russia . . .	115	56	24	72	4	4
Total for Moscow . . .	3	8	36	21	14	1

What the Soviet Government Has Done for Public Health

In examining the results attained by the People's Commissariat of Health, the difficult conditions under which this work has been carried out must again be emphasized. Numerous diseases were called forth by the war and by the starvation conditions. Under these awful conditions, which are serious even for people in good health, it was impossible to employ good, systematic treatment. It was only the methods introduced by the Soviet Government that made it possible to move effectively against these conditions.

We have spoken above of the work done in suppressing epidemics; the money spent in this endeavor during one and a half years by the People's Commissariat of Health was over one milliard rubles (about 1,200,000,000 rubles). Never before had so many patients been admitted to hospitals shortly after their infection.

At present there are 150,000 special beds for civilians suffering from epidemics. In addition, there are 250,000 beds for soldiers.

The organization of treatment has made great progress. The report of the All-Russian Conference of Health Boards shows that during two and a half years the number of treatment beds for civilians increased forty per cent (we must point out that the figures include only permanent beds in therapeutic, surgical, special and other hospitals; special beds for the infected, as above indicated are not included); there are now four provincial physico-mechanical-therapeutic organizations at Kazan, Saratov, Orel, and Kostroma. No fee is taken in any Soviet hospitals or medical institution for treatment. The ambulatories and the hospitals deliver medications free of charge. The drug stores are nationalized and all medical goods are distributed in the most economical and systematic manner.

Special forms of medical attention are perhaps best illustrated by the example of the development of denistry.

Before October, 1917, free dental ambulatories were very few in number and were found only in the large cities, particularly the capitals. By May 1, we already had 1,406 free national dental ambulatories, uniformly distributed throughout the Republic, including even institutions in villages, which employ 1,776 dental surgeons for free dental care of the population. In addition, 160 dental ambulatories have been organized in the Red Army, for which purpose 1,500 dentists have been mobilized.

There is also a free dental ambulatory in each provincial capital. The expenses for the organization of dental treatment in 1920 are about 352,000,000 rubles.

The government has been particularly effective in the work done in health resorts. Before the October revolution the health resorts were under the direction of various departments and institutions, such as, for instance, the Ministry of Trade and Commerce, Home Office, the Irkutsk Mountain Department, local government of the Caucasus, military direction of the Cossack Army, and even the clergy. At present, however, all health resorts without exception are under the direction of the People's Commissariat of Health. Formerly, health resorts existed only for the rich; now not only treatment, but board and lodgings at these health resorts are at the expense of the government. For 1920, the estimated expenses allotted for the maintenance of health resorts are about two and one-half milliard rubles.

At resorts where formerly there appeared the members of a capitalist society in order to cure their bloated stomachs and gouty limbs, the working people are now restoring their health. According to the statistics of one of the big health resorts, that of Lipetsk, the patients were distributed last year as follows: workers and working members of the intelligentsia, 70 percent; Red Army soldiers and invalids, 25 percent; others, 5 percent. The People's Commissariat of Health has made considerable efforts to broaden the work connected with health resorts, and now that the Crimea has been cut off by the White Guards, we have in Central Russia 20,000 beds at these health resorts, in the Ukraine 35,000; in the Caucasus 40,000; on the coast of the Black Sea, 30,000; in Siberia, 18,000; total, 143,000 beds.

Special attention is paid to health in general. Free feeding of children below the age of sixteen was decreed by the Council of People's Commissars. Thousands of children in winter, and many more in summer, enjoy a stay in the children's colonies and sanitariums, for which purpose the estates of the former landed proprietors are used. The People's Commissariat is particularly interested in children. It is about to install special institutions, to be called "Institutions for Defective Children," in all provincial capitals. This decree of the Council of People's Commissars delegates that children below the age of eighteen are not subject to trial in court. These cases are examined by a special committee composed of officers and teachers, which decides either to send them to an educational or a medical institution of the People's Commissariat of Health, or the People's Commissariat of Instruction.

What Could Not Be Done

There are many problems still remaining unsolved in spite of the two and a half years of work and the results which have been already obtained.

Under the rule of the tsar, every inhabitant paid about one ruble in health taxation. Of this sum ninety-five kopeks went for purposes of general treatment, and only five kopeks for sanitary prophylaxis. In other words, all effort was directed toward curing diseases, while only a very insignificant labor was devoted to their prevention. Furthermore the appropriation for health protection was quite insufficient. Of course, this ridiculous condition obtained even under the Kerensky Government, where more attention was given to cure than to prophylaxis. But all this now is changed. More than sixty per cent of the appropriation of the People's Commissariat of Health for 1920 (the total appropriation for the Commissariat runs into several milliards) will be spent for sanitary prophylaxis. The People's Commissariat of Health will consider it its duty to combat unsanitary health conditions, ignorance, dirt, lice, those wretched vestiges of tsarism and slavery; the Commissariat will do all it can to accustom the people to cleanliness, to improve the sanitary conditions of living, particularly the housing conditions, to put an end to the terrible infant mortality (under the tsar one child out of every four died before the age of one year), to improve the medical systems and make it really accessible to the population and of a nature to be useful to the population. Such are the aims of the People's Commissariat of Health. The economic disorganization, the war and the mobilization, to be sure, have offered very serious obstacles to the full realization of this program.

HOW CAN WE PROTECT THE CHILDREN?
The Mother of a Child

Dear Comrades!

There are many of us, a great many, but not all of us struggled the way I did. Just recently, I have entered a blind alley and can see no way out other than the death or dangerous illness of a child. Do not think that I am one of those neurotic individuals, belligerent, always complaining, and so on. Truthfully, my background is distasteful (I am the daughter of a priest), but that cannot be blamed on me. While I was still in the gymnasium, at the age of twelve, I started tutoring, distributing books, and so on, in a word, working. In 1905 I began to work as a teacher in a factory school. At first I was indiscriminately sympathetic with all revolutionary parties, then with the SR's (there were lots of them). Then I got to know SD's (Bolsheviks) and started sympathizing, then working with them. I did not become a party member, largely out of cowardice; that is, not out of fear of prison, but out of fear of speaking at meetings and the difficulties then, for me, of political economy. Somehow, it was very incomprehensible to me then. Later the reaction set in. One could only offer shelter to party comrades, and keep guard over the literature. In 1914 I married a Bolshevik. You know him—N.N. In 1914 I had a child. Then came the 1917 Revolution.

Everybody who was left after 1905 reacted. And I did, too. I began to attend meetings. So did my husband. But still I had the school and a great deal of work. My husband put the question this way: either he should stay with the child or I should. Of course, I gave him priority. He was, after all, an underground worker and could make speeches. While I, alas, even now will not say two words in front of a crowd. I cannot, after all, I am not cut out to be a party worker! But they thought of me as a good teacher. I worked a lot on the school and pre-school. I worked, studied, and tried to always have a hot meal for my husband when he came home from work. I thought that if I created quiet working conditions for him and if I taught communism to our child and others, that was enough.

My husband and I did well together until he left to spend the winter in another city. There he took up with another woman, but when she found out there was a family, and after talking with me, she decided to break off with him, and she did so.

Letter to *Izvestiya*, from L. Sosnovskii, ed., *Bol'nye voprosy (zhenshchina, sem'ia, i deti)*, Leningrad, 1926, pp. 7-12.

Once again, we got along reasonably well. The child loved his father tremendously. At first, he grew up healthy, but because of the famine and bad living conditions, he became sick and could not recover even in the better conditions of 1922. He came down with a severe case of malaria. I dropped all my work to look after him.

At this point, my husband was sent to another city and there acquired a new wife. He began to find fault with me. When I asked him, the answer was that he had nobody but me. We continued as before. Finally, he began to find fault with my son. I could not restrain myself and demanded an explanation. It appeared that the other woman got tired of playing a secondary role and she demanded legal ties. I was pressured to agree to separation. I found a place to work and prepared to leave. My son, having discovered that his father could no longer live with us, fell ill of inflammation of the cranial membranes. His father broke off with the other woman and soon returned to his family. Because of illness, he was sent to a health resort. We went with him. Life began to improve.

Suddenly the other woman reappeared (we lived, separately, in the same sanatorium). We began once more to be in the way. He suggested that I leave, and said that I turn my son against him. He stubbornly continues to suggest this. My son clings to his father even more than usual. He sees that things are not going well. Besides, children today know too much. My son is nine years old. He is still forbidden to study, but that does not prevent his being knowledgeable about politics, to try to propagandize among his friends, to carry on anti-religious debates with them, and so on. His father either is proud of him or begins pushing him away.

Now, my son began to eat his heart out, to cry, to become pensive. If we were separated it would kill him. If the inflammation were to reappear, that would be the end, and he has the same symptoms as last fall. The main thing is the widening of his pupils. Well, what does one do now? I repeat, I am not alone, there are thousands of deserted children, and they are all suffering. Comrades, do not replace the family for them yet. To embitter my son, as his father suggests, and as many do, I cannot. It would not help much and it would just kill the child faster.

His father's other relationship goes on before his son's eyes. He cries about some other "Aunty" taking Daddy away, clings to him even more closely. What should I do? I have been told that I do not understand because I am not a party member. But could the party tell me to kill a child?

My husband is a good man, sympathetic, kind, but susceptible to the influence of women and to obeying their instructions. The more one tells him what to do, the better. I am too proud to hold on to him underhandedly. If it had been a matter of just myself, I would have left a long time ago. But a sick child, that is why I have humbled myself. But it is impossible, after all, to let the child see how his father is making up to another woman before his very eyes. The child loves both mother and

147

father. Tell me, how are the children to blame in all these dramas? If there were public educational institutions it would be a different matter. But there is not room in them even for complete orphans. And how is such care organized? It depends, by and large, on the personal characteristics of the directors. And what should one do with children now? "Embitter" them? Against his father, a Communist, who was held up to him as an example, as soon as he was old enough to understand that "your father was deported," Daddy is working so that it will be better for poor people, Daddy is for truth and against the bourgeois? How can I tell him now?

If you have got anything to say about this case, drop me a line.

I have been meaning to write you for a long time, but the fact that you know my husband held me back. But you are not going to publish my letter, it is nothing extraordinary. It is just one stage in women's lot and children's fate.

Later, it will be fine. But what about now, in the interim period? What is it like? In a month, if not sooner, my son will find out that his father has left him. And it will kill him.

You say, come to an agreement with my husband?—It will not work, because they do not hear me, they do not believe what I say. At the moment as usual, I am worse than anyone. That I understand, that is the way things are. But the child? What has he done? He is ill. The Pioneers will not take him; he is weak and sick. The school will not either. I had hoped that his father would sooner or later listen to reason and the child would again have a family. But I am still alone. His father does not help in raising him. Or rather occasionally he makes scenes, says all this is nothing but my fantasies. But that is temporary. Until now, this father loved his son and was proud of him; now he is a burden to him.

I am not a party member. How would a Communist have acted in my place? Would she have stopped to fight for a child? To go away is to kill him. What can I do? Work, earn his bread, his subsistence (they do not pay teachers very much). That I can do, but I cannot replace his father for him and he needs his father, too.

When someone talks to me about separation, the first thing they mention is material welfare (payments). For one thing, it is not all that much, even if he will agree to give it, and how can one take it from a man who rejects his own son, and he is rejecting him. I am not grieving for money. It is not as if I have to get used to working. I will manage to feed us, but the child needs his father.

Sorry. The letter is long. But probably you have not gotten many letters of this kind. Tell me, should we let such children die? The doctor said my son would be completely healthy if he were taken care of for two or three years.

The Mother of a Child

PROTECTION OF MOTHER, BABY, AND CHILD IN RUSSIA
N. Semashko

Before the November Revolution, Russia was the classical country of child mortality. One-fourth of all newborn babies died even before they reached their first year. Every year about two million babies were buried in Russia. Child mortality was especially great in the villages among the peasant population.

There were two fundamental causes which contributed to this extraordinary mortality of babies. In the cities, it was the terrific exploitation of the labor of mothers and of pregnant women. It happened frequently that women went on with their work till the very last day of their pregnancy, and sometimes it even happened that women were delivered of their children within the walls of the factory. Thus children have been crippled even while in their mothers' wombs. When the child was born, the mother could not nurse it; she had to leave it at home and feed it with substitutes for food.

In the villages, to these main causes—poverty and exploitation—was added the frightful ignorance of the peasant women, who have no idea of the most elementary rules of hygienic nursing.

The Republic of the toilers first of all concerned itself with the protection of the labor of pregnant and nursing women. A decree was issued to the effect that women cannot be allowed to work eight weeks before and eight weeks after confinement. During all this time the mother receives her regular wages and her full food-ration. Pregnant women receive, besides, better food and a number of privileges in daily life. When the child is born, the mother receives linen and warm clothes for the baby. Nursing mothers are relieved from work several times during the day. Special products, such as milk, eggs, sugar, etc., are given for children on their special children's food-cards.

The greatest attention was given by the Soviet Government to the work of creating a sufficient number of establishments for the protection of mother and child: large model "Homes of Mother and Child", confinement homes, milk dispensaries, nurseries, children's homes, etc. There are at present thousands of such institutions all over Russia, in the cities, at factories and even in many villages. We have already passed through the period when it was necessary to explain to the population the use of these

From *Soviet Russia*, Jan. 29, 1921.

establishments. At present, we are unable to keep up with the constantly growing demand for such institutions, because of the shortage of medicines, food products for the nourishment of children, and various necessary appliances.

Children of a more advanced age have also been an object of constant care on the part of the Soviet Government. Children's homes exist not only in the cities but even in many villages. Children's colonies have been established in many of the best residences of the landlords. During the past summer, about 50,000 children lived in the colonies in the vicinity of Moscow alone. In the schools, the pupils receive hot breakfasts. It is quite touching to see how the population of the cities, frequently suffering from hunger and feeding on substitutes, is giving away the last food supplies for the children. Hired labor of children up to the age of 14 years is prohibited altogether. For children of the age of 14-16 years, the working day is limited to four hours. No child labor is allowed in harmful production. The trade unions pay special attention to the protection of the labor of women and young persons. Their interests are considered also in the carrying out of labor duties.

For weak and sick children there are special establishments, so-called "Forest Schools", which are situated in healthy forest localities. At present there are 33 such schools. Besides, there are 34 sanatorium-schools and sanatorium-colonies for children inclined to consumption, and 37 sanatoria for consumptive children.

Further, children under the age of 18 years, who have committed some offense, are not considered as criminals. On the contrary, we look upon them as victims of capitalist society, who require proper education and cure. Such child offenders are not liable to the general courts, but there are special committees consisting of physicians and pedagogues, to decide whether they are to be placed in institutions of the Public Health Commissariat or of the Commissariat of Public Education. The Public Health Department has 134 such institutions for mentally and physically defective children. There are also 41 schools for deaf and dumb, and 15 schools for blind children.

The difficult conditions in which the Republic was put by the war and blockade had their destructive effects upon the organizations for the children. But the toiling population of the suffering Republic gave away its last piece of bread and the last yard of cloth for the children, because the toilers of the Soviet Republic are conscious that the children represent our better future, that upon their health depends the success of our Socialist construction work. And as soon as the pressure which is exerted upon us by our numerous enemies is made somewhat easier by the efforts of our Red Army, and as soon as our economic and food situation is somewhat improved, the first to feel the benefits of these improvements will be our children, our hope and future.

IV. PROLETARIAN LEGALITY

INTRODUCTION

Early in 1919, ragtag elements of the Red Army entered Riga, the cosmopolitan capital of Latvia. The very appearance of the Bolshevik troops was enough to strike terror in the hearts of the city's bourgeoisie, which had recently lived in relative comfort under the Germans. "We are the Vandals of Justice," one popular account reports the Bolsheviks as declaring, "we are the Barbarians of Right . . . wandering with heavy tread in ironspiked sandals along the Highway of the Future!"[1]

For some in Riga, what made this pronouncement so frightening was the fact that the head of the Soviet administration in Latvia, P. I. Stuchka, was also the Bolsheviks' first Commissar of Justice. The combination of positions gave credence to the idea that Lenin's supporters were vengeful anarchists in the area of law, bent on destroying all traditional legal precepts, and totally without respect for even the most elementary concepts of legality. To many, law was what Bolshevik officials wanted to make it; the courts and their wide range of punitive sanctions were simply another of the party's coercive instruments.

Without diminishing in the slightest the arbitrary horrors of the Bolsheviks' secret police, the wanton disregard for civil rights in the Western sense of the term, or such occurrences as the use of "Peoples' Courts" as an instrument of political terror in the early years of Soviet power, it can still be argued that such a view was very wide of the mark. As the materials of this chapter suggest, early Soviet jurists were deeply concerned with the problems of law and jurisprudence in a proletarian society. They approached theoretical issues with considerable sophistication, and developed a clear and in many ways remarkably progressive approach to problems of nonpolitical crime and punishment, grounded on discrete perspectives of human personality and behavior. Indeed, a number of the innovative concepts of early Soviet jurisprudence have now found widespread acceptance in the West.

A review of the writings of P. I. Stuchka, and especially Evgeny Pashukanis, the leading Soviet legal theorist of the early period, suggests that the crux of the Bolshevik approach lay in a conception of law as a derivative of economic relationships, serving essentially the function of regulating "commodity exchange." Both Stuchka and Pashukanis approach the question historically. In his *General Theory of Law and Marxism*, excerpted below, Pashukanis stresses the role of law in bourgeois society as essentially the guarantor of contractual relationships involving private property. The apparatus of state law is an extension of these guarantees into the public realm. As Stuchka puts it, law in bourgeois society constitutes the apparatus of "protection," which serves to "preserve" a particular (bourgeois) social order. Law in these circumstances can be refined or "improved" (the role of precedent), or extended as an instrument of protection (the role of legislation), but not altered in its social objectives without, in effect, provoking or involving revolutionary change.

The meaning of "equality before the law" thus stems directly from the right of equal protection afforded by bourgeois society to each holder of property. Property becomes the basis for legal status (citizenship), even if many citizens are not, in fact, property owners, since the law enables "legal persons" to acquire property, and affords them protection. Pashukanis extends this notion somewhat by arguing that the "equivalency" of contracting parties in economic relationships is actually carried over into the public areas of crime and punishment, whereby civil compacts (constitutions) become contracts between individuals and the collective social order (state), even to the extent that punishments for crimes are set essentially in terms of the relative "damage" incurred as a result of the contractual breach.

This approach involves an equally important critique of what Pashukanis labels the concepts of "natural law," or "neo-Kantian deontology," that is, the notion that law also derives from some set of transcendent moral values. Neo-Kantian (bourgeois) "dualism" distinguishes the realm of the practical (material) from that of the ideal, postulating distinct (although connected) realms of reality. In this perspective, the *idea* of law, based on moral concepts of right and wrong, precedes experience both logically and epistemologically. The foundations of legality are thus ethical precepts (and assaults against the law are "immoral"), although the specific content of legal systems develop in response to practical necessity.

Pashukanis attacks this view directly in the selection below, calling it a "prescriptive" theory of law which "seeks to explain nothing." As a Marxist, he rejects the Kantian distinction between material reality and the reality of idea (ideals, values), and hence the notion of law as moral imperative. As Stuchka insists, societies are not founded on laws, laws are founded on societies. But unlike many of their Bolshevik colleagues, Pashukanis and Stuchka both reject the "anarchist" notion that proletarian jurisprudence should be "theory-free," i.e. exclusively practical in formulation and execution. On the contrary, such an approach could only lead (and in fact, *did* lead, in innumerable instances) to arbitrariness in regulation and enforcement. It also facilitated a juridical "superstructure" bearing little relationship to the new socio-economic patterns of Bolshevik socialism.

In spite of criticism against their "theorizing," therefore, Pashukanis, Stuchka, and others attempted after October to articulate "transcendent" juridical norms appropriate to the transition period in which Soviet Russia found itself. Full communism would involve the withering of law, essentially a coercive, regulatory instrument, just as it would involve the withering of the state and other "superstructural" elements. Meanwhile, Soviet jurists had to identify those norms by which proletarian law and "Peoples' Courts" could be functionally integrated into the tasks of socialist construction.

At first, as Stuchka points out, an effort was made to maintain pre-revolutionary legal standards, "insofar as those laws have not been changed by the revolution or do not contradict revolutionary conscience and revolutionary legal consciousness." The difficulty here, however, was not only the way in which such a formulation encouraged, rather than reduced, arbitrariness in judicial proceedings, but also the recognition that pre-revolutionary laws necessarily reflected tsarist socio-economic relationships and their protective cover of values, however indirectly. Better in the view of some simply to overturn the tsarist codes and start from scratch. Kozlovsky, for example, in the essay below, argues that codification in any form is essentially "wasted work." But Stuchka and others struggled to develop a set of "Guiding Principles," designed to circumscribe the limits of juridical proceedings, and intended as a foundation for the development of a new set of proletarian legal norms and laws. Published in December 1919, the "Guiding Principles," translated below, have rightly been called "the first systematic exposition of Soviet conceptions of law."[2]

The "Principles" differ dramatically from preceding official conceptions of law in at least three ways (although it should be pointed out that many of the concepts and ideas they express had been discussed by progressive European jurists for a number of years, particularly in Italy, and in this sense were not completely original): first, they admit unabashedly that law "is a system of social relations corresponding to the interests of the ruling class," and that Russian law, developed in the interests of the autocracy and the gentry, must now be systematically reformulated to protect and defend the interests of the proletariat. Law as a partisan social instrument thus replaces law as a transcendent body of ethical (but politically and socially neutral) principles, a concept which was not, of course, supported by the tsarist regime, but for which the Russian bar had been struggling for years, and which the Provisional Government had tried to implement after February 1917. Such notions as "universal civil liberties" and "equality before the law" were thus reduced to contingent principles, subordinate to the defense of proletarian state interests.

Second, the "Principles" attempt to remove any ethical considerations from the concepts of crime and punishment. Crime becomes a "socially harmful act," rather than retribution. Neither notion, of course, eliminates society's need to repress criminals, and the law is clearly seen in this respect as an instrument of coercion. At the same time, however, there is no effort

155

to blame the criminal for his act, or to exact any form of social "atonement." In subsequent Soviet criminal legislation, in fact, until Stalin reverted to traditional language in the early 1930s (a period which also saw the arrest of Pashukanis and other leading Bolshevik jurists), the word "crime" was replaced in statutes with the ethically neutral phrase "social harm," and "punishment" became "penalty".

Third, the "Principles" speak directly to the issue of a criminal's "social background," and consequently reflect a fundamental optimism about the role of criminal law in social reconstruction. It is assumed (Articles 9 and 10) that *all* criminals are capable of being "rehabilitated," but that some, because of deeply ingrained social prejudices, will "refuse" socialization, in which case incarceration or capital punishment might be warranted. Thus the question of punishment is theoretically tied to the criminal's "level of consciousness." Similarly, (Article 12) the question of social background must also be considered by a court before imposing sentence, in an effort to distinguish whether "socially harmful acts" were the consequence of material deprivation or persistent "bourgeois" values (greed, avarice, etc). In the vagueness of these prescriptions there was, of course, enormous latitude for subjectivity on the part of Soviet courts, but at their core, as Kozlovsky's essay shows clearly, was enormous optimism. There was little doubt in many Soviet jurists' minds that crime as it existed in pre-revolutionary society would eventually fall away, as changing social conditions eliminated the objective causes of criminal behavior.

Although the "Guiding Principles" were expressly to cover criminal law, the concepts they reflected carried into other judicial areas as well. Goikhbarg's essay on civil law shows, for example, how early Soviet jurists hoped to replace the "private individual" basis of pre-revolutionary civil law with one based on "collectives," as juridically responsible parties. "A laboring society" he writes "must eliminate all private-legal relations of ownership and individuality—in other words, all civil law."

In some areas, as Goikhbarg indicates, it was relatively easy to "proletarianize" civil law. Rights of property ownership could easily be modified or eliminated; contracts, mortgages and other legal instruments based on private ownership concepts could be changed; and such principles as "the right of inheritance" could simply be replaced with a confiscatory escheat. This "destructive" task of early Soviet law, as Goikhbarg labels it, required only some general sense of purpose, which the decrees of the Bolshevik regime itself readily supplied. In other areas, however, the issues were more subtle. Proletarian civil law could not eliminate the need for contracts, particularly in industry, where specific goods had to be ordered and delivered on a regular basis and according to mutually agreeable prices. If collectives, rather than individuals, were the only acceptable contracting parties, the problem of sanctions for contract breaches became acute in cases (such as large factories) where the size of the collective membership or the complexity or number of specific contracts precluded general awareness of their terms. Criminal sanctions for non-fulfillment made little sense, since they were bound to deprive the economy of needed workers and technicians. And the lack of any sanctions at all (as was often the case in these early years) essentially reduced the civil contract to an unenforceable agreement.

Somewhat similar problems emerged in the area of the courts and the ministry of justice. On one hand, as Stuchka indicates in his essay on "The Old and New Court", it was impossible to eliminate overnight all pre-revolutionary judicial institutions, but necessary at the same time to alter the basis on which many decisions traditionally were made. One way to do this was to dissolve the Senate, which served as Russia's Supreme Court, and replace it with a Soviet body capable of reviewing cases according to Bolshevik values. Another was to replace the bar with a system of state (party) appointed procurators and public defenders. On the other hand, the expertise of Russia's pre-revolutionary judiciary was still needed in matters of evidence, trial procedure, and especially court administration, where the strike of chancellery workers in the ministry of justice caused administrative havoc in the weeks after October, and undoubtedly burdened the fledgling Soviet regime with scores of criminal offenders who might otherwise have been incarcerated.

To solve these problems, the Soviet government adopted what at first seemed an appropriate solution: the elevation of ordinary workers and laymen to the status of judges in a new system of "Peoples' Courts," where they heard cases together with professional jurists. Procedures governing the relevance of evidence and testimony were also altered to allow the introduction of wide-ranging material concerning social background, political attitudes, character, and the like. Assuming ordinary workers genuinely shared the social and political objectives of the new proletarian dictatorship, Stuchka and others initially felt confident that such modifications would alter Russia's court system in a progressive manner while preserving legitimate (i.e. politically neutral) court procedures.

From the start, however, like the tsarist courts after the judicial reform of 1864, the Soviet "Peoples' Courts" did not behave in predictable ways. For example, the former Assistant Minister of Education, Countess Panina, was accused of sequestering 93,000 rubles from the ministry to prevent their being used by the Bolsheviks (a charge she readily admitted), and was tried late in 1917 as a counter-revolutionary and "enemy of the people." In testimony presented to the Peoples' Court, a parade of ordinary workers testified to her humanitarianism and concern for their welfare, which impressed the panel of judges enough to render a very mild sentence. The money was soon repaid through contributions, and Countess Panina was freed, much to the government's embarrassment.[3]

This and other cases suggested the "imperfections" of early proletarian courts, just as popular resistance to many of the Bolsheviks' early economic and social policies raised serious questions about its legitimacy as a workers' and peasants' regime. And Stuchka's Peoples' Court was easily corrupted. All one had to do was assure the views of lay judges corresponded to the goals of the government attorney or prosecutor, and the court's decision could be readily pre-ordained. This, of course, violated the basic principle of workers' justice articulated by Stuchka and others, but here, as in many other areas, "progressive" institutions often acted in repressive ways.

Still, from the viewpoint of some Soviet jurists, this first phase of the cultural revolution was generally a success in the area of law and jurisprudence. Many of the ideas expressed in the following selections, particularly those relating crime to social conditions and substituting rehabilitation for punishment, have found general acceptance in the West. The achievements of Russia's "revolution in law" over the first five years are summarized in the final selection by P. I. Stuchka.

PROLETARIAN LAW
P. Stuchka

Understanding law in the bourgeois sense, we cannot speak of proletarian law, since the very goal of the socialist revolution consists of doing away with laws and their replacement with a new socialist order. For the bourgeois jurist, the word "law" is inseparably bound with an understanding of the state as an organ of protection, a tool of coercion in the hands of the ruling class. With the fall, or more correctly, the dying off of the state, law in the bourgeois sense falls naturally, atrophies. So, we can speak of proletarian law as the law of a transitional period, the period of the dictatorship of the proletariat, or even of the law of a socialist society in a completely new sense of that word, since with the elimination of the government as an organ of oppression in the hands of one or another class or interdependent people the socialist order will not be regulated by force, but by the conscious good will of working people, that is, by the whole of the new society.

The tasks of the bourgeois revolution in this respect were considerably easier than those of the socialist revolution, as it was set forth by Voltaire in his well-known revolutionary statement, "If you want to have good laws, burn your old ones and make new laws." But we know how little these words were fulfilled by bourgeois upheavals, even the most decisive of them, the great French Revolution. It mercilessly burned the castles of feudal lords and the deeds of purchase of those castles. It abolished privileges and their holders, it replaced the entire feudal order with a bourgeois one. But the oppression of humans by other humans remained, and even the old laws turned out not to have been burned, and continued to be applied. The legal monument of the French Revolution, the Napoleonic "Civil Code," was written only ten years after the Revolution (in 1804) when the counter-revolution triumphed, not to mention purely counter-revolutionary codexes, like the Statutes on Legal Proceedings and Criminal Regulations (in 1808 and 1810).

From *Oktiabr'skii perevorot i diktatura proletariata,* Moscow, 1919, as republished in P.I. Stuchka, *Izbrannye proizvedeniia po marksistsko-leninskoi teorii prava,* Riga, 1964, pp. 256-72. Petr Ivanovich Stuchka helped found the Communist Party of Latvia, and after serving as Commissar of Justice (1917-18), became Chairman of the Latvian Soviet regime. After 1919 he was also Deputy Commissar of Justice and between 1923 and 1932, chairman of the Supreme Court of the RSFSR.

In one of his first pieces (1843) Marx clearly draws the basic distinction between socialist and bourgeois revolutions. The bourgeois revolution dissolves old feudal forms of organization through the political liberation of independent individuality, but does not add new forms of economic ties and subordination of that individuality. It divides the personality in the citizen and the individual, so that all socio-economic relationships of a citizen are related to his personal matters, which are outside the interests of the state. "A person leads a double life, not only in thoughts and consciousness, but a double life in reality as well, a heavenly and an earthly life; a life in the political community, in which he recognizes himself as a social being, and a life in a citizen's society, in which he acts as a private individual, looks at others as means, lowers himself to the role of means and becomes the plaything of alien forces."

Private interests do not matter, because whether or not a person is satisfied with a bourgeois state, whether or not he has to tire himself out in unsuitable work for a meager existence until overtaken by extreme age, whether or not he has enough time for the satisfaction of his spiritual needs—that is a private matter, the egotistical interest of every individual person, with which the state has no business. "The state can be a republic without people being free."

For the bourgeois revolution, depending on the degree of its resoluteness, it was enough to put one class in power, instead of or jointly with another, in order to change the form of organization of state power. And the form of oppression could be easily changed without any substantial change in the text of the laws. The permanence of a law seems to be the most significant basis for human society, insofar as it is based upon the principle of exploitation of man by man. Thus, the laws of slave-owning Rome survived not only the feudal order, but also all phases of developing capitalism, including imperialism. "Law and right continue through inheritance like an eternal disease."—Goethe.

The bourgeois revolution not only did not always listen to Voltaire's words, and did not burn the old laws quite so decisively, but in those cases in which the old laws were destroyed, this turned out to be insufficient to uproot them from memory and their usage by people. "People's minds are dependable storehouses in which the stone tablets of Moses with their legacies are facts just as real as all the newest state directives about bread rations. Ancient history is closely interwoven in them with contemporary history to form an indivisible and equivalent reality."—Renner. Here is the source of all theories about the divine origin of such institutions as sacred ownership, of the "inborn" character of class privilege or of the "natural rights" of owners to the service of workers, and so on.

Just as socialism, in theory, is an unrelenting critic of all existing institutions, so the proletarian revolution is, above all, the relentless destroyer of the entire existing state and social order. It immediately

160

destroys two statutes of tsarist criminal legislation, Statutes 100 and 126, and frees prosecutors of the counter-revolution from unnecessary discussions about whether to invoke the given revolution under Statute 100 (punishing for a bourgeois or political revolution, for "subversion of governmental power") or under Statute 126 (referring to a socialist upheaval, "overthrowing the social order").

And, as in everything, so in the field of law, the proletarian revolution, for the first time in history, consciously and irrevocably puts into practice the demand for true democracy. It brings to life the words of Voltaire and solemnly throws all sixteen volumes of "The Collected Laws of the Russian Empire" on the bonfire, along with the empire itself and imperialism. In vain have some of our revolutionaries begun to cut "Codes of the Russian Revolution" from those few burnt sheets which survived this blaze, instead of securing in statutes the real achievements of the proletarian revolution or of noting landmarks for the rightness of its course, in other words, to create new, really revolutionary laws.

The proletarian revolution is committed to creativity. It must be daring not only in the work of destroying, but in its law-creating role. And references to the former laws of war or peacetime seem to be completely out of place in the decrees of a Worker-Peasant government, as these laws of earlier governments should mean nothing to us.

But the socialist revolution is not just a leap into the unknown. It is a lengthy, more or less continuous process of civil war, as a result of which, the bourgeois social order, with its division into classes of oppressors and oppressed, will become a socialist order. This transitional period demands a special law for a transitional time, in part because the social order itself does not change all at once, in part because the old order continues to live in people's minds as a tradition of the past. This is being felt in the ranks of all levels of the proletariat, which is just now awakening and which still adheres to traditional ideology and which still feeds on the leftovers of the bourgeois.

The Worker-Peasant Revolution has found a means of resolving the problem. In the Decree on Courts we read that new courts should be "guided in their decisions and sentences by the laws of the overthrown governments only insofar as those laws have not been abrogated by the Revolution and do not contradict revolutionary conscience and revolutionary legal consciousness."

This, on one hand, was the answer to all attempts to save the old laws, even though they had been burned, but were still living in people's heads; "only insofar as," and "on the other hand," were an answer to those who reproached us about anarchistic tendencies, precisely for having rejected the laws of previous governments, and these people, who reproached us with this, were our own Marxists (of the Right). I respond to these our opponents with the following citation:

161

"But what do you understand, gentlemen, by this preservation of legal grounds? The saving of laws which belong to the preceding social epoch, issued by representatives of social interests which have disappeared or are in the process of disappearing— that means the introduction into law of only those interests which directly oppose common need. But society is not founded on laws. That is a jurist's fantasy. Quite the opposite, law should be founded on society; it should be an expression of society's general interests and needs, proceeding from a given material means of production of interests and demands. These unavoidably change with the changing conditions of life. To save old laws in defiance of the new demands and needs of social development is, in truth, nothing other than to uphold obsolete private interests concealed by pious phrases against mature common interests. This retention of legal foundations has the purpose of making such private interests the ruling interests at a time when they are no longer the ruling ones. It has the purpose of imposing laws on society which are condemned by the very conditions of life in that society: by its way of providing a livelihood, its exchange system, its material production... And proceding from this phrase concerning legal elements, they substantiated the convocation of the United Landtag on the basis of either conscious trickery or unconscious self-deception."— K. Marx, F. Engels...

What did you expect? There were Marxists who found this passage to be anarchistic as well, and I have had to let them in on a secret, that this citation is taken word for word from a famous speech of Karl Marx before the Cologne jurors. No, we are not anarchists. Quite the contrary. We attribute a great deal of significance to laws, perhaps even too much at the moment, but only to laws of the new order. And those laws correspond to the old laws only insofar as the new order can agree with the atrophying, repudiated order.

"Henceforth, all power belongs to the Soviets. The commissars of the Provisional Government are deposed. The chairmen of the Soviets will communicate directly with the Revolutionary Government." Such was the decree (No. 5) of the Second All-Russian Congress of Soviets, giving foundation to proletarian law in its full extent. There is no reason for us to dwell on the ways in which the Soviets, during the period of eight months when the government was first purely bourgeois, and then a revolutionary coalition, repeatedly encountered moments when the question of taking full power was put to them point-blank. Naturally it was only the Soviets, which shared the perspective of dictatorship of the proletariat and of the socialist revolution, which could actually take all power into their own hands, because no one supposed that the bourgeoisie, or their colleagues in counter-revolution, the landowners, with Prince Lvov at their head, would freely give up power without a fight. "That will be the final and decisive battle."

If we remember the days of the first revolution in February, we will notice a certain resemblance. At that time, power at the local level was transferred to commissars recruited by the Provisional Government automatically, with one stroke of the pen, from the ranks of chairmen of the former zemstvo and town councils. As a result of this measure, local power came to be in the hands of bourgeois and agrarian leaders who were organized in the zemstvo-town unions with Prince Lvov, as the president of Zemgor* at their head. Only gradually were some of the commissars at the local level, under pressure from revolutionary people, replaced by purely bourgeois or even revolutionary elements; and in July Prince Lvov was forced to leave. The replacement of the Provisional Government by a worker-peasant government, and on the local level, replacement of the power of bourgeois commissars by proletarian-peasant Soviets, removed the bourgeoisie from power and replaced it with the proletariat and the poor peasantry. And that is all! The rights of ownership were replaced with the rights of labor. Capital in power was replaced by labor; "He who was nothing will become everything."

For a long time all proletarian state law was confined to a decree two lines in length (No. 5). Only in January did a new name for Soviet Russia appear, "The Russian Socialist Federated Soviet Republic." At the same time the declaration of the Congress established certain founding principles of Soviet power. And only at the Fifth All-Russian Congress on July 10, 1918, was the *Constitution* of the RSFS Republic *ratified*. But that Constitution only repeats and reinforces that which existed and which was a simple conclusion from Decree No. 5 regarding the transfer of all power to the Soviets. It was only a written summary statement of proletarian creativity.

But the transfer of all power to the Soviets simultaneously destroyed not only state order, but also social order. The worker-peasant Soviet Republic, like any other state, is a class-based state, but its task is not the oppression of non-possessors in the interests of a small group of rich persons, but quite the opposite: the dictatorship of the non-possessors (that is, the great majority), "the suppression of the numerically negligible minority (that is, the bourgeoisie) with the aim of eliminating the exploitation of man by man and establishing socialism, under which there will be neither division into classes, nor state power." In the Soviet Republic the unification of the working citizen with the working person into a single entity is taking place.

Any proletarian revolution begins with the actual smashing of Montesquieu's theory of the division of power. Look at the Soviet of Workers' Deputies in Petrograd or at the Federated Committee in Riga in 1905: Everyone went there, not only for political defense and advice, for laws and governmental instructions, but even for judicial matters, not excluding civil quarrels. The investigative commissions of the Military-Revolutionary committees in 1917 were the same organs of power to which one turned even in matters of marriage and separation. And Soviet

* Zemgor: "The Union of Zemstvos and Towns," formed in 1915 by the imperialist bourgeoisie and the landowners for the purpose of mobilizing the strength of the country to pursue the imperialist war. [P.S.]

authority from October 25, 1917, in the RSFSR has been *simultaneously the legislative and executive authority, as well as the judicial.* It does not reject the technical division of labor, but it denies hypocritical theories regarding the independence of one authority from another. The dictatorship of the proletariat and poor peasantry is an *indivisible, powerful, Soviet power.*

GUIDING PRINCIPLES OF CRIMINAL LAW IN THE R.S.F.S.R.
People's Commissariat of Justice

Introduction

   Having taken power in the October revolution, the proletariat broke
up the bourgeois governmental apparatus, which had the aim of oppressing
workers through all of its agencies, its army, its police, its courts, and its
church. It is self-evident that such an aim was also served by all codes of
bourgeois law, as systems of norms (rules, formulae) of organized force to
establish a stability of interests among social classes designed to serve the
ruling classes (the bourgeoisie and the landowners). But just as the
proletariat could not immediately transform the bourgeois state machine
to serve its own ends, and smash it, as it should have, into pieces, creating in
its place its own state apparatus, so it also could not adapt for its own aims
the bourgeois legal codes of past epochs, and consign them, as it should
have, to the archives of history. An armed people tries to cope with its
oppressors without special rules, without codes. In the course of struggling
with class enemies, the proletariat adopts various forceful measures,
applying them at first without a special system, randomly, from case to
case. The experience of struggle, however, trains the proletariat to follow
general rules, leads it to systematization, creates, in other words, a new law.
Almost two years of such struggle has now given us the ability to develop
concrete formulations of proletarian law and to draw appropriate
generalizations. In the interest of economic might and in accordance with
the centralization of various activities, the proletariat must work out rules
to keep its class enemies in check, develop methods to struggle with its
enemies, and govern them. And first of all, this must be done by means of
criminal law, the task of which is to struggle with those who violate the
conditions laid down by the new social order in the transitional period of
the dictatorship of the proletariat. Only when the resistance of the deposed
bourgeois and propertied classes has finally been broken, and a communist
order established, will the proletariat be able to do away with the state as
organized force and law, as a function of the state. To assist in this task by
aiding the organs of Soviet justice fulfill their historic mission in the area of
struggling with class enemies of the proletariat, the People's Commissariat
of Justice issues the following guiding principles of criminal law for the
R.S.F.S.R.

   Order of the People's Commissariat of Justice, Dec. 12, 1919, from *Sobranie uzakonenii
i rasporiazhenii rabochego i krest'ianskogo pravitel'stva*, No. 66, Dec. 18, 1919.

I. *Criminal Law*

1) *Law* is a system (order) of social relations corresponding to the interests of the ruling class, and secured by the organized power of that class.

2) *Criminal law* has as its content legal norms and other legal measures by which the system of social relations of a given class society protects itself from violations (crimes) by means of repression (punishments).

3) *Soviet criminal law* has the task, by means of repression, of protecting the system of social relations corresponding to the interests of the laboring masses, organized into the ruling class under the dictatorship of the proletariat in the transitional period from capitalism to communism.

II. *Criminal Justice*

4) Soviet criminal law in the R.S.F.S.R. is carried out by organs of Soviet justice (People's Courts and Revolutionary Tribunals).

III. *Crime and Punishment*

5) *Crime* is a violation of the order of social relations protected by criminal law.

6) A crime is an act of commission or omission dangerous for the given system of social relations, and makes struggle by governmental power necessary against the person (criminal) who perpetrates such acts or allows them to occur as a result of a failure to act.

7) *Punishment* consists of those compulsory measures by which the government protects a given order of social relations against the actions of those who violate its rule (criminals).

8) The purpose of punishment is to protect the social order from those who commit crimes or attempt to commit them, and from future possible crimes of these or other individuals.

9) To protect the social order from future criminal acts by persons attempting to commit crimes, a person can either be socialized into the given social order, or isolated, if that person refuses socialization, or, in exceptional circumstances, physically eliminated.

10) *In selecting a punishment* it should be kept in mind what crime in a class-based society means in terms of the order of social relationships in which the criminal has lived. Punishment is not retribution for blame, nor atonement of guilt. It is only a *defensive* measure which should be expedient, and at the same time lack any traces of martyrdom, and it should not cause the criminal useless and extraneous suffering.

11) In determining the *measures to be applied* against those who

commit crimes, the court must evaluate the *degree and character* (nature) *of the danger for society* of both the *criminal* himself and the *act.* To these ends the court must first, conduct an unrestricted investigation of all circumstances surrounding the commission of the crime; clarify the personality of the criminal insofar as it will help explain the commission of the crime and its motives, and insofar as it will help explain the crime on the basis of the criminal's life and past; and second, establish how much that act, in the given conditions of time and place, violated the bases of social security.

12) In determining the *measures of punishment* in each instance it is necessary to distinguish a) whether the crime was committed by a person belonging to the propertied classes in the interests of restoring, saving, or obtaining some kind of privilege linked with the rights of ownership, or by a propertyless person, in hungry or needy circumstances; b) whether the act was committed in the interests of restoring power to the deposed class, or in the personal interests of the person committing the act; c) whether the act was committed consciously, or in ignorance and unconsciousness; d) whether the act was committed by a professional criminal (recidivist) or by a first offender; e) whether the act was committed by a group, gang, band, or by a single person; f) whether the act involved bodily harm; g) whether the act involved premeditated intent, cruelty, maliciousness, cowardice, or was committed in a burst of passion as a result of ignorance or a lack of thought.

13) Minors under 14 years of age are not subject to the courts and their punishment. Rehabilitative measures are to be used for them. Such measures are also to be used against those in the transitional ages of 14 to 18 who act unconsciously.

14) Judgment and punishment are not to be applied against persons who have committed crimes in a state of chronic mental illness, or who are in such mental straits that in committing the crime, they are not aware of their own actions, or who, although in their right senses at the time of the act, are, at the time of sentencing, mentally deranged. To such persons, only medical and preventative measures can be applied.

15) Punishments shall not be applied when the acts were committed in order to prevent a danger which in the circumstances could not have been prevented by any other means, provided that the harm caused does not exceed the limits of necessary defense.

16) If conditions have changed such that an act or the person who committed it is no longer a danger to the established order, punishment shall not be applied.

IV. *Stages in the Commission of a Crime*

17) A crime is considered *to have taken place completely* when an

167

intentionally committed criminal act is perpetrated in its entirety.

18) An *attempt* to commit a crime shall be considered equivalent to a crime when the criminal has done everything considered necessary for the perpetration of the crime, but failed due to circumstances beyond his control.

19) Criminal *intent* is the search for, acquisition of, or adaptation of tools, weapons, etc. needed for the completion of a crime by a person preparing to commit it.

20) The stage of commission of an intended crime shall not by itself influence the measures of repression, which are to be determined by the degree of danger posed by the criminal.

V. *Complicity*

21) In the case of an act committed jointly by a group of persons (gang, band, crowd), the perpetrators as well as the initiators and accomplices shall be punished. Their punishment shall depend not upon the degree of their participation, but upon the *degree of danger* represented by the criminal and the act committed.

22) Perpetrators shall be considered those who take part in the implementation of a criminal act however it turns out.

23) Initiators shall be considered those who incite crimes.

24) Accomplices shall be considered those who, while not taking direct part in the completion of a criminal act, assist in its completion by word or deed, by advice, the elimination of obstacles, concealing the criminal or the traces of the crime, or by acquiescence, that is, by not hindering the accomplishment of a crime.

VI. *Types of Punishment*

25) In accordance with the task of protecting the social order from being violated, and considering the necessity of reducing as much as possible the personal suffering of the criminal, punishment should vary in accordance with the particular characteristics of the situation and the personality of the criminal.

Examples of types of punishment:
   a) reprimand
   b) social censure
   c) compulsory activities, without physical hardship
   d) boycott
   e) temporary or permanent exclusion from an association
   f) restitution, or, if this is impossible, indemnity
   g) suspension of duties

h) restrictions on filling apost, or doing other kinds of work
i) confiscation of all belongings
j) deprivation of political rights
k) being declared an enemy of the revolution or of the people
l) compulsory labor without imprisonment
m) imprisonment for a set period or for an unspecified period until the occurrence of certain events
n) being declared outside the law
o) execution by firing squad
p) combination of the above forms of punishment.

Annotation: People's Courts may not apply the death penalty.

VII. *Conditional Sentences*

26) When a court has ordered imprisonment for a crime committed (a) as a first offense; (b) under exceptionally difficult personal circumstances; (c) when the convicted person poses no danger to those around him sufficient to require immediate isolation, the court may substitute a conditional sentence, that is, issue a suspended sentence for a period corresponding to the conviction or appropriate to the crime. On repetition of such an act, the suspended sentence loses its conditional character and the primary sentence immediately takes effect.

VIII. *Territory Covered by Criminal Law*

27) The criminal law of the R.S.F.S.R. applies to the whole territory of the Republic, both in terms of the action of its citizens and also those of foreigners who commit crimes on its territory, and likewise shall affect citizens of the R.S.F.S.R. and foreigners who commit crimes on the territory of another government, but avoid judicial punishment in the location where the crime was committed, and subsequently are found within the boundaries of the R.S.F.S.R.

12 December 1919.
Signed: Deputy Commissar of People's Justice, *P. Stuchka*

THE PROLETARIAN REVOLUTION AND CRIMINAL LAW
I. Kozlovsky

Among ideologies by which ruling classes keep oppressed masses within their sphere of influence, the law has always been given an especially honored place. Evoked to protect productive relations and to strengthen the exploitation of labor by capital, the law naturally had to be imparted with a higher mystical authority, turned into a fetish. It is not difficult to verify this *a priori* conclusion by a quick glance at the "theories" concerning the origins and essence of law. From the moment of its birth and up to now, official scholars have explained the origin of law metaphysically. At the dawn of history, society, dividing itself into classes, attributed the establishment of law to god, in the literal meaning of the word. With the development of knowledge, the concept of the divine origin of law has been replaced by teachings concerning its origins from other mystical forces or metaphysical beings, such as "nature," "the popular spirit," "the objective spirit," "the common will," "the joint will," "the will of the state," "reason" as the supreme being, and other similar fictions. And to this very day, among the luminaries of bourgeois jurisprudence, these fantastic theories dominate (the historical schools of Savigny, Pukhta, which consider law to be the product of "popular spirit"), and it is extraordinarily portentious for bourgeois science that up to now it has no scientific basis for the origins of law...

The "naturally progressive process of the development of law" thus comes down to the following short formula: the Communist order does not know law. Law is born out of economic inequality, with the schism of the population into classes. The legal system of ancient times reflects in itself the exploitation of the lords over slave labor. Feudal serf law existed fully up to the Nineteenth Century with the exploitation of the serfs. Bourgeois law from the time of the French Revolution presented itself as the reflection of the exploitation of "free" labor by capitalists. The transitional period from capitalism to socialism, experienced for the first time on the face of the earth after the October Revolution in Russia, creates in the process of socialist revolution a special law hitherto unseen, not a law in the literal sense of the term (a system of the oppression of the majority by the

From the collection *Oktiabr'skii perevorot i diktatura proletariata*, Moscow, 1919, pp. 231-40. A prominent early Soviet jurist, Kozlovsky later opposed such measures as "Peoples' Courts" and worked to establish uniform norms of socialist law.

minority), but a proletarian law, which is nevertheless the law, in the sense of a means of suppression of the opposition of the minority by the working classes. (In this period, law is not a code, it is not a written compilation of laws. Without any laws, without special rules, the armed people struggle with class enemies.)

In the sense of external protection of productive relations, law exists and functions even under a socialist form of society, but it will gradually atrophy, and with the transition to communism, precluding any economic inequality, it will completely disappear. Born of economic inequality (after primitive communism), law will die in communist society with the death of economic inequality. Such is the life course of law. An enormous portion of this path has already been traversed by mankind. Now our country is going through the epoch of proletarian law. What are to be its further fortunes?

It is perfectly clear that proletarian law, first of all, will be significantly simplified. This is most readily explained. Since the law until now has defended the economic rule of the minority over the majority, it has had to be a complicated, refined system of all sorts of clichés, innumerable rules meant for an anarchistic condition of the economy, providing for the disordered "free" play of individual forces. This is why bourgeois law is a heap of separate statutes, such a motley diversity. On the other hand, in suppressing the majority the ruling minority has had to be especially concerned with having the complicated complex of rules produce the impression of objective justice, so that it would have, in the eyes of the suppressed majority, the authority of generally useful norms, of non-class benefits, equal for all. From this comes the necessity of fiction in law, concealing its true meaning. Thus in accordance with the significant easing of the task of the suppression of the minority by the majority, proletarian law will be considerably simplified. And already, with a revolution in the sphere of productive relationships taking place, and with the socialization of the means of production, entire fields of so called civil law have fallen away as unneeded. Traditional family law has disappeared, a vestige of a patriarchal system. There is no extremely confusing and intricate system of inheritance law. The bourgeois law of estates has been scrapped. The basis of public law, the personal employment agreement, has collapsed. With the steady conversion of the latter into labor conscription, this area of civil law will disappear entirely. With the final socialization of the means of production our *Corpus Iuris Civilis,* v. X, part 1, will be razed to the ground.

And it goes without saying that the old state law already represents the ruins of an old building. With the final suppression of the bourgeoisie, proletarian "law" will gradually lose its own functions and will be changed into rules for the organization of economic life—production, distribution and consumption. Organs of law will be turned into economic and administrative organs. Workers, overseers and bookkeepers will more and more supplant judges.

That ruling and prohibiting law will gradually be reduced in extent and sphere of application, and that the legal order will gradually be turned into an organization of economic character—with this even the representatives of the so-called "sociological" school of law agree; however, not one of them, including Menger, can agree that it will disappear entirely; and chiefly, they draw arguments for the defense of this scientifically hopeless position from the sphere of criminal law, from the sphere of crimes.

I will now turn to this.

As was indicated above, the stumbling block for the socialist-opportunists to which Menger belongs, and over which their thought trips, is the metaphysical idea of human nature as an absolute given. It is, generally speaking, their dualism.

Just as Menger stops halfway in his investigation of the evolution of the state when he asserts that future society will be only predominantly an economic and administrative organization and will never die out as an organization of coercion, as a state, so he also stops midway in the question of crimes. He stops with the basic instincts of human nature, which, in his assertion, exclude the possibility of the disappearance of crimes in any system of society whatsoever. He grants only that crimes will be encountered more and more rarely.

In this he has in view exclusively crimes directed, according to his own terminology, "against the person" and crimes "against the law,"—that is, crimes against the laws recognized by the legal system. Menger conceives of the occurrence of these crimes in any system; the bad instincts of human nature serve as a guarantee of this for him.

Without touching on the question of the artificiality of the division of crimes into these categories, one must say that in these assertions is hidden a superstitious prejudice, the fetishism of law as something eternal. After all, if the state, the law, crime, have as their prerequisite economic inequality, if law is born out of the differentiation of society into classes, then with the disappearance of the class system, with the disappearance of inequality, all these categories will disappear, too, and among them crimes. For the Marxist, any crime is the product of the irreconcilability of class antagonisms.

The anarchy of capitalist production, creating the instability of separate existence and provoking a struggle for separateness in the individual, gives birth to excesses, extremes, crimes, including the most savage. Exploitation of the masses creates need, poverty, ignorance, running wild, vices. No struggle with them can be so fruitful as the removal of the possibility of their appearance. They will disappear only in the later phase of the Communist system, remaining during the transition to communism as a rudimentary vestige of the past.

172

Mankind will not free itself right away from this accursed legacy of many centuries of slavery.

It long will weigh upon him, until finally mankind passes from the condition of necessity to the condition of "freedom."

That transitional system to socialism which the October Revolution brought Russia received an extremely rich legacy of criminality from imperialism, having led to the unheard of carnage of the people, to hunger and, in connection with it, to extreme brutalization. The extraordinarily heavy task of coping with this evil was put before the proletarian government. What measures must it take to struggle with this evil during the transitional time? First, our punitive policy will break completely with the principles of retribution. Torture and cruelty of punishment must be abolished. Possible achievements in the direction of reforming the criminal seem insignificant to us. That which will determine the driving forces of his feelings has been acquired once and for all from his environment. Sentimental means of reformation, practiced in several transatlantic prisons, such as increased diet, prolonged walks, massage, swimming, gymnastics etc. can only at best arouse a smile in us. The only aim of an imposed punishment must be, in accordance with our views on the reasons for criminality, self-defense or protecting the community from encroachment, and in terms of these views the authorities must act with decisive surgical measures, measures of terror and isolation.

There is no need to speak of general preventative measures, since life will work for us, bringing us closer to communism, under which crime and all sorts of violence will pass into history together with punishment and law itself.

And in the meantime, until we cannot, paraphrasing the old jurists, exclaim, "pereat justitia, fiat mundis," it is not bourgeois hypocrisy, individual "humanity" which will direct our work in the area of punishment, but rather the class interest of the unbending suppression of the incursions of the parasitical minority on society, corresponding to the interests of the working masses of the population.

To make this work concrete, to establish in advance a detailed plan of measures in the struggle with crime, to compile them in a code, would amount to contriving a more or less amusing utopian system. It is necessary to present to the revolutionary masses the possibility of their manifesting legal creativity, and with the strengthening of the system gained by the revolution, to sum up this formerly concealed work in the midst of the masses. The healthy class instinct of the workers will show them the appropriate path. The independence of the masses must be our slogan in this respect, too. The implementation of the functions of power, when the working people have power, must become national.

Leaving the chief role in legal creativity in the transitional epoch to the independence of the masses, and maintaining that so-called codification of criminal law during a period of socialist revolution is wasted work, I think that the task of the authorities in the legal area comes down chiefly to guidance, to instructing the masses.

It is the armed people themselves who govern in a time of revolution. They do not yet have patterns, and there can be no code of special rules. People will cope without them. But having defeated the bourgeoisie and consolidated its rule, the working class must work out, temporarily, until the full destruction of inequality, special norms of law for the preservation and defense of socialist production, distribution of labor and material benefits. Encroachments upon this sphere of relations now must be considered serious crimes. So-called political crimes (against the political system) will fall away, since they will cease to be dangerous. Attempts of separate individuals or their insignificant groups do not frighten the people, since they have gained victory and strengthened the new system. Another section of criminal law must occupy their place—violation of the economic order, of equality of labor and equality of the sharing of products. Incursions on socialist production, the exploitation of labor above the norm, determined in accordance with the economic necessity of a given moment, violations of the rules of distribution, laziness and idleness—these will comprise the most serious crimes. So-called crimes against "property rights," obviously, will remain crimes in this transitional system, born from the capitalist system, until the time that economic inequality disappears; this can be expected only at the highest stage of technical development in the Communist phase. In regard to so-called crimes against the person the same thing holds. In this area conflicts and excesses will naturally become more rare; the grounds for them will gradually disappear; the motives will be reduced. But until the disappearance of the remnants of the capitalist system, which gave birth to savagery, brutality, moral coarseness, ignorance, superstition and other delights of that accursed regime, proletarian courts will have to conduct a decisive, punitive policy in defense of the individual existence of citizens against incursions on their personal inviolability.

One thing is clear. With the establishment of a new order of things, with a fundamental reform of the social system, when the economic existence of each individual person is secured, the punitive functions of the law will be more and more reduced, since the attack on this order of things, and opposition to it, will be carried out on the part of an insignificant minority. More and more law will be turned into rules for the management of economy; judges will become its managers.

Such is, to me, the "program minimum" of the punitive policy of the Soviet government. Just as the revolution in the sphere of productive relations is revolutionizing the law and destroying it, so the development of productive forces will lead to the establishment of genuine humanism in human relations, and will return real meaning to this word, which has been

174

debased by liberal-philistines.

Turning from these general observations of a theoretical nature to a review of the so-called positive legislation of the Worker-Peasant Government in the sphere of criminal law, it is necessary to keep two things in mind: first, one should not forget that although the legal superstructure is being reformed more or less rapidly with the change of the economic base of society, it will not finally perish until new economic relations have fully developed. Second, one must take account of the fact that in criminal law the revolution in economic relations is reflected more remotely, and not as directly, as it is in the other spheres of law (for example, "civil" or "state"). That is why one cannot expect fundamental reforms in the sphere of the criminal law policy of Soviet authorities during the transitional period.

The Worker-Peasant Government must develop its activities in an extremely unfavorable environment, in an environment of the final agony of a dying capitalism. Aside from the criminal legacy left from the old regime, it must struggle as well with the unbelievable growth of criminality which usually accompanies the fall of the old world, and which is expending all efforts, perpetrating all crimes, in order to defend the right of its own existence.

It is perfectly obvious that the workers' government had to respond with merciless repression. And this has happened. Independent of the establishment of special militant organizations for the struggle with counter-revolution, such as the extraordinary commissions, which quickly and decisively, without special rules, react to direct incursions against the conquests of the workers' revolution, special laws were published, preserving the new organization of distribution and punishing opposition to the implementation of the government's individual resolutions and general measures. Among these legislative acts in the sphere of criminal law, the decrees on speculation and bribery attract attention. Directed against the propertied classes, they carry the definite stamp of class proletarian justice. They wear no bourgeois finery, whose purpose it is to create the illusion of a law under which all are equal, and in this way to cover up its class essence. On the contrary. With complete openness, the decree (for example, on bribery) declares that if a person guilty of giving or taking a bribe belongs to the propertied class and uses the bribe for the preservation of privileges connected with the right of property, then he will be sentenced to the most unpleasant and difficult forced labor, and all his property will be subject to confiscation. In contrast to bourgeois legislation, the decree strikes the giver and the taker equally.

The decree on speculation is directed against the commercial class and puts a leash on "freedom of trade," first of all on objects of mass consumption. Together with the positive organization of work in the implementation of socialist distribution of products, and in defense of this,

175

the Soviet authority was forced to enact a merciless law against the orgy of speculation. According to this law, the punishment threatening the speculator is greater than the punishment which the old law gave to the thief, swindler, or robber. And this is understandable, since the speculator, undermining the system of just distribution of objects of primary necessity, inflicts with his criminal actions incomparably greater harm on the community than does the intruder on separate property. The distinctive characteristic of these two laws, just as with all criminal laws enacted by the Soviet government, is that in determining punishment, the law proceeds from considerations of objective harm caused by the actions of the criminal and from a defense of class interest, and rejects the traditional classical principle of the subjective responsibility of the guilty party.

Another typical peculiarity of criminal legislation of the transitional period, flowing, however, from the same principle, is the rejection of weighing the "free will" displayed by the criminal, carried out with unusual scrupulousness by bourgeois jurisprudence. Soviet legislation, standing on the objective ground of the defense of the social system and of the merciless struggle with incursions against it, ignores the question of how much "criminal intent" took place in the carrying out of a criminal activity, and thus accomplices, instigators and even simply those privy to the activity are punished equally with the chief offenders. (See the decrees on bribery, speculation, private trade, etc.)

The sanctions of the criminal law are also unique.

As a general rule, one must note that sanctions are lacking. The descriptive part of the criminal act ends with a general resolution on bringing the culprit to trial or before a tribunal. And only in especially important instances does the sanction define a minimum punishment (not less than so and so), thus giving to the court unlimited discretion in increasing the punishment. This system of criminal sanctions, unusual for bourgeois jurisprudence, is deeply meaningful. The mathematically exact yardstick "from-to," adopted by bourgeois legislators, rests on the fiction of a "normal," "average person"...on which criminal norms are computed.

Proletarian justice does not need fictions for concealing its class character, as does the bourgeoisie, and does not operate with a fictitious "median," lacking correspondence to a living and diverse reality.

Proletarian justice, guided in the defense of the socialist system only by the principle of expediency, grants a free hand to its court in calculating the amount of repression, in accord with the diversity and many-sidedness of criminal activities, of the "forms of social life," according to the apt expression of List.

However, the peculiarities of the transitional period, evoking furious opposition of the overturned classes, contributes, as was said above, to the unusual growth of incursions against the still unsecured system, and forces

176

the government in especially dangerous cases to give guiding orders from the center for its defense, and to define the amount of repression, not subject to lowering by the court.

The traditional scale of punishments has not been left inviolable. The confiscation of all or part of property has taken the place of the fine. The fine, "equal" for all classes of the population under economic inequality, appeared to be a measure unjust in the highest degree from the point of view of socialist legal consciousness. Replacing the fine with the confiscation of property at the order of the court appeared an especially flexible means of equalizing the responsibility of individuals of different property statuses for one and the same act. In conformity with the new contingent of criminals recruited from among the bourgeoisie, the new criminal legislation normally combines the given punishment of deprivation of freedom with the confiscation of the property of the guilty.

The next step of the old ladder of punishments, the short term arrest, is abolished as an absolutely inexpedient measure.

Rejecting the "classical" theory of "responsibility" and "culpability" as metaphysical, the Soviet government has naturally destroyed the division of places of incarceration into detention centers, prisons, work homes, corrective arrest divisions, and penal convict prisons, replacing them with uniform places for deprivation of freedom, always accompanied by compulsory labor. It goes without saying, of course, that compulsory labor, in contradiction to the demands of bourgeois justice, affects those under investigation, too. At the same time it is worth noting that the measure contemplated by the government, the levying of the cost of maintenance in prison on the prisoners, is seen as correct in light of the fact that first, representatives of the propertied classes are beginning to predominate among the criminals, and secondly, there is no basis for putting the burden of maintaining their class enemies in prison on the shoulders of the workers.

The Soviet government, merciless toward the enemies of socialist law and order, is working out a far-reaching plan for the construction of corresponding educational institutions for the reform of the victims of the capitalist regime (reformatoriums), and it has already placed juvenile criminals into the special institutions of the People's Commissariat of Enlightenment, removing their files from the sphere of judicial agencies, its task being not to punish, but to protect children from the influence of an unfavorable environment.

Such are the transformations produced by Soviet power in the sphere of criminal law during a time of intensifying struggle with its enemies. A quick survey of the changes outlined once again indicates what colossal devastation the proletarian revolution produces when it invades economic relations, even in an area as remote from this field as the sphere of criminal law.

177

THE PROLETARIAT AND CIVIL LAW
A. Goikhbarg

To write in a jubilee collection dedicated to the anniversary of the ongoing proletarian revolution about proletarian and civil law, about what has been done by the proletariat in the area of civil law, or more exactly, in the area of those relationships which are governed by civil law in the bourgeois order, is to write about all the domestic economic and even social policies of the ruling proletariat. Indeed, all productive economic relationships under a bourgeois state are regulated on the basis of civil law in general, and on the basis of its constituent parts—industrial and commercial law—in particular. The bourgeoisie, throwing off at the time of its revolution the yoke of a feudal-guild order, which obstructed the development of productive forces, strove for the establishment of "free" conditions for the development and strengthening of its class. It strove for the unhindered accumulation in its hands of great wealth, for the general exploitation of all natural resources in the interests of private enrichment, and for the unlimited exploitation of the laboring class, which it bought and sold like a commodity, and which was necessary to the accumulation of wealth. Therefore the bourgeoisie demanded private ownership of land with all its appurtenances, free circulation of productions (of others' work) as goods, the organization of mutual relationships between people on the basis of an economy of free competition, that is, free (in form) agreements and treaties. To maintain the stability and continuity of the individual accumulation of wealth in the hands of certain persons, it upheld the transmission of wealth by right of inheritance and the freedom of will-making, the freedom of posthumous distribution of personal belongings. In other words, the bourgeoisie made demands and successfully introduced into practice a purely civil law which granted "freedom" for the possessors.

All of a nation's material and even spiritual demands were to be satisfied on this basis of free competition, through personal initiative. And if that free competition was precluded for many members of society, if they were unable to display initiative due to material poverty, so much the worse for them. It was not for them that the rising third estate was striving to

From *Oktiabr'skii perevorot i diktatura proletariata*, Moscow, 1919, pp. 221-30. A former professor of law, A.G. Goikhbarg served in the Commissariat of Justice after 1917, and gained prominence as the official primarily responsible for drafting the first Soviet Civil Code.

create good, "free" conditions of life. It was even willing not to count them as citizens of the "free," "legal" state, as members of the new society. The ideologues of the third estate were not reluctant to declare this openly, in spite of all their writings about the rights of man and the citizen. "We are all equal as people," said Voltaire, "but we are not identical members of society." Catherine's teacher Diderot went further, exclaiming "It is property which makes the citizen." The conclusive "dot-on-the-i" was offered by Dupont de Nemours at the height of the French Revolution, when, apropos of the discussion concerning the electoral census, he openly defined the limits of bourgeois society: "He who has no property is not a member of society. . . . "

A labor society faces entirely different tasks, especially in its early years, than those of a society of owners. A laboring society cannot strive for the strengthening of some at the expense of the weakness and deprivation of others. It does not recognize the privileges of individuals; it recognizes living people, who are, in the overwhelming majority, capable of work and who, without exception, have certain material and spiritual needs which can increasingly grow. To ensure the employment of available manpower and to completely satisfy all human needs and requirements—such is the fundamental task of a new society built on the foundation of labor.

This task can be completed only through the systematic organization of production and distribution, organization which clearly takes into account all available and possible powers, resources and needs of the entire population of a given place and later of all humankind. A laboring society cannot in any circumstances, and especially in its earliest period of existence, retain the anarchy of productive and related relationships. Moreover, it cannot allow that, thanks to their judicial titles received by sheer luck, certain persons will have at their disposal (on the basis of private ownership) means and implements of production which are completely incompatible with their personal physical strength and exceed their reasonable needs beyond all limits. It cannot allow that the accident of birth or fancy, or even the reasoned wish of a living person, can serve as the basis for the acquisition of things left by the dead, who are no longer in need of them (on the basis of inheritance law). It cannot allow the exclusive possession by certain individuals of products of the mental work some-times of generations (on the basis of family or other trusts). It cannot disregard care for the birth and upbringing of a new healthy generation either. In a word, a laboring society must eliminate all private-legal forms of economic relations which existed in a bourgeois society, all the private-legal relations of ownership and partly of individuality, in other words, all civil law.

The proletariat, accordingly, has immediate tasks in two directions: a negative task, the task of destruction in the area of private-legal titles (ownership, inheritance, agreements, and so on); and a positive task, a task of creation in the area of organizational construction. And these two tasks of the proletariat, organized in a ruling class, are inextricably bound up with one another. The proletariat cannot confine itself to the removal of the private-ownership of already accumulated assets, without worrying about the proper use and distribution of those assets. It cannot limit itself to the removal of private, accidental means of acquisition for purposes of individual support, without trying to design a common, organized support for everyone. In the bourgeois order, one relied basically upon individual capacity for the satisfaction of all kinds of needs. Not only one's daily bread, but all necessities were obtained on this basis. Needs for health support and medical care could also be obtained by private individuals at certain doctors or hospitals, with the more or less reliable help of talented, outstanding, learned doctors available only for large sums of money, that is, only to representatives of the ruling classes. This satisfaction of the need for knowledge, a full, more or less well-rounded education was also available only to the possessors. The fulfillment of demands for cultural satisfaction and enjoyment was also obtained only through private, unregulated efforts on the part of separate individuals (tickets to theaters, exhibits, the purchase of books, library memberships, and so on), and at great expense. Excellent representation of interests and defense in court were likewise available on the basis of private agreements with generously paid talent-monopolists. If the masses received anything in this area, it was only of a secondary or lower quality. The proletariat must organize the fulfillment of all these needs (insofar as they will exist in the new order) and of all newly emerging needs, so that it is not separate individuals whose needs are accidentally fulfilled, but so that the whole laboring collective is satisfied. It should strive to expand, to the greatest possible extent, the fund for the support of demands, so that every member of that collective can receive complete and all-around satisfaction of all his needs. As long as this fund is insufficient, incomplete satisfaction will be the result, but it will be organized so that this is true for everyone...

What has the Russian proletariat, organized into a ruling class, done in this direction in so short a time? (Less than a year, for when this article is being written there has not yet been an anniversary of the proletariat's seizing the apparatus of state power.)

In the sphere of destruction and in the sphere of the creation of principle and compromise, so much has been done that, disregarding the unprecedented and unforeseen, unfavorable environment, there can be no place for pessimism. Without any hesitation it can be said that we are nearing the moment when, if one judges by Russia's example, every living person will be a real member of a new, future, harmonious and happy collective, the name of which is *humanity*. We are approaching this moment with giant steps.

In the period from the February to the October Revolution, the foundations of the order of private enterprise remained untouched. The foundations of civil law were also untouched. But, as soon as power became the proletariat's, the crack of the destructive ax aimed at the very roots of the bourgeois order was heard. In the first days of the proletarian upheaval, the landlords' ownership of the land was abolished by decree, immediately and without any reimbursement. Then a law was issued regarding the socialization of all land, which ended forever any private ownership of land, minerals, water, forest and the living forces of nature. The end of private ownership specifically of all forest land was reaffirmed in a later decree about forests on May 27, 1918. In this way, the attachment of property through private law to individuals and the possibility of handling property through private law were eliminated from one of the principal means of production—from the land with all its "appurtenances." Instead of private law, what has been introduced is the social, organized distribution among the agricultural population of the land with its "appurtenances" for the use of those who work it. Organized distribution has been completed by means of those decrees and others, which established the organs of distribution—land committees and then land departments of the Soviets. This distribution is being improved by means of various kinds of instructions, developed by central and local Soviet authority, and likewise in the code of law on land that is being prepared for publication. In addition, in the interests of an actual allocation of the possibility of applying one's work to the land, in the interests of the working people, a number of organizational measures have been taken, the most important of which are the announcement of the Republic as the exclusive owner of all agricultural machinery tools already manufactured, those being manufactured, and those being imported from abroad—in order to provide agriculture with tools and to meet the demands of the working peasantry; the decree about the creation of village poverty committees and their being furnished, among other things, with agricultural implements free, or at low cost; the decree already prepared for publication about the organization of village communes.

Buildings, which are primarily meant to satisfy the need for housing, have been almost completely withdrawn from private circulation. At first, already in December, 1917, as a preparatory measure, all transactions for sale, pledges, and so on, of all immovable property and land in the cities was forbidden. Then in August, 1918, an end was put to the right (which had already been legally ended once in the law on the socialization of land) of private ownership of all built and unbuilt lots in urban settlements, and in cities with a population of over 10,000, of all buildings which yielded profits higher than those set by the local soviet. Private ownership survived only so long as there was no apparatus for the transferral of all buildings into the hands of the government. Besides that, in October, it was still granted to city self-governments (or their

181

Soviet replacements) to requisition empty buildings, suitable for housing, and to settle into living space those people needing space or living in overpopulated or unsanitary apartments. The amounts of living-space (the number of rooms and so on) to which the inhabitants could lay claim, was established (this measure was extremely widely used by official Soviets). All buildings of lower, intermediate, and higher educational institutions were allocated for the use of the population for cultural-enlightenment purposes at times when there were no classes. Finally, a whole group of organizations was created, among them state agencies, for the development of construction, in order to provide the whole population with housing.

To a significant degree, the means of production of extractive and processing-type large-scale industry have been removed from private circulation. At the beginning, still in November 1917, workers' control was established in all industrial establishments. Then the entire holdings of separate large-scale industrial enterprises were confiscated and declared the property of the Republic, mainly due to their refusal to submit to workers' control, (the first to be turned into the possession of the republic back in December, 1917, were the holdings of the joint-stock society of the Bogoslovsk and Simsk mining regions, Russo-Belgian metallurgical association, "The 1886 Electrical Light Society," the Serginsko-Ufaleino and Kyshtymsk mining regions and the Putilov plants). After this, the payment of dividends to stockholders (December 29, 1917) was discontinued and all dealings in securities were forbidden, with the intention of furthering the nationalization of production. Then industrial firms of specific branches of industry were turned over to the ownership of the Republic. Match and candle factories were nationalized (March 7), then sugar and petroleum industries (May 3 and June 22). Finally, on June 28, in the interests of a decisive struggle with economic and productive devastation and of the consolidation of the dictatorship of the working class and the very-poor peasantry, all the largest-scale firms of all branches of industry were declared the property of the Russian Socialist Republic...

Almost all transportation businesses with almost all their subsidiary firms were also removed from the private sphere. Still in January, it was announced that the whole merchant marine was the nationalized, unalienable property of the Soviet Republic; then all the largest graneries were declared state property. Finally, all the large-scale firms of railroad transport were declared to be the property of the Russian Socialist Republic. On the other hand, a whole series of decisions was made which touched on the development and improvement of transportation businesses. Decrees were handed down about protecting roads and about the increase of their vehicle capacity, about the building of supply railroads, in the interests of restraining the unbelievable ruin in transportation created by the demobilization of the tsarist army. Supervision of the expansion of the railroad network was made the responsibility of the Committee on State Defense. A Department of Water Communications was established for the direction of trade, sea, and river fleets and water communications. The organization of road construction was turned over to road departments formed in the Soviets.

All external trade (in the interests of the immediate and systematic supply of products to the population) and almost all internal trade was removed from the sphere of private circulation. According to the law on the socialization of land, all grain trading, internal and export alike, had to be part of a state monopoly. Similarly, the agencies of soviet authority monopolized trade in agricultural machinery and seeds. Then, on April 23, all export trade was nationalized, meaning that all trade dealings, the buying and selling of all kinds of products from foreign governments and with firms abroad, could take place only through the Russian Republic's representatives. A whole series of preparatory measures were taken with relation to internal trade, moving toward its full nationalization (in general and for separate branches of industry). Then some branches were completely nationalized. Thus, all agricultural machinery and tools were to be under monopolistic supervision of the state. Back in December, the sale of manufactured goods from the factory to private individuals was forbidden. All wholesale enterprises dealing in rice, pepper, coffee, and spices were nationalized. Price committees were formed to supervise trade and the just distribution of goods among the population. "Tsentrotkan" was formed to keep track of products of the textile industry. It has resolved to obtain all available reserves of material within the boundaries of the Republic and determined that all future production of material at the disposal of the RSFSR will be for fair distribution to the population. Finally, it has determined that all materials found in wholesalers' and factories' storage within the RSFSR will come under the control of the state. A decree has been issued about obligatory barter.

Private control has been turned out of almost all banking business. Banks based on private means, which hold in their hands commercial industry, transport and other enterprises, thanks to subsidies, have been nationalized. Only in December all banks were transferred to the state and in January, all the joint-stock capital of private banks was confiscated for use by the Soviet Republic and bank stocks abolished.

State controls have been established over all sorts of nonsocialized insurance in preparation for the nationalization of all private insurance businesses. A General Commissariat on Insurance, Business and Fire-fighting was formed. The transfer of all insurance organizations into the hands of the Soviet Republic was prepared.

Private management has been almost completely eliminated in the sphere of using labor for private income purposes. Working conditions in privately owned places are determined by collective agreements, unilateral or bilateral, but in the final analysis are dependent upon approval by the organs of soviet power (the People's Commissariat of Labor). Similarly, the conditions of labor in soviet institutions and enterprises will not be set according to the principles of private law. In addition, the majority of the population (factually) obtained the right to apply their labor to agriculture according to the law on the socialization of land, which was proclaimed in the January Declaration of Workers' Rights, and in the July Soviet Constitution, which proclaimed labor to be obligatory. Labor exchanges were organized for the proper and systematic distribution of manpower...

An entire enormous section of civil bourgeois law has thus been eliminated by the proletariat. The rights of inheritance have been abolished without any exceptions. Even in cases when private property has not been confiscated, it has ceased to be property in the sense that this was understood by bourgeois law. It cannot cast its shadow beyond the lifespan of its present possessor. This abolition of inherited property and its transfer to other private individuals, either according to the will of the dead person or by law, will strike a blow at the very concept of private ownership, as something that can be perpetually attached to private individuals from generation to generation. The rejection of laws of inheritance thus has tremendous educational significance for the proletariat and those elements which side with it, freeing them from the power of proprietary ideology instilled by the bourgeois classes. But in totally rejecting the laws of inheritance without exception, one had to deal with the current lack here of general social welfare, systematically organized for everyone, in particular for those who had not attained or who lost their ability to work. These conditions being taken into account, a primitive surrogate for social welfare was created from the possessions of the dying for the use of their relatives, based, however, not on their degree of closeness (in relation to the dead person) but by the degree of their need and incapacity for work.

The proletariat has also greatly changed the former area of family private law...

Concluding this necessarily incomplete overview (the theme being such a large one) of what has been done by the proletariat in the space of less than a year (in the area of those relations which are regulated in the bourgeois order, if one can express it that way, by civil law), one can boldly state that hardly anything is left of so-called civil law. In almost all areas (economic, for the most part), the life of the proletariat has either approached or come close to approaching the substitution of a planned state of affairs pertaining to social welfare for the unorganized anarchy of former private law relationships....

THE OLD AND NEW COURT
P. Stuchka

Our counter-revolutionary press still cannot calm itself in regard to the Decree of the Soviet of Peoples' Commissars on the Court. [November 22/December 5, 1917] Lacking serious arguments against the decree, they resort to the usual gossip and slander, or simply mock the name of the author of the decree, as if such methods of polemic against the author could discredit the content of the decree itself. In fact, they demonstrate a complete lack of familiarity with the matter and often go in for conjecture and supposition about the content of the new law, instead of simply reading the eight points of the brief decree.

The elimination of the honored institution of the governing Senate by the decree has evoked more animosity than anything else. [The Senate served the function of a Supreme Court. (ed.)] In its own day the bourgeois press wasted much paper and ink in destructive criticism of this same Senate, as an organ of the court and as an organ of surveillance, both against its individual departments as well as against the institution in its entirety. But bourgeois criticism did not touch on the class character of this institution. For the proletarian and peasant revolution, this aspect of the question played the primary role.

In reality, the court, after the permanent armed forces and the bureaucratic police, was the most trustworthy defender of the bourgeois-landowner system. Under the guise of the illusory defense of truth and justice, the supposedly independent judicial authority of the bourgeois state was the most trustworthy defender of the capitalist system and the interests of the propertied classes. This was not only because these judges were the direct agents of the state and state authority as instruments of the enslavement of the oppressed classes, but also because by their own class position they belonged to the class of oppressors. They understood truth and justice, as well as freedom and equality in a way prompted by the interests of their class. Thus, for example, the very same Senate which "stands above politics," which after the bourgeois revolution of February 27 of this year [1917], immediately sanctioned the new revolutionary authority as fully legal, then after the proletarian-peasant revolution of

Pravda, January 3, 4 and 5, 1918. On early Soviet courts, see esp. John Hazard, *Settling Disputes in Soviet Society*, New York, 1960, chapter 6. On the role of lawyers, see Eugene Huskey, *Russian Lawyers and the Soviet State: The Origins and Development of the Soviet Bar, 1917–1939*, Princeton, 1986.

October 25, openly declared this revolution to be a heinous crime. On the next day after the first revolution, our courts pronounced decisions not in the name of overthrown tsarism, but in the name of the new government: "By decree of the Provisional Government"; while after the second revolution, during the course of an entire month, they continued to administer justice in the name of that very same deposed Provisional Government. And even the most perfect form of our pre-revolutionary court, a trial by jury, composed of residents from the Nevsky Prospekt, undoubtably would justify Kornilov and condemn the Bolsheviks. After all, we are familiar with the decisions of bourgeois jurors in England (against Maklin and others) and in other Western European countries. Inevitably this stems from the class composition of the court and the juries of the old system.

The proletarian revolution, while taking the regular army into its own hands and destroying its foundations, put in the place of the bourgeois police-militia its own Red Guard or democratic militia. Could it stop before the stronghold of judicial authority which continued to hold in its clutches the revolutionaries of July 3-5 or simply ignore the events of October 25? But the age-old bourgeois ideology stubbornly wielded power over the minds of even our own revolutionaries. Conceptions of bourgeois truth and justice outlive their own real foundations and introduce more than a little confusion into the speeches and even the actions of otherwise true revolutionaries. This is why at the first moment, the suggestion of breaking the entire old structure of the class court evoked doubts even in the heads of several rather left-inclined comrades, and, however strange it might have seemed, chiefly in the ranks of the theoreticians. Really, I can scarcely believe that in the beginning the project of the decree on the court evoked greater doubts and united more voices against itself than such an extremely decisive step as the breaking up of the entire banking business. Not for nothing did people speak during the course of centuries about "the temple of justice."

For me, from the first day of the Revolution there was never any doubt that only on the ruins of this temple of bourgeois justice would we succeed in raising a structure of socialist justice, more modest in its outward appearance, but infinitely sounder in its substance. The arguments that it is first of all necessary to create a new law code, a new book of justice for the new court, are based on a purely mechanistic view of the character of the legal relations between people. And hopes for the gradual transformation of the old class court into a genuinely democratic one are founded on the typical illusions of reformism. For revolutionary law is not a simple reform of the former order, and the tsarist-bourgeois class court cannot, by a simple change in personnel, be turned into a genuinely popular, just court...

Reproach for the destruction of the free legal profession of lawyers still remains. I, again, never spoke of the "rotten lawyers' bar" in general and never will say that our law profession stood at a lower level than in other countries. I will not dwell here on the natural conservatism of professional jurists in general and lawyers in particular. But really, would that mutual relation between the bar and magistrates (judicial staff), such as existed in former times, be tolerable in the future system? At the time when the democratization of the entire system takes place, leading to an equalization of large and small incomes, it will be impossible for this reason alone to leave this privileged layer untouched. But by its further behavior, the bar declared itself, almost without exception, to be the class enemy of the Worker-Peasant Government.

Such was the old system, which we have in part already broken, and are still breaking apart. But we are not only breaking down, we are at the same time building, and although we are building according to principles unarguable in the programs of all socialists, it is namely from the direction of our socialists that the most undeserved reproaches for this are heard.

When we introduced the Decree on the Court, in the first instance we were asked the question, "But according to which laws will the revolutionary courts be judging?" They convinced us that first of all it is necessary to create a new revolutionary material law, both civil and criminal, by which the new court can be guided. And until then? Judge in the old court according to the old laws?

I have already noted that such discussions are distinguished by a purely mechanistic view of law as an arbitrarily published statute, and not as a superstructure growing naturally out of existing and changing economic and social relations. If even in normal times this written law embraces much less than all existing legal relationships and especially often only very incorrectly reflects real law, that is law "recognized" and really carried out by living people, then it would be funny to dream of the stability of written law at a time of a great upheaval. To speak of an immutable written civil, that is in essence, bourgeois law, during a transitional moment on the way to a socialist system! Or regarding a compulsory criminal law, that is, a law securing, first of all, the legal relationships of the existing system, at a time when this whole system is going to oblivion!

However, not only our phony socialists, but even some of our friends have been horrified, while reading Point Five of the Decree on the Court, to the effect that the court must be guided by the laws of the overturned governments only insofar as they are not abolished by the revolution and do not contradict revolutionary legal concepts or the revolutionary conscience of the peoples', that is, the elected court! There were arguments to the effect that to use the written laws of the overturned regime was unrevolutionary, and in this argument there is much truth. Except that, unfortunately, in their legal consciousness the people themselves are too firmly tied to the written law, which is transferred, "like an eternal disease to posterity." But chiefly they have pounced on us from another side, directly accusing us of anarchism and many other sins. Now they have already become accustomed to our formula and even in the ranks of our primary opponents is heard the admission that "the revolution punishes and pardons its enemies neither by written nor by affirmed law."

From the first days of the Revolution of 1917, as early as March and later, I had to argue constantly against the conscious or involuntary hypocrisy of those revolutionaries who were used to talking of strict legality at the very height of the Revolution. I remember those Kadet or still more rightist authors who identified spontaneous revolutionary acts with crime. They were completely sincere and recognized the now-toppled Provisional Government only insofar as it received sanction from the highest authority, that is, from Nicholas and Michael. I see a similar reference in a most solemn decree now lying before me of the now abolished "Ruling Senate." But I maintain that even the most moderate socialist recognizes the patent counter-revolutionary nature of such a view...

Turning to the question of what law will be implemented in our new court, we have had to pause on the issue of so-called political crimes. We Marxists categorically reject the very concept of political crime, but we are far from rejecting the struggle against counter-revolution. Therefore, in creating a special revolutionary tribunal, we definitely declare that it is not a court for political criminals, but rather a special organization "for the struggle against counter-revolutionary forces by means of taking measures for protecting the Revolution and its conquests from them." Those special methods which our united counter-revolution uses (from Purishkevich, Kornilov and Milyukov to the Avksentyevs and Co.), demand public inquiry with the participation of elements from society, since public exposure of these matters will remove the masks from their heroes.

With what do we propose to replace the abolished class-based court? There can be only one answer: *an elected people's court*. And if only the revolutionary proletariat and peasantry had in their ranks a sufficient number of judicial specialists, then the question would be resolved quite easily. But it is on the basis of this insufficiency of specialists that the "bourgeoisified intelligentsia" decided to conduct a battle with the proletariat. In one field after another this intelligentsia began to declare strikes, but strikes not with their own means, not with their own strike funds, but with the funds of bourgeois imperialists supporting, as always, with an open hand, all those who would weaken the forces of the proletariat and the Proletarian Revolution.

To this struggle, which only a cadre of specialists waged consciously, were attracted the semi-intelligentsia, semi-proletarian mass of clerks, those pariahs of the judicial world, who, existing on beggarly pay scales and chance extra tips, were still so permeated with the atmosphere of the bureaucratic "way of life," that they looked at the proletarians in part with envy, in part with hatred. They considered themselves intellectually above the popular masses, but in reality thought more narrowly in their own kingdom of the twentieth of the month* than did the "factory rabble" they so scorned. This is the difference between the world view of *Pravda* and the world view of *Novaya Rus* or *Zhivoe Slovo!*

I find that, despite all the difficulties arising from such strikes, the results will be rather beneficial, since they will destroy that thick wall of alienation between, for example, the bureaucratic, judicial world and so-called active life. The court system will right away free itself from the mass of untalented careerists planted here from above by the various Muravyevs and Shcheglovitovs, and will produce in the lower ranks that natural rejuvenation which is necessary for the future great democracy.

Before us is the task of immediately replacing the courts we have destroyed with the new People's Court, and the execution of this task has already begun. The local People's Court, as the court of first instance and the one closest to the needs of the population, has already been elected and has begun work in some places. In major cities it is lacking the specialist element, for jurists did not want to put themselves up for candidacy, and those elected were thus almost exclusively workers and soldiers. Are they coping with their task? To all appearances, yes. And in vain do the gullible bourgeois jeer at the lack of special knowledge in these people's judges. Look for a moment at the essence of the matter! The People's Court must thrash out normal commonplace interrelationships among people. Is their comprehension really so difficult and inaccessible to the normal intelligence of a normally conscious person? Those laws and legal norms which can be understood only by the jurist-specialist are bad, and to the highest degree inappropriate. Such law, as non-people's law, clearly "contradicts the revolutionary legal consciousness of the people" and must be discarded. And if affairs of the specialist-bourgeois world which are less appropriate to the People's Court come up for analysis then there is a simple solution: to call in specialists, experts. The former bourgeois judge called in experts quite often on questions of working, professional life; now it is the reverse. The task of the People's Court, therefore, is not insurmountable, and the only thing here which is disadvantageous for the Revolution is the necessity of wasting so many of our best workers for a new, at first sight, less important, field of social labor.

But the proletariat and working peasantry, after the victorious Revolution of October 25, cannot stop in the presence of this task. And the new work may turn out to be of such creative force that legislative institutions will not, in any event, be able to replace it....

---

* The twentieth of every month was a pay-day in pre-revolutionary Russia. [ed.]

189

FIVE YEARS OF REVOLUTION IN LAW
P. Stuchka

Revolution has nothing in common with law. From the point of view of law, all revolutions are subject to unquestionable condemnation. That is what bourgeois jurists believe. The continuity of law is to them an unshakable principle. The Russian Revolutionary Provisional Government acted according to the orders of the deposed Nicholas; the German Provisional Government of 1918 acted in the name of the deposed Wilhelm, or rather, due to a transfer of the power of attorney, in the name of his chancellor Max Baden.

The October Revolution, as a revolution of the proletarian masses, could not stand on such a formal point of view; it carried out a revolution in law, too. In truth, it was more revolutionary in this respect in deed than in words. The revolutionary courts were formed before general laws were made about the courts; the old laws were abolished before decrees were issued about this. The old courts had already lost all authority in the eyes of the broad masses, when party comrades, revolutionaries of conscience rather than fear, still vacillated at signing a decree about their abolition. Once again, this time in the greatest revolution in the world, we received ostensible proof that the strongest fortress, the last refuge of any ideology, of all idealistic survivals, is the law...

Of course, the bolsheviks did not reject the significance of laws. They perhaps even believed in them too much. But before the revolution, they, like all social democratic Marxists, thought too little about questions of law, and legislation did not take place very regularly in the beginning. Along with the resolutions and decrees of the Second Congress (on the power of the Soviets, on peace, on land) decrees were signed in the name of the government of the Russian Republic, "the President of the Soviet of People's Commissars." But at that time, in the "Newspaper of the Provisional Worker-Peasant Government," a "Resolution by the Worker-Peasant Government About the Eight Hour Day" was printed with the signature "in the name of the Russian Republic, by the Deputy Commissar of Labor, Yu. Larin," or "On the Moratorium on Living Space," with the

From *Ezhenedel'nik sovetskoi iustitsii*, No. 44-45, 1922, as republished in P.I. Stuchka, *Izbrannye proizvedeniia po marksistko-leninskoi teorii prava*, Riga, 1964, pp. 282-89.

signature "The People's Commissar of Land Affairs, V. Milyutin," and so on. "The initiative of legislation" was not limited, and thus one fine day, Comrade Kozlovsky and I, then still not in Narkomyust [The People's Commissariat of Justice], sat down and wrote and presented before the Sovnarkom, on a half-sheet of paper, the project of the decree "regarding the elimination of titles and civil ranks," and in a few days, on November 10 (23), the decree had passed the Sovnarkom and was published.

At that time, all courts with the "Governing Senate" at the head, just ignored our revolution. If in February, on the second day of our revolution, the courts had already written their decisions "by the order of the Provisional Government," then after the October Revolution, even temporarily (even as a provisional one)* they did not want to recognize the Worker-Peasant Government.

In hundreds of chambers of Justices of the Peace and other kinds of courts, they proclaimed decisions by decree of the deposed governments. This was intolerable, and again Comrade Kozlovsky and I outlined the project of the first "Decree on the Courts."

At this point I received the appointment of Provisional Commissar of Justice. In the Ministry of Justice, as in all departments, there was a strike by the employees. This was opportune for me, because I did not think for a minute that I would have to chase out the whole senior staff of the Ministry of Justice. I discovered from party sources that out of the whole staff of chancellery employees, only three were willing to continue working (one of them calling himself a bolshevik). The day after my appointment, I set off on foot, without any extra ceremony, to the Ministry building on Ekaterinskaya Street.

It may have seemed a little strange to the door-keepers and messengers that a representative of the new "terrible" power came alone, without an escort, on foot, and shook hands with them all in greeting. But I must admit that, in my turn, I was somewhat surprised by their welcoming greeting, not only in the Ministry, but later in the Senate and other places. This was the only element close to the proletariat in the whole of the old court system, and evidently their class-instinct showed them that this power was specifically in their class interest. One has to be just; they were of great service to the republic in protecting the belongings and the buildings. And, of course, it was not the republic's fault that it had to pay them insufficiently, and even the opposite, to reduce their numbers, re-locate them, and in general place them in a very unpleasant position. But I must emphasize once more that this was not the fault of the new power.

---

* It hurriedly called itself provisional even though it did not intend to relinquish its power voluntarily and fully believed in its own strength. Therefore, we at Narkomyust in the heading, "Collection of Laws and Decrees of the Worker-Peasant Government," introduced a small correction into the resolution; we just left out the little word "provisional." [P.S.]

I found no other employees in the chancellery, but at the same time I was informed that all the employees showed up very punctually in the dining-room for dinner and meetings. Out of prudence they had left two of their representatives at work, old employee-diplomats, one of whom I met there in the corridor. He explained to me that he was willing to continue work, and thus took away the reason for my firing him, which I would have done that very day, accidentally finding out his attitude toward the new power, and not only to the new power. I told him that I was firing all the higher staff of the Ministry's employees for evasion of work, and that I invited all the rest of the personnel to come to work the next day, with the warning that if the opposite was the case, they would be fired. At the same time, I gave instructions about closing the dining-room and the building as a whole to those who were not coming to work. The lower ranking employees asked me to send some armed protection, but although I did indeed take certain measures in this respect, there was none of that kind of protection, at least on that day, and it turned out to be unnecessary in general. Thus, we won the center of the whole apparatus of justice without bloodshed, the historical building of the Ministry of Justice. I would say, fortunately, without its bureaucrats, because, with the exception of three or four people, indeed, no one showed up for work until the main citadel, the Governing Senate, was broken.

I have already said that the first project of the Decree on Courts was put together by us before my appointment as People's Commissar. Its passage encountered entirely unexpected opposition in our own ranks. I am not talking about the left SRs [Socialist Revolutionaries] already represented in the VTsIK [All Russian Central Executive Committee (of Soviets)]. No, even in the Sovnarkom, where only communists sat. I do not know if the majority was set against that idea from the beginning or just a minority, since the project was not put to a vote. But Vladimir Ilich, to whom the bold project was agreeable, did not want to push it through this way, with one swoop, since there was 'opposition' in our own ranks. He correctly reasoned that the progress of the revolution would do its own work in this respect as well.

What was the point of their objections? The original project of the Decree on Courts was found in the papers of Narkomyust and published in 1918 in the second edition of "Materials of the People's Commissariat of Justice." It consisted of nine clauses and its introduction read: "The great worker and peasant revolution destroys the foundations of the old bourgeois order, which rested upon the exploitation of labor by capital; this creates the necessity for uprooting old judicial institutions and establishments, the old codes of law, suitable for obsolescent social relations (of the past), and also the need to create new, truly democratic institutions and laws." Anyone who has read Karl Marx (his speech before the jurists at Cologne) will notice that expressions of the 'destructive' part

192

of this first statement of revolutionary law were taken from there. As early as the pre-October era of our Revolution, in the Petersburg Executive Committee, we put forward this thought, but when I once cited Marx's words from this speech, our social-democrats, the mensheviks, found that evidently these were the words of some anarchist or other. When this outlook on law was introduced into court by Comrade Kozlovsky during the Kshisinskaya trial about the removal of the TsK and PK [Central and Party Committees] of the bolshevik party from her palace he was laughed at not only by the mensheviks, but also, of course, by the Kadets. And now the same idea met with a certain opposition in the ranks of the Bolsheviks themselves. Especially this statement of the decree, "to do away with general court institutions, namely, district courts, judicial chambers, the Governing Senate, with all its departments, military courts of all names, as well as commercial courts and the institution of justices of the peace, chosen through indirect election."

If in our first words we talked about "truly democratic institutions," here we repeat the same thought about indirect elections.

Statute Six of our project read, "for the resolution of judicial matters, both civil and criminal, local workers' and peasants' revolutionary courts will be formed, created by local regional, district and volost courts, and where these do not exist, by the regional and provincial soviets, and consisting of the chairman and no less than two members, to be guided in their decisions and sentences not by the written laws of deposed governments, but by the decrees of Sovnarkom, with revolutionary conscience and revolutionary legal consciousness." This is, we proclaim class principles of justice in the very first project, without looking back.

The thought of how courts would get along without laws scared our comrades most of all. "Let's write the new laws first," they said, "and then we can dismiss the old courts and appoint new ones." "And until then," we asked, "are the justices of the peace, the judicial chambers and Senate to continue their counter-revolutionary activity?" Evidence about this counter-revolutionary activity of theirs was being received daily; the Senate was particularly militant. At the same time we showed our comrades how slowly new codes were put together during revolutionary times. "The Civil Code of Napoleon" came out only in 1804. Some comrades began to incline favorably toward the decree, but with one reservation, that not all the courts be eliminated at once. Some suggested starting from the bottom, others from the top, that is with the Senate, and continuing with the elimination process gradually. The idea was obviously poorly grounded and lacked reasonable foundation.

Comrade Lunacharsky was a dangerous opponent to the decree. But a miracle took place. At a session of Sovnarkom, in view of his objections, the question was postponed to the next session. Comrade Lunacharsky took the legal project with him and overnight was changed from a Saul into a Paul.* At the next session, Comrade Lunacharsky gave a brilliant supporting speech in favor of the project and the project became a decree. It was not passed for confirmation by the VTsIK, since new delays of matters on the part of our allies, the left SR's were feared. The Decree on Courts was published and took effect on November 24th.

If the project and the final decree are compared, then we can see that the decree left one matter half undone. It *abolished* all courts, but only matters for peaceful judgment were given over to the *local* (that is people's) courts, the matters of other courts being put off until a special decree. The local courts "will be chosen by the Soviets, until arrangements are made for direct democratic elections." That meant that only the so-called "minor business" of the justices of the peace was given over by this decision to the workers' courts. As far as democratic elections went, the illusions of the Constitutent Assembly had not been lived down in the first place, and in the second place, one had to count somewhat the opinion of the left SRs, as yet unbeaten.

Life was more decisive than we were. Long before October in Kronstadt, in the Vyborg region and in other areas, people simply boycotted the old courts and formed their own revolutionary courts. Even Kerensky made a concession to "public opinion" and sat two representatives, a worker and a soldier, next to the justice of the peace. The revolutionary courts did not judge by law, but according to their convictions. This appeared absurd to the intelligentsia; they were more entangled in the fetters of legal mysticism. They could not get over all at once the old ideology of law as the creation of the age-old human mind. And when Comrade Lunacharsky made his ardent speech in defense of the revolutionary decree, and Sovnarkom offered to set forth his thoughts in a special article in *Pravda,* we were convinced that we were aided in our revolution by the theories of the counter-revolutionary professor Petrazhitsky, not by the theories of Marx. All this, of course, is not to reproach those comrades. No, it is only important for me to note that we all, without exception, change slowly toward a revolutionary outlook with regard to law.

That paragraph of the project which concerned laws also had to be softened a little bit. "The local courts ... should be guided in their decisions and sentences by the laws of the overthrown governments only insofar as those laws have not been abrogated by the revolution and do not contradict revolutionary conscience and revolutionary legal consciousness." The meaning of the paragraph did not change the outlook on abolition of the old laws as it was expressed in the project, but it softened the wording and for the sake of greater concreteness, a note was introduced with reference to the program-minimum of the victorious revolutionary parties. Our friends

---

* See his article "Revolution and the Courts," in *Pravda,* Dec. 1, 1917. [P.S.]

on the right mocked this notice quite a bit, which only showed how alien the revolutionary viewpoint was to them.

At that point, while all the other courts submitted to the decree, the Senate and the estate of barrister-attorneys declared an uprising against the decree. The Council of Barrister-Attorneys of the Petersburg district avenged themselves on me by 'demonstratively' excluding me from the ranks of barrister-attorneys, a group which had just been abolished by us in that same Decree on Courts, after which the Soviet was in an 'illegal position.' The Senate was preparing a counter-revolutionary appeal, left unprinted only because the workers in the Senate printship refused to set it. With difficulty they found a machinist who would print this appeal in a few copies. Unfortunately, this historical document turns out to have still not been published. At any rate, we had to shut the Senate building, though without any armed resistance. The procedure of closure was accomplished on December 4, 1917. The Kadet paper *Rech,* which was still coming out, described quite wittily how Senate Commissar Comrade Damberg called together all the doorkeepers and messengers and, sitting in the armchair of the presiding-officer, stated that while until now the senators had sat in armchairs and the messengers had stood near the doors, now it was to be the reverse (citation from memory). One has to be fair to the witty reporter, and we all laughed whole-heartedly at this description, but it did not save the Senate. The thought expressed in this description was the same as that in the successor *Russkie vedomosti* (*Svobodnaya Rossiya*) when it wrote regarding the People's Courts that "the landed gentry have been replaced by the proletariat, that is all." But the exchange of the Senate and Justice of the Peace for a proletarian court—that is a revolution of the law.

We have lived through five years since then. Without closing our eyes to the weaker side of our People's Court, we have to recognize that it has completely justified itself and that all proletarian revolutions should take the same path. But luckily all these future revolutions will have the experience of our revolution to go by. That the revolution in law has only penetrated the realm of theory after five years is hardly strange since in this period we have found ourselves in a state of "retreat" in the area of law.

To many our words in honor of the revolution of law will be incomprehensible at the moment, when they see how we "are returning to 'burned out' laws." For the procuracy, the advocates, the "red" tenth volume, that is, the "Civil Code," is it not simply a reprint? I take the law on the implementation of the Civil Code of the RSFSR and read, "The interpretation of the regulations of this Code on the basis of the laws of deposed governments, of the practice of pre-revolutionary courts or reference to them is forbidden." That means, not a return, but only a retreat, a strictly controlled retreat with a preservation of the power of the victorious Revolution. This is from a purely practical point of view.

But at the moment we are living through a whole revolution even in the ideology of law. The impetus to that revolution of ideology was given by the actual deeds of the Revolution. The human mind often enough follows along after events, which does not prevent it from creating new wonders when it is illuminated with the enlightenment of class consciousness. And it is not surprising that it is the field of law which lags behind everywhere in this fight with obsolete ideology. In 1917, when we boldly enunciated the principles of "revolutionary legal consciousness," it did not have that specific class content which we put into these words today. Only by remaining true to the accomplishments of these five years of revolution in law can we avoid having "our red procurators turned into pre-revolutionary procurators," "red" defenders turned into former Balalaikins, and Soviet People's Courts turned into simply bureaucratic courts.

The Revolution of the Law is not complete. It continues now, after five years of struggle, but with new methods.

THE GENERAL THEORY OF LAW AND MARXISM
E. Pashukanis

Introduction

Tasks of a General Theory of Law

A general theory of law might be defined as the development of fundamental, that is, most abstract, juridical concepts. In addition, this includes such definitions as "juridical norm", "juridical relations", "the subject of right," etc. As a result of their abstract nature, these concepts have the same applicability to any branch of law, and their logical and systematic meaning remains the same regardless of the concrete circumstances in which they are applied. No one will deny, for example, that the concepts "subject of civil law" and "subject of international law" are both subordinate to the more general concept "subject of law", and that consequently, this category can be defined and developed independently of any particular concrete content. On the other hand, if we remain within the bounds of a single branch of law, we can assert that these fundamental juridical categories are not dependent on the specific content of legal norms in the sense that they preserve their meaning despite any changes in that concrete material content.

It is self evident that these most general and simple juridical concepts are the result of the logical development of the norms of positive law, and represent *per se* the latest and highest product of conscious creativity in comparison with spontaneously forming legal relationships and the norms which express them...

Despite what the Neo-Kantians assure us, that the "idea of law," in their view, precedes experience not genetically, that is, not in terms of time, but logically and epistemologically, we must still recognize that such so-called "critical philosophy" takes us back to medieval scholasticism on this point, as with many others.

One might therefore consider it established that advanced juridical

From *Obshchaia teoriia prava i marksizm,* 4th. ed., Moscow, 1928, pp. 11-18, 20-24, 31-32, 45-46, 55-57. Evgeny Bronislavovich Pashukanis was, with Stuchka, Soviet Russia's most prominent legal theorist. Before being purged by Stalin, he was Director of the Moscow Law Institute and Vice-Chairman of the Communist Academy. See Robt. Sharlet, "Pashukanis and the Withering Away of the Law in the USSR," in S. Fitzpatrick, ed., *Cultural Revolution in Russia, 1928-31,* Bloomington Ind., 1978, pp. 169-88.

thinking, regardless of the material to which it is addressed—cannot do without a certain quantity of the most abstract and general definitions.

Nor can our soviet jurisprudence do without them, as long as it remains such, that is, as long as it remains responsive to its direct practical task. Fundamental (that is, formal) juridical concepts continue their existence in our codes and in corresponding commentaries. There also remains in force the method of juridical thinking with its specific modes.

But does this mean that a scientific theory of law must concern itself with an analysis of the above-mentioned abstractions? It is a widely held view that these basic and most general juridical concepts have a purely conditional and technical meaning. We are told that dogmatic jurisprudence uses these designations only for convenience, that they can have no other theoretical meaning. However, the fact that dogmatic jurisprudence is a practical, and in a certain sense technical discipline, is no basis for the conclusion that its concepts cannot be integrated into the structure of corresponding theoretical disciplines. We might agree with Karner* that the science of law begins where jurisprudence ends, but it does not follow from this that the science of law ought simply to throw overboard the fundamental abstractions which express the principled essence of legal forms. For political economy also began its development with practical questions, primarily the circulation of money, and it, too, originally set for itself the task of showing "the means of making governments and peoples wealthy." Nonetheless, we already find in these technical counsels the foundations of concepts which, in a deepened and more generalized form, become part of the structure of the theoretical disciplines of political economy.

Is jurisprudence capable of developing into a general theory of law, without simply replicating psychology or sociology in the process? Is it possible for there to be an analysis of basic definitions of legal forms, similar to the analysis of the fundamental and most general definitions of value in political economy? These are the questions whose resolution will determine whether it is possible or impossible to regard a general study of law as an independent theoretical discipline.

For bourgeois philosophy of law, whose representatives in the main reflect a neo-Kantian point of view, this problem is resolved by a simple antithesis of two categories: the category of that which is, and the category of that which ought to be. According to this conception, two categories of science are recognized: causal and normative. "Whereas causal or explicative science," we read, for example, in Wunte, "strives to seek out the laws of nature, according to which the process of real life factually flows, and must flow, with natural necessity, the aim and object of the normative

---

* See Karner, "Social Functions of Law," Russ Trans., 1923, p. 11. (E.P.)

198

disciplines, which do not try to explain what is happening, are exclusively those norms on the basis of which something ought to occur, although it factually sometimes does not happen."* In Simmel, the category of "ought" defines a special form of thinking, separated by an impassable boundary from the logical order in which we think of being as occuring with natural necessity. The concrete "you should" can be demonstrated only by reference to another moral imperative. Remaining within the boundaries of logic, we cannot infer morality from necessity, or vice versa.** Stammler, in his basic work "Economy and Law", runs through all the possible variations of this same thought, that the regularity of law [*zakonomernost*] can be established by two different methods, the causal and teleological. Thus jurisprudence acquired, so to speak, a regular methodological base as one of the normative disciplines. Furthermore, attempts to deepen this methodology—for example, by Kelsen—led to the conviction that it is precisely jurisprudence which is the principal normative science, since it can be kept within the framework of the formal logical meaning of the category "ought" more than any other of the disciplines of its type. Moreover, in morality and aesthetics both, the normative is impregnated by the psychological, and may be regarded as a qualified volition, that is, as a fact, as existent: the viewpoint of the causal connection intrudes at every moment, violating the purity of the normative comprehension. On the contrary, in law, the highest expression of which Kelsen considers the law of the state, the principle of moral imperative emerges in an unconditional heteronomous form, broken completely from the factual, from that which exists. It is enough to transfer the legislative function itself to the realm of metaphysics—and this Kelsen does, too—and to jurisprudence is left the pure sphere of the normative. Its task consists exclusively in putting various normative contents into a strictly logical order...

Such a general theory of law, which does not undertake to explain anything, which turns its back in advance on the facts of reality, that is, on social life, and concerns itself with norms while remaining uninterested in either their origins (a metajuridical question) or their connection with any form of material interests, can, to be sure, pretend to the name of theory only in the sense, for example, that there is a theory of playing chess. Such a theory has nothing at all in common with science. It does not take care to investigate law, the legal form, as an historical form, because it does not, in general, investigate that which exists. Therefore, to use a common expression, there is nothing to be gotten from it.

So called sociological and psychological theories of law are another matter. One can demand more of them, since because of the method they

---

* Wundt, "Ethik," p. 1 (E.P.)
** See Simmel, "Einleitung in die Moralwissenschaft" (E.P.)

use, they undertake to explain law as a phenomenon in terms of its emergence and development. But here another disillusionment awaits us. Sociological and psychological theories of law usually leave the form of law, as such, outside their purview, since they simply do not see the problems involved. From the very beginning they operate with concepts which are essentially outside the juridical realm; and when they do investigate purely juridical definitions, it is only to declare them "fictions," "ideological phantasms," "projections," and the like. This naturalistic or nihilistic approach undoubtedly evokes a certain sympathy at first glance, particularly if one contrasts it with idealistic theories of law impregnated with teleology and "moralism." After high-flown phrases like "the eternal idea of law" or "the absolute significance of personality," the reader searching for a materialistic explanation of social phenomena will turn with special satisfaction to theories which treat law as resulting from a struggle of interests, as a manifestation of state compulsion, or even as a process acting in real human psyches. Many Marxist comrades thought that they only had to introduce the elements of class struggle into the above mentioned theories in order to obtain a genuine, materialist, Marxist concept of law. However, the result one gets from this is a history of economic forms with a more or less faint juridical hue, or a history of law, but certainly not a general theory of law.* Moreover, if bourgeois jurists such as Gumplovich, who attempt to develop more or less materialistic views, consider themselves bound, so to speak, by duty, to review the arsenal of basic juridical concepts, albeit in order to declare them artifically and provisionally constructed, Marxist writers, as persons who owe no allegiance to jurisprudence, most frequently simply pass over in silence the formal definitions of a general theory of law, devoting all their attention to the specific content of legal norms and to the historical development of legal institutions. In general it must be noted that Marxist writers, speaking of legal concepts, have in view primarily the concrete content of legal regulation, pertaining to this or that epoch, that is, what people at a given stage of development consider law to be. This is apparent

---

* Even the book by comrade P. I. Stuchka, *The Revolutionary Role of Law and the State,* while treating an entire series of problems in the general theory of law, does not treat them in a systematic, unified way. The historical development of legal regulation, in terms of its class content, is set out in the exposition in the foreground, in comparison with the logical and dialectical development of the form itself. One must, however, qualify this, in the sense that anyone who compares the third edition of this book with the first will note, of course, that our esteemed author has taken a step forward in terms of directing his attention to questions of legal form. This developed from the viewpoint from which Stuchka began: he understands law as a system of relationships of production and exchange in the first instance. If, from the very beginning, law is treated as a form of any social relationships one pleases, its specific aspects will certainly remain outside the field of vision. On the contrary, law, as a form of relations of production and exchange, readily reveals its specific feathers with more or less elaborate analysis. (E.P.)

even in the following formulation: "On the basis of a given state of productive forces, certain relations of production are formed, which receive their ideal expression in the legal concepts of human beings, and in more or less 'abstract rules', in unwritten customs and written laws." (Beltov, "On the question", etc. p. 140). Here legal concepts are regarded exclusively in terms of their content; the question of the form of law, as such, is never considered. At the same time it is undoubtedly the case that Marxist theory must investigate not only the material content of legal regulation in various historical epochs, but give a materialistic interpretation to legal regulation itself, as a definite historical form.

Moreover, if we reject analysis of basic juridical concepts, we are left only with a theory which explains for us the origins of legal regulation from the material demands of society, and consequently, the correspondence of legal norms with the material interests of one or another social class. But legal regulation itself, despite the richness of the historical content which we pack into this concept, will remain unanalyzed, as mere form. Instead of the completeness of internal formations and ties, we will be forced to use insufficient juridical concepts with roughly formed contours, so rough that the boundaries between the juridical and contiguous spheres is completely erased.*

To a certain extent, it is impossible not to recognize such a method as being in conformity with law. The history of an economy can be laid out completely aside from the subtleties and details of, say, the theory of rent or of wages. But what would one say of an historian of economic forms for whom the basic categories of theoretical economics—value, capital, profit, rent, etc.—were used diffusively, in a hazy and undifferentiated concept of economy? We are not speaking of the type of reception an attempt to foist off such an account as a theory of political economy would receive. Moreover, in the field of Marxist legal theory, the situation is as follows. One can, it is true, take some consolation from the fact that even jurists themselves are still seeking, and cannot find, a definition of their concept of law. For while courses on the general theory of law begin with a formula which is superficially exact, for the most part, and definite, even this simply provides us with a hazy, approximate, unanalyzed idea of the juridical in general. One must affirm as an axiom that we learn least of all about the law from these definitions and, conversely, that the less attention the scholar gives to his own definition, the better grounded he will make us in law as a form.

The reason for this is perfectly clear. A concept as complicated as law

---

* An example of how a wealth of historical exposition can coexist with the most imperfect rough draft of legal forms can be found in the book by M. Pokrovsky, "Essays in the History of Russian Culture", where the definition of law is reduced to a sign of immobility and stagnation, in contrast with the dynamism of economic phenomena. (E.P.)

cannot be completely understood by a definition according to the rules of school logic *per genus et differentia specifica.* Unfortunately, even the few Marxists who concerned themselves with the theory of law did not avoid the temptations of scholasticism. Thus for example, Renner, (*Marx-studien,* I, 1905) puts as the basis of his definition of law the concept of an imperative addressed from the person of society to an individual. This artless construction seems to him a perfectly adequate exploration of the past, present, and future of legal institutions.*

The fundamental vice in formulae of this sort is their inability to regard the concept of law in its actual movement, which reveals the completeness of internal mutual relations and ties. In place of presenting a concept of law in its most complete and discrete form, and thus demonstrating the significance of that concept for a specific historical epoch, we are offered a purely verbal commonplace about "external authoritarian regulation" equally suitable to all epochs and stages of the development of human society. There is a perfect analogy to this in political economy, in efforts to give a definition of the concept economy which would itself embrace all historical epochs. If all economic theory had been made up of such fruitless scholastic generalizations, it would scarcely have deserved to have been called a science.

... The general theory of law, as we understand it, cannot be criticised on the grounds that this discipline is solely concerned with formal and conventional definitions and artificial constructions. No one doubts that political economy studies something actually existing, although Marx himself warned that such things as value, capital, profits, rent and so forth "cannot be discovered with the help of a microscope and chemical analysis." The theory of law operates with abstractions no less "artificial": "juridical relationships" or "the subject of right" also cannot be revealed by the investigative methods used by natural science. However, behind these

---

* Compare also Ziber (*Collected Works,* Vol. II, p. 134): "Law is nothing but a set of coercive norms which serve to express a typical instance of the accomplishment of economic phenomena—a set whose task is to avert and cut short any variations from the ordinary course of affairs." We find an analogous definition of law as compulsory norms issued by state authority in the book by comrade Bukharin (*Historical Materialism,* 2nd edition, p. 175). The difference between Bukharin and Ziber, and especially Renner, consists of the fact that Bukharin stresses heavily the class character of state authority, and consequently, of law. A more expanded definition of law is found in [the work of] one of Bukharin's pupils, Podvolotsky: "Law is a system of coercive social norms reflecting economic and other social relations of a given society, introduced and protected by the state authority of the dominant class in order to sanction and safeguard these relationships, and consequently to make secure also the dominance of a given class."(Podvolotsky, *Marxist Theory of Law,* p. 156). All these definitions underscore the connection between the concrete content of legal regulation and economics. At the same time, however, they strive to eradicate law in terms of it being a form of external, state-organized compulsion, that is they do not in essence go farther than the crude and empirical methods of the most practical or dogmatic jurisprudence, the conquest of which must be the task of Marxism. (P.S.)

abstractions are also concealed perfectly real social forces.

From the point of view of a person living in the milieu of a natural economy, the economics of value relationships will seem just as much an artificial perversion of simple and natural things as does the juridical mode of thinking to the healthy reasoning of an "average man."

It is necessary to note that the juridical point of view is incomparably more alien to the consciousness of the "average" man than economics, for in the case where the economic relationship is realized simultaneously with the juridical, it is the economic side of that relationship which has reality for those involved in the vast majority of cases, while the juridical relationship remains in the background, and emerges with all its definiteness only in special and exceptional cases (legal proceedings, disputes about the law). On the other hand, the bearers of the "juridical function" at the stage when it is active are usually representatives of a special caste (jurists, judges). Therefore, for the "average" man, thinking in economic categories is more usual and natural than thinking in juridical categories.

To think that the basic concepts which express the meaning of legal forms are products of some sort of arbitrary thinking is to fall into the mistake which Marx noted about 18th century teachers. Since the latter, in Marx's words, did not yet know how to explain the origin and development of mysterious forms of social relations, they tried to remove from them their unexplainable character by stating that they were human inventions, and had not come down from heaven (*Kapital,* I, p. 61).

It is impossible, however, to deny that an important segment of juridical constructions, in fact, bears an extremely unstable and conditional character. Such, for example, are the majority of constructions of public law. We will try below to explain the causes of such phenomena. Meanwhile, we shall restrict ourselves to the observation that in the conditions of a developed commercial economy, the form of value becomes universal, and takes on a series of derivative and imaginary expressions together with primary ones, emerging as the selling price of goods, which are not the products of labor (land) and even entirely unrelated to the process of production (for example, military secrets bought from a spy). This does not interfere with the fact that value, as an economic category, can be understood only from the point of view of socially-necessary labor costs, required for the production of this or that product. In exactly the same fashion, the universalism of legal form should not stop us in the quest for relationships which constitute the real foundation of that form. We hope to show below that the relationships which are labelled those of public law *are not* that real foundation.

Another objection to the tasks of a general theory of law put forward by us is that the abstractions which lie at the basis of analysis are recognized as inherent in bourgeois law only. Proletarian law, we are told, ought to find other general concepts, and the search for these ought itself to be the task of a Marxist theory of law.

This objection seems at first glance to be quite serious. It stems, however, from a misunderstanding. In insisting on new general concepts for proletarian law, this tendency appears to be revolutionary *par excellence*. However, in fact, it proclaims an important form of law, since it tries to express this form outside of the defined historical conditions which allowed it to flower fully, and declares it capable of constant renewal. The dying off of categories (but of categories, and not any injunctions) or bourgeois law certainly does not signify their exchange by new categories of proletarian law, since the dying out of such categories as value, capital, profits, etc. in the process of transition to developed socialism will not mean the appearance of new proletarian categories of value, capital, rent, etc.

The dying out of categories of bourgeois law in this circumstance will mean the dying out of law in general, that is, the gradual disappearance of the juridical moment in human relations.

As Marx pointed out in his *Critique of the Gotha Program,* a characteristic aspect of the transitional epoch is that human relations for the duration of that period will be necessarily restricted by "the narrow horizon of bourgeois law." It is interesting to analyze what Marx conceived this narrow horizon of bourgeois law to be. Marx takes as a given condition a social structure in which the means of production belong to the entire society, and in which producers do not exchange their products. Consequently, he assumes a stage higher than our transitional NEP. The market link is replaced entirely by an organized one, and in conjunction with this "labor used in the manufacture of a product is not reflected in the form of value, as an attribute of the product itself, since here, in contrast to capitalist society, the labor of the individual is directly, and not indirectly, a part of collective labor" (*Critique of the Gotha Program,* 1919 ed., Petrograd, p. 15). But even if the market and the market exchange system were completely eliminated, the new communist society would have to bear for a certain time "all relationships—economic, moral, and intellectual—in which existed the sharply defined imprint of the distinguishing attributes of the old society, from whose core it came to be." This is stated in the principle of distribution, whereby "each producer personally receives (after certain deductions) precisely what he contributed to society." Marx emphasizes that despite the fundamental changes of content and form, "the dominant principle here is the same as that which prevails in the exchange of goods equivalents: a definite quantity of labor in one form is exchanged for the same quantity of labor in another form." Insofar as the relationships of the individual producer and society continue to keep the form of an equivalent exchange, they continue to that extent to preserve as well the form of law, since "by its very nature, law is merely the application of an identical pattern." However, since the natural difference of individual capabilities are not taken into consideration in such circumstances, "the content of this law, as with any law, is the law of inequality." Marx says nothing about the necessity of state authority, whose coercive powers would guarantee the fulfillment of these norms of "unequal" law, which preserves the "bourgeois limitations" of law, but this is self-evident. Lenin offers this conclusion: "Bourgeois law in relation to the distribution of products of *consumption,* inevitably presupposes, of course, the existence of a *bourgeois state,* for law is nothing without an apparatus capable of *compelling* observance of legal norms. The result not only is that bourgeois law remains for a certain time under communism, but that the bourgeois state remains as well, without the bourgeoisie!" (Lenin, *State and Revolution,* p. 93). Once the form of an equivalent relationship is given, a form of law is also given, as well as a form of public (that is, state) power, which is thereby enabled to remain in force for a certain time even in conditions where division into classes no longer exists. The withering away of law, and together with it, the withering of the state, will be completed, according to Marx, only when "labor," having ceased to be a means of life, becomes itself the primary demand of life, "when together with the multi-faceted development of the individual there is an expansion of production forces, when each will work voluntarily according to his abilities, or, as Lenin says, "shall not connive like Shylock so as not to work an extra half hour more than someone else," in a word, when *an end shall finally be put to the form of the equivalent relationship.*

Consequently, Marx conceived the transition to developed communism not as a transition to new forms of law, but as the withering of juridical forms in general, as the liberation of this heritage of the bourgeois epoch, which was destined to outlive the bourgeoisie itself.

Together with this Marx points out the fundamental conditions of existence of the legal form, conditions rooted in the economy itself, and particularly, the unification of labor efforts according to the principle of equivalent exchange, that is, he opens up the profound inner relationship between the form of law and the form of goods. Society, which according to the condition of its productive forces is compelled to preserve an equivalent relationship between expenditures of labor and compensation in a form which is reminiscent, although only remotely, of the exchange of good values, will be *compelled* to preserve the form of law as well. It is only if we start from this basic element that we can understand why a whole range of other social relations takes on juridical form. On the contrary, to reason that courts and laws will always remain, even under conditions of maximum economic security, because certain crimes against persons and so forth will not disappear, is to mistake secondary and derivative elements for principal and basic ones. For even progressive bourgeois criminal theoreticians have become convinced that the struggle against crime should be seen in and of itself as a medical-pedagogical task, for the resolution of

205

which the jurist, with his "list of crimes," his codes, with his conception of "guilt," his "full or mitigated criminal responsibility," with his subtle distinctions between participation, complicity, and instigation, and so forth, is altogether unnecessary. And if this theoretical conviction has not yet led to the abolition of criminal codes and criminal law, this is, of course, only because overcoming the form of law is tied not only with going beyond the framework of bourgeois society, but also with radical deliverance from all the surviving elements of that society.

A critique of bourgeois jurisprudence from the point of view of scientific socialism must take as a mode the critique of bourgeois political economy as Marx gives it. For this purpose it ought first of all to venture on to the enemy's territory, that is, it should not cast to the side those generalizations and abstractions which have been worked out by bourgeois jurists, starting from the demands of their time and their class; but having analyzed these abstract categories, reveal their true significance, that is, in other words, demonstrate that historical conditionality of the legal form.

Any ideology dies out along with the social conditions which created it. However, this final disappearance is preceded by a moment in which the ideology, under the blows directed at it by critics, loses the capacity to cover over and obscure the social relationships out of which it emerged. Exposure of the roots of ideology is the true sign of its approaching end. For, as Lassalle says, "Das Anbrechen einer neuen Zeit besteht immer nur in dem erlangten Bewustsein über das, was die bisher vorhandene Wirklichkeit an sich gewesen ist."*

Ideology and Law

The problem of the ideological nature of law played an important part in the polemic between comrade P. I. Stuchka and Professor Reisner.** Basing his argument on a whole string of citations, Professor Reisner tried to demonstrate that Marx and Engels themselves considered law one of the "ideological forms" and that this view was maintained as well by many other Marxist theorists. Certainly one must not quarrel with his references and citations. It is similarly impossible to deny the fact that law is experienced by human beings psychologically, in particular, in the form of general rules or norms. However, the task most certainly does not consist of recognizing or refuting existing legal ideology (or psychology), but in

---

* "The onset of a new epoch consists of the increasing attainment of a consciousness about what actually constituted the previously existing reality." Lassalle, *System of Acquired Rights*. (E.P.)

** See *Journal of the Socialist Academy*, No. 1. (E.P.)

demonstrating whether or not legal categories have other than ideological meaning. Only in the latter case do we recognize the "necessity" of Reisner's conclusion that "the Marxists can study law only as one of the sub-species of the general species of ideology." The entire essence of the matter lies in this one little word "only." We will clarify this with an example from political economy. The categories "goods," "value" and "exchange value" are undoubtedly ideological conceptions: distorted, somewhat mystical forms of ideas (as Marx described them) in which an exchange society thinks in terms of a labor bond between individual producers. That these forms are ideological is demonstrated by the fact that it is sufficient to move to other economic constructions in order for the categories of goods, value and so forth to lose all significance. Therefore we have a full right to speak of a goods ideology, or, as Marx called it, a "goods fetishism," and to relate this phenomenon to the category of psychological phenomena. But this certainly does not mean that the categories of political economy have an *exclusively* psychological meaning, that they indicate *only* transient experiences, ideas, and other subjective processes. We know quite well, for example, that the category of goods despite its clear ideologism, reflects an objective social relationship. We know that the degree to which this relationship has developed, the greater or lesser degree of its universality, is in essence a set of material facts, susceptible to being examined as such, and not only in the form of ideological-psychological processes. Thus, the general concepts of political economy are not only elements of ideology, but also a type of abstraction, from which we might scientifically, i.e. theoretically, construct objective economic reality. Speaking the words of Marx, "these are socially significant, and therefore objective, forms of thought within a framework of the production relationships of a given, historically defined social means of production—goods production." (*Capital*, I, p. 36).

Consequently, it is necessary for us to prove not that general juridical concepts can, and actually do become integrated into the structure of ideological processes and ideological systems—there is no dispute about that—but that in them, in these concepts, it is impossible to reveal the social reality from behind that certain mysteriousness with which it has been covered. In other words, we are forced to investigate whether or not legal categories constitute those objective forms of thinking (objective for the given historical society), which correspond to objective social relationships. Consequently, our question, as we formulate it, is *whether or not it is possible to understand law as a social relationship in the same sense in which Marx designated capital a social relationship.*

Such a formulation of the question eliminates in advance any reference to the ideological nature of law, and our entire investigation is transferred entirely to another plane . . .

Relationship and Norm

... If we lay out the problem we are analyzing in the terminology of
the Marxist materialistic conception of history, it comes to the same thing
as the problem of the correlation of juridical and political superstructures.

If a norm is seen as the primary factor in all relationships, then before
we search for some kind of juridical superstructure, we must suppose the
presence of a norm-establishing authority, that is, in other words, a
political organization. Thus we should have come to the conclusion that
the juridical superstructure is a derivative of the political one.

Moreover Marx himself emphasized the fact that the basic, most
deeply set stratum of the juridical superstructure—property relations—is
so closely associated with the base that it is "the very same relations of
production expressed in juridical language." The state, that is, the
organization of political class dominance, grows up on the basis of given
production relations or relations of property. Production relations and
their juridical expression form that which Marx, following Hegel, called
civil society. The political superstructure, and in particular, the official
polity, is a secondary, derivative feature.

How Marx himself views the relationship between civil society and the
state is evident from the following citation:

The egotistic individual in bourgeois society can, in his abstract
reasoning, in lifeless abstractions, conceive of himself as an atom, that is, as
an unrelated, self-sustaining being, who needs nothing and demands
nothing in order to lead a fulfilled, blissful existence. Cruel reality, revealed
to our sensory perceptions, does not trouble his fantasies. Each of his
feelings compels him to believe in the reality of the external world and other
individuals, and even his lowly stomach reminds him daily that the external
world is not a void, but is precisely that which fulfills him. Each of his
inherent activities, each of his aspects, each stimulus of life, becomes a
demand, a need, which turns his egoism into a thirst for the things and the
people of the outside world. But since the need of a single individual does
not have any perceptible meaning in and of itself for another egotistical
individual, who possesses the means for satisfying that demand, and since,
consequently, the need is not tied directly to the satisfaction, each
individual is forced to create this tie, becoming in turn an intermediary
between another demand and its object. In this way, natural necessity, the
attributes of human existence (however alien they seem to each other) and
interest binds members of civil society together; *civil, and not political life:
that is its real bond.* Thus it is not the state which unites the atoms of civil
society, but the fact that they are atoms only in imagination, in cloud-like
fantasies—whereas in actuality their existence is far from resembling
atoms, and they are, to be precise— not divine egos but egotistical human
beings. *Only political prejudice still compels one to believe that civil life*

208

must be tied with a state, while on the contrary the state is bound in unity with civil life.*

... It is not difficult to show that the idea of unconditional obedience to external norm-establishing authority has nothing in common with legal form. It is sufficient to take examples of such structure which have been thought out thoroughly and are therefore the most distinct. Let us suppose some sort of military order where a large number of people are subjected in their movements to a common order, in which the sole active and autonomous principle is the will of the commander. Or another example: a jesuit community, where all members blindly and without protest fulfill the will of the leader. One need do little more than think about these examples very carefully in order to come to the conclusion that the more consistently the principle of authoritative regulation is applied, excluding any inkling of a separate and autonomous will, the less grounds for the application of the category of law. This is felt with particular sharpness in the sphere of so-called public law. Here juridical theory meets the greatest difficulties. Generally speaking, the very same phenomenon characterized by Marx as the separation of the political state from civil society, is expressed in the general theory of law in the form of two independent problems, each having its special place in the system and each solved independently of the other. The first of these has a purely abstract character, and consists in the splitting of the basic concept into two aspects, which we discussed above. Subjective law is a characteristic of egotistical man, a member of civil society, "concentrated on his private interests and his private whim, isolated from society." Objective law is an expression of the bourgeois state as a whole, which "feels itself a political state and declares its principle of universality, merely contrasting itself to its elements."

The problem of subjective and objective law is the problem of man-as-bourgeois and man-as-member-of-a-state, expressed in the most general philosophical form. However, the very same problem is revived a second time and already in a more concrete form, as a problem of public and private law. Here the problem is reduced to the delimitation of several actually existing areas of law, and the distribution according to the rubrics of institutions which have been formed historically. It is self evident that dogmatic jurisprudence, with its formal-logical method, is not able to resolve either the first or the second problem, nor to explain the link between them.

The division between public and private law poses specific difficulties because it is only possible to draw a line between the egotistical interests of man as a member of civil society, and the universal abstract interests of the political whole in terms of abstractions. In actuality, these elements

* Heilige Familie (Fr. Mehring—"Gesammelte Schriften von Karl Marx and Fr. Engels," II, p. 227. (E.P.)

mutually infiltrate each other. It is therefore impossible to designate those concrete legal institutions in which this notorious private interest is completely embodied without residue and in pure form.

Another difficulty consists of the fact that in more or less successfully delimiting the boundary between the institutions of public and private law, the jurist clashes once again, within the limits of each of these areas, with the very same problem which he had supposedly solved but which now emerges in a different and abstract form: this problem stands before him in the form of the contradiction between subjective and objective law. Subjective public rights are, of course, those same private rights, resurrected and somewhat transformed (and consequently, also private interests), which intrude into the area where an impersonal and universal interest should be dominant. But whereas the civil law jurist, whose concern is with fundamental and primary legal strata, employs the concept "subjective rights" broadly and assuredly, the application of this theory in public law gives rise at every step to misunderstandings and contradictions. Therefore the system of civil law is distinguished by simplicity, clarity, and completeness, while state law theory abounds in conceptions which are distorted, artificial and one-sided to the point of deformity. The form of law, with its aspect of subjectively giving power to rights, is born in a society consisting of isolated possessors of private, egoistic interests. When the entire economic life is built on the principle of an agreement between independent wills, any social function takes on legal characteristics, as if it is a reflection. That is, it becomes not simply a social function, but also the right of the person who is carrying out that function. However, since in a political organization, by its very essence, private interests are unable to obtain that full development and that overwhelming significance that they obtain in the economy of bourgeois society, it follows that subjective public rights also emerge as something ephemeral, without genuine roots, and are constantly being doubted. At the same time, the state is not a juridical superstructure, but can only be *thought of* as such.*

Juridical theory cannot identify "the right of parliament," the "right of executive authority," etc. with the right, for example, of a creditor to receive payment for a debt because this would mean putting an isolated private interest where bourgeois ideology assumes the hegemony of a general impersonal state interest. But at the same time every jurist knows that he cannot give to these rights any other principled content without the juridical form in general sliding through his fingers. State law can assist only as a reflection of the private law form in the sphere of political

---

* "For juridical cognition, it is exclusively a matter of an answer to the question: how ought I think of the state juridically." Jellinek, "System der subjektiven öffentlichen Rechte", p. 13. (E.P.)

210

organization or it ceases in general to be law. Any attempt to depict a social function in terms of what it really is, that is, simply as a social function, and a norm, as simply an organizing rule, means the death of legal forms. However, the real precondition for this overcoming of legal form and legal ideology is the condition of society in which an end has been put to the contradiction between the individual and social interest. . . .

V. RELIGION, LANGUAGE, AND OTHER "AWKWARD HABITS" OF EVERYDAY LIFE

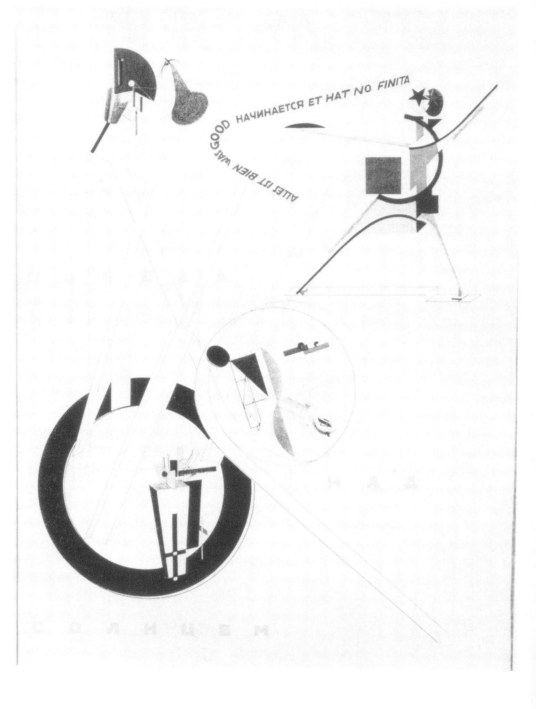

INTRODUCTION

Habits are difficult to change, much more so even than attitudes and ideas. The way we eat or talk, the way we dress and go about our daily affairs seems intrinsically a part of life itself, rather than customs related directly to particular forms of social or political organization. Habits thus are powerful conservative forces. As "necessary" parts of daily life which reflect traditional values, they stand as "awkward" impedimenta to revolutionary social change. After all, what could Bolsheviks do about such "bourgeois" patterns as the way ordinary Russians spoke deferentially to their "betters."

As Trotsky notes in his essay "Habit and Custom," and as many have pointed out elsewhere, taking power was relatively easy for the Bolsheviks compared with the task of building socialism in backward, agrarian Russia. Not the least reason for this was the incompatibility of deeply ingrained habits and outlooks with socialist rationality and conceptions of community. In addition to formulating effective social and economic policies and a workable system of proletarian law, Lenin and his comrades also had to encourage suitable behavior patterns if these policies were to be implemented.

This was difficult and risky. Among other things, the party had to identify those everyday habits which were genuinely incompatible with the tasks of socialist construction, explain their choice, and mobilize appropriate resources to change them without provoking mass resistance. Anti-Bolshevik armies during the Civil War posed a big enough threat without unnecessarily provoking popular animosity over trifles. But what was a trifle? Religion? Prostitution? Alcoholism? The habit of thinking of one's own needs before those of the broader community?

Some everyday patterns were relatively easy to identify and to legislate about, but difficult to change. Alcoholism was "clearly the consequence of oppressive social conditions," which would die out as these conditions were eliminated, but which in the meantime had to be controlled. But while the party could and did control the sale of spirits (which in any case were in short supply because of the grain shortage), it was impossible to implement strict controls even in such groups as the Red Guards, and hardly popular to do so.

Difficulties with language were more subtle. The personal form of address (*ty* — thee) was traditionally used either among close friends or by a member of a higher social group (noble, army officer, industrialist) in addressing a lower one (peasant, soldier, worker). Class deference and respect was reflected in the impersonal form (*vy* — you). As Trotsky's brief

215

essay indicates below, the Red Army could hardly inculcate a sense of social equality if officers reinforced traditional estate distinctions in their language.[1]

The problems of coarse language, and especially of prostitution, were more difficult to define. What, after all, was the matter with swearing? And given the necessity of establishing new relations of equality and respect between men and women, how could prostitution be defined as socially harmful if sexual relations took place privately between consenting adults? Kollontai's essay on "The Fight Against Prostitution," like Trotsky's on "Cultured Speech," is interesting in part because it indicates the logic underlying the proscription of undesirable behavior. Bolsheviks recognized prostitution as a "bourgeois evil," inculcating anti-socialist attitudes, but it was not especially easy to determine why. At first there was a tendency to arrest and punish prostitutes as deserters from work, but on one hand, redefining "desertion from work" in conditions of massive unemployment was virtually impossible; and on the other, it turned out that many gainfully employed women, even within the party apparatus, engaged in prostitution simply to supplement their incomes. What in the end was determined as genuinely harmful about prostitution was "the element of material calculation," i.e., the fact that it was private trade and "crassly materialistic," and hence incompatible with the attitudes and values of socialism.[2] In the case of vulgar speech, as Trotsky's essay suggests, the party fell back to condemning a habit as "uncultured" and "undignified" essentially because of its prevalence under capitalism, rather than because of any clearly demonstrable incompatibility with socialism. But here, clearly, there was a dangerously thin line between simple disapproval on essentially aesthetic grounds, and the unnecessary authoritarianism of official proscription, with consequent popular resistance.

Most difficult of all was the question of religion. There was no doubt that superstition, belief in magic, reverence for religious symbols, obedience to the clergy, and a powerful, propertied Orthodox church were all incompatible with socialist values and institutions. But there was also no doubt that spiritualism met a deep human need, and that assaulting the "faithful" might have serious consequences in terms of popular support. Marx himself was sensitive to these problems. He wrote, of course, that religion was the "opium of the masses," but he prefaced this famous aphorism with a statement clearly recognizing religion's comforting qualities: "religion is the sigh of the oppressed creature, the heart of a heartless world, the spirit of soulless stagnation."[3] Destroying an oppressive, "heartless world" would end humanity's need to "drown itself in spiritual gin," to use Lenin's phrase, but social revolution took time.

Western writers often dwell on the anti-religious attributes of "atheistic Bolshevism," but if one couples the church's own political stance in the revolution and civil war with the Bolsheviks' deep feelings about the falsity of religious consciousness, the party's attitude actually seems remarkably mild. Virtually without exception, the Orthodox clergy scathingly attacked Bolshevism during the 1917-1921 period. Even before October, the All-Russian Sobor (Congress) of Church leaders called on "the All-Russian, Christ-loving people" to destroy the "German spies and hirelings, the betrayers and traitors in the rear who have poisoned the army's mind and torn out its heart."[4] Openly supporting General Kornilov's attempt at a right-wing coup, the Sobor elected a Patriarch, Tikhon, who regarded the Bolsheviks as "open and concealed enemies of Christ... Satan's henchmen... who will burn in hell-fire in the life hereafter and be cursed for generations... "[5] Tikhon's views were widely circulated in 1918, as the church openly appealed for support for the Whites against the "Jewish-Masonic slavemasters."[6]

The Bolshevik response to all this— and it essentially was a *response*, rather than an aggressive campaign— was to move where necessary against the church as an institution, and to leave aside for the time being the question of an individual's personal religious beliefs. Church land was nationalized with all other landed property in 1917, and alloted to the peasants (who were already seizing it in any case); control over marriage and family matters was abolished, along with the teaching of religion in public or private schools (private teaching and study was permitted, although officially proscribed for persons under 18 years of age by a law of March 3, 1919); church cash reserves, securities, and non-religious property was confiscated (but not, for the most part, religious "valuables"); in sum, every effort was made to eliminate completely the church's role in public affairs, and weaken its institutional power. But not only was little done about the question of private religious beliefs, the Patriarch was placed only under mild house arrest as a result of his vitriolic anti-Bolshevik speeches, and many of the party's specific decrees were not enforced. Instead, Bolsheviks generally followed the posture of Article 13 in the Party Program, adopted in 1918, which called for "systematic anti-religious propaganda to free the masses from their prejudices, but without irritating the feelings of believers."

As the leading Western historian on this question points out, little was actually accomplished on the "anti-religious front" during the Civil War. While the church hierarchy itself grew more accommodating, the Bolsheviks for their part simply lacked the money, resources, and energy to do more than distribute posters, a few issues of *Revoliutsiya i tserkov,* and an occasional film. In some quarters, inside both the church and the communist movement at large, it seemed possible that the party and organized religion might reach a *modus vivendi.*

The selection below by S. Kheglund (Zeth Höglund), a member of the Central Committee of the Swedish Communist party, shows just how far

217

this thinking had gone by the early 1920s. Kheglund did not regard religious convictions as at all incompatible with communism, insofar as they were private, and not manifested in "class-political institutions." Religious consciousness might even encourage revolutionary politics. It was therefore "undoubtedly rash" for the party to label itself as anti-religious, since this "detaches from us elements which can be useful in our movement." Material betterment, not anti-religious propaganda, would eventually lead to "spriritual emancipation."

Such views seriously alarmed militant Bolsheviks. Party figures like Emilyan Yaroslavsky, a left-communist in 1918 and future head of the League of Militant Atheists, saw Kheglund's "softness" as a potentially fatal separation of theory and practice, dangerously undermining socialist construction. Any party which regarded itself as "a union of conscious vanguard fighters for the liberation of the working class" could not remain indifferent to the "unconsciousness, ignorance, and obscurantism represented by spiritual visions." The Communist party was anti-religious precisely because the falseness of religious teaching was an ideological buffer for capitalist institutions, values and habits. Religiosity was consequently a dangerous legacy of the past.

The publication in 1923 of Yaroslavsky's response to Kheglund (see below), signalled the beginning of an organized anti-religious movement. Many in the party still urged caution; the "League of Militant Atheists," formally a "private union" rather than a party body, was not permitted to function until 1925, and the 13th party congress in 1924 "strongly condemned" such measures as the arbitrary closing of churches. But a resolution on "The Setting of Anti-Religious Agitation and Propaganda" urged a deeper and more systematic effort "to show workers and peasants that their interests were not served by religion, and to give them a scientific outlook in place of religious conceptions."[8] Some of the party's efforts in this regard, short editorials from the journal *Bezbozhnik* (*Atheist*), are given below.

Many party leaders still recognized, however, that the task of changing habits and outlooks was an enormously difficult undertaking—that cultural revolution, in other words, was serious work. Habits could only be changed effectively by practice, and by careful example: peasants and workers had to be shown clearly that such changes genuinely benefited their interests. With this in mind, party propaganda increasingly took on the character of the final selection in this chapter. Readers of Soviet pulp literature will undoubtedly recognize the art-form: a "memoir," perhaps entirely fiction, of "one day in the commune," in which peasants are gradually persuaded of the utilitarian and ethical value of "behaving like Bolsheviks should."

HABIT AND CUSTOM
L. Trotsky

In the study of life it is peculiarly manifest to what an extent individual man is the product of environment rather than its creator. Daily life, i.e., conditions and customs, are, more than economics, "evolved behind men's backs," in the words of Marx. Conscious creativeness in the domain of custom and habit occupies but a negligible place in the history of man. Custom is accumulated from the elemental experience of men; it is transformed in the same elemental way under the pressure of technical progress or the occasional stimulus of revolutionary struggle. But in the main, it reflects more of the past of human society than of its present.

Our proletariat is not old and has no ancestry. It has emerged in the last ten years partly from the petty townspeople and chiefly from the peasantry. The life of our proletariat clearly reflects its social origin. We have only to recall *The Morals of Rasteryaev Street,* by Gleb Uspensky. What are the main characteristics of the Rasteryaevs, i.e., the Tula workmen of the last quarter of the last century? They are all townsmen or peasants who, having lost all hope of becoming independent men, formed a combination of the uneducated petty bourgeoisie and the destitute. Since then the proletariat has made a big stride, but more in politics than in life and morals. Life is conservative. In its primitive aspect, of course, Rasteryaev Street no longer exists. The brutal treatment accorded to apprentices, the servility practiced before employers, the vicious drunkenness, and the street hooliganism have vanished. But in the relations of husband and wife, parents and children, in the domestic life of the family, fenced off from the whole world, Rasteryaevism is still firmly implemented. We need years and decades of economic growth and culture to banish Rasteryaevism from its last refuge—individual and family life—recreating it from top to bottom in the spirit of collectivism.

Problems of family life were the subject of a particularly heated discussion at a conference of the Moscow propagandists, which we have already mentioned. In regard to this everyone had some grievance. Impressions, observations, and questions, especially, were numerous; but there was no answer to them, for the very questions remain semi-articulate, never reaching the press or being aired at meetings. The life of the ordinary

Article in *Pravda,* July 11, 1923, reprinted by permission from *Problems of Everyday Life* by Leon Trotsky, Monad Press, New York. Copyright 1973 by the Anchor Foundation, Inc.

workers and the life of the communists, and the line of contact between the two, provide such a big field for observation, deduction, and practical application!

Our literature does not help us in this respect. Art, by nature, is conservative; it is removed from life and is little able to catch events on the wing as they happen. *The Week*, by Libedinsky, excited a burst of enthusiasm among some of our comrades, an enthusiasm which appeared to me excessive, and dangerous for the young author. In regard to its form, *The Week*, notwithstanding its marks of talent, has the characteristics of the work of a schoolboy. It is only by much persistent, detailed work that Libedinsky can become an artist. I should like to think that he will do so. However, this is not the aspect which interests us at the moment. *The Week* gave the impression of being something new and significant not because of its artistic achievements but because of the "communist" section of life with which it dealt. But in this respect especially, the matter of the book is not profound. The "gubkom" is presented to us with too much of the laboratory method; it has no deeper roots and is not organic. Hence, the whole of *The Week* becomes an episodic digression, a novel of revolutionary emigrants drawn from the life. It is, of course, interesting and instructive to depict the life of the "gubkom" but the difficulty and significance come when the life of communist organization enters into the everyday life of the people. Here, a firm grip is required. The Communist Party at the present moment is the principal lever of every conscious forward movement. Hence, its unity with the masses of the people becomes the root of historic action, reaction, and resistance.

Communist theory is some dozen years in advance of our everyday Russian actuality—in some spheres perhaps even a century in advance. Were this not so, the Communist Party would be no great revolutionary power in history. Communist theory, by means of its realism and dialectical acuteness, finds the political methods for securing the influence of the party in any given situation. But the political idea is one thing, and the popular conception of morals is another. Politics change rapidly, but morals cling tenaciously to the past.

This explains many of the conflicts among the working class, where fresh knowledge struggles against tradition. These conflicts are the more severe in that they do not find their expression in the publicity of social life. Literature and the press do not speak of them. The new literary tendencies, anxious to keep pace with the revolution, do not concern themselves with the usages and customs based on the existing conception of morals, for they want to transform life, not describe it! But new morals cannot be produced out of nothing; they must be arrived at with the aid of elements already existing, but capable of development. It is therefore necessary to recognize what are these elements. This applies not only to the transformation of morals, but to every form of conscious human activity. It is therefore necessary first to know what already exists, and in what manner its change of form is proceeding, if we are to cooperate in the re-creation of morals.

We must first see what is really going on in the factory, among the workers, in the cooperative, the club, the school, the tavern, and the street. All this we have to understand; that is, we must recognize the remnants of the past and the seeds of the future. We must call upon our authors and journalists to work in this direction. They must describe life for us as it emerges from the tempest of revolution.

It is not hard to surmise, however, that appeals alone will not redirect the attentions of our writers. We need proper organization of this matter and proper leadership. The study and enlightenment of working class life must, in the first place, be made the foremost task of journalists— of those, at any rate, who possess eyes and ears. In an organized way we must put them on this work, instruct, correct, lead, and educate them thus to become revolutionary writers, who will write of everyday life. At the same time, we must broaden the angle of outlook of working class newspaper correspondents. Certainly almost any of them could produce more interesting and entertaining correspondence than we have nowadays. For this purpose, we must deliberately formulate questions, set proper tasks, stimulate discussion, and help to sustain it.

In order to reach a higher stage of culture, the working class— and above all its vanguard— must consciously study its life. To do this, it must know this life. Before the bourgeoisie came to power, it had fulfilled this task to a wide extent through its intellectuals. When the bourgeoisie was still an oppositional class, there were poets, painters, and writers already thinking for it.

In France, the eighteenth century, which has been named the century of enlightenment, was precisely the period in which the bourgeois philosophers were changing the conception of social and private morals, and were endeavoring to subordinate morals to the rule of reason. They occupied themselves with political questions, with the church, with the relations between man and woman, with education, etc. There is no doubt that the mere fact of the discussion of these problems greatly contributed to the raising of the mental level of culture among the bourgeoisie. But all efforts made by the eighteenth century philosophers towards subordinating social and private relations to the rule of reason were wrecked on one fact— the fact that the means of production were in private hands, and that this was the basis upon which society was to be built up according to the tenets of reason. For private property signifies free play to economic forces which are by no means controlled by reason. These economic conditions determine morals, and so long as the needs of the commodity market rule society, so long is it impossible to subordinate popular morals to reason. This explains the very slight practical results yielded by the ideas of the eighteenth century philosophers, despite the ingenuity and boldness of

221

their conclusions.

In Germany, the period of enlightenment and criticism came about the middle of the last century. "Young Germany," under the leadership of Heine and Boerne, placed itself at the head of the movement. We here see the work of criticism accomplished by the left wing of the bourgeoisie, which declared war on the spirit of servility, on petty-bourgeois anti-enlightenment education, and on the prejudices of war, and which attempted to establish the rule of reason with even greater skepticism than its French predecessor. This movement amalgamated later with the petty-bourgeois revolution of 1848, which, far from transforming all human life, was not even capable of sweeping away the many little German dynasties.

In our backward Russia, the enlightenment and the criticism of the existing state of society did not reach any stage of importance until the second half of the nineteenth century. Chernyshevsky, Pisarev, and Dobrolyubov, educated in the Belinsky school, directed their criticism much more against the backwardness and reactionary Asiatic character of morals than against economic conditions. They opposed the new realistic human being to the traditional type of man, the new human being who is determined to live according to reason, and who becomes a personality provided with the weapon of critical thought. This movement, connected with the so-called "popular" evolutionists (Narodniks) had but slight cultural significance. For if the French thinkers of the eighteenth century were only able to gain a slight influence over morals—these being ruled by the economic conditions and not by philosophy—and if the immediate cultural influence of the German critics of society was even less, the direct influence exercised by this Russian movement on popular morals was quite insignificant. The historical role played by these Russian thinkers, including the Narodniks, consisted in preparing for the formation of the party of the revolutionary proletariat.

It is only the seizure of power by the working class which creates the premises for a complete transformation of morals. Morals cannot be rationalized—that is, made congruous with the demands of reason—unless production is rationalized at the same time, for the roots of morals lie in production. Socialism aims at subordinating all production to human reason. But even the most advanced bourgeois thinkers have confined themselves to the ideas of rationalizing technique on the one hand (by the application of natural science, technology, chemistry, invention, machines), and politics on the other (by parliamentarism); but they have not sought to rationalize economics, which has remained the prey of blind competition. Thus the morals of bourgeois society remain dependent on a blind and non-rational element. When the working class takes power, it sets itself the task of subordinating the economic principles of social conditions to a control and to a conscious order. By this means, and only by this means, is there a possibility of consciously transforming morals.

The successes that we gain in this direction are dependent on our success in the sphere of economics. But even in our present economic situation we could introduce much more criticism, initiative, and reason into our morals than we actually do. This is one of the tasks of our time. It is of course obvious that the complete change of morals—the emancipation of woman from household slavery, the social education of children, the emancipation of marriage from all economic compulsion, etc.—will only be able to follow on a long period of development, and will come about in proportion of the extent to which the economic forces of socialism win the upper hand over the forces of capitalism.

The critical transformation of morals is necessary so that the conservative traditional forms of life may not continue to exist in spite of the possibilities for progress which are already offered us today by our sources of economic aid, or will at least be offered tomorrow. On the other hand, even the slightest successes in the sphere of morals, by raising the cultural level of the working man and woman, enhance our capacity for rationalizing production, and promoting socialist accumulation. This again gives us the possibility of making fresh conquests in the sphere of morals. Thus a dialectical dependence exists between the two spheres. The economic conditions are the fundamental factor of history, but we, as a Communist Party and as a workers' state, can only influence economics with the aid of the working class, and to attain this we must work unceasingly to promote the technical and cultural capacity of the individual element of the working class. In the workers' state culture works for socialism and socialism again offers the possibility of creating a new culture for humanity, one which knows nothing of class difference.

THE FIGHT AGAINST PROSTITUTION
A. Kollontai

Commission to Fight Prostitution

Already last year, at the suggestion of the Central Organ of the People's Commissariat of Social Welfare, there was organized an Interdepartmental Commission to Combat Prostitution.

For a number of reasons, the work of the Commission was temporarily abandoned, but in the autumn of this year the Commission was again formed, and with the active cooperation of Dr. Golman and the Central Organ, this Commission was already beginning an organized activity in accordance with a carefully elaborated plan. In the Inter-departmental Commission there are representatives of the People's Commissariats of Justice, of Health, of Labor, of Social Welfare, Education, of the Working Women's Sections, and the League of Communist Youth. The Commission drew up a set of theses (printed in its Bulletin No. 4), sent out a circular letter to all the provincial sections of the People's Commissariat for Social Welfare, caused the creation of similar commissions in the provinces, which carried on their work under the guidance of the Central Commission, and went about the task of elaborating a number of great measures for a systematic struggle with the sources that feed prostitution...

The Inter-departmental Commission makes the statement that in Soviet Russia prostitution appears in two forms: 1) in the form of professional prostitution; and 2) in the form of secret earnings. The first form of prostitution is very little developed among us, and is of very slight extent. In Petrograd, for example, where raids were undertaken against prostitutes, this mode of combating prostitution yielded practically no results. The second form of prostitution, although it is highly developed and extremely extensive in bourgeois capitalistic countries (in Petrograd, for example, there were from 6,000 to 7,000 registered prostitutes before the revolution, whereas as a matter of fact more than 50,000 women were actually practicing prostitution), also assumes a great variety of forms in our country. Prostitution is practiced by the Soviet office employees, in

From *Soviet Russia*, Sept. 1921, pp. 118-122 (abridged).

order to obtain, by the sale of their caresses, boots that go up to the knee; prostitution is resorted to by mothers of families, working women, peasant women, who are out after flour for their children and sell their bodies to the manager of the rations division in order to obtain from him a full bag of the precious flour. Sometimes the girls in the offices associate with their male superiors not for manifestly material gain, for rations, shoes, etc., but in the hope of advancement in office. And there is an additional form of prostitution—"careerist prostitution"—which is also based in the last analysis, however, on material calculations.

Inadvisability of Legal Penalty

How shall we fight these conditions? There was proposed to the Inter-departmental Commission the question of a *punishment of prostitution by law*. Many of the representatives in the Inter-departmental Commission were inclined to favor the method of subjecting the prostitute to legal prosecution, by reason of the fact that the professional prostitute is a frank deserter from work. A recognition of the culpability of the prostitute logically led to an admission of the legality of the hunts for the prostitutes, of their internment in concentration camps, etc.

The Central Organ came out clearly and resolutely against this conception of the matter. If it is proper to permit hunts for prostitutes, it follows that similar hunts should be made for such lawful wives as are existing on the means of their husbands and are of no use to the state. The latter are just as much deserters from work as are the prostitutes. It is proper and logical to put prostitutes into concentration camps only in cases where lawful wives, not occupied in productive labor, are also interned for similar reasons.

Such was the viewpoint of the Central Organ, which was supported by the representatives of the People's Commissariat of Justice. If we take the factor of desertion from labor as the defining element of the crime, we shall have no other outlet: all the forms of desertion from labor will be rendered equal by the same punishments.

The factor of conjugal relations, of a relation between the sexes is eliminated. That factor cannot serve as the defining element of a crime in the Workers' Republic.

Bourgeois Objections to Prostitution

In bourgeois society the prostitute was branded and persecuted not for the fact that she did not engage in productive and useful labor, and not for selling her kisses (two-thirds of the women in bourgeois society sold themselves) to her lawful husband, but for the informality of her conjugal relationship, for the shortness of its duration.

225

The basis of marriage in bourgeois society was its *permanence and formality, its registration.* This registration was for the object of securing proper inheritors of property. The absence of formality, the short duration of the relation between the sexes,—that is what was despised by the bourgeoisie in extra-marital relations; it was that which was branded with contempt by all the sanctimonious hypocrites, the standard bearers of the bourgeois morality. Can the short duration, the informality, the freedom of the relation between the sexes be regarded, from the standpoint of working humanity, as a crime, as an act that should be subject to punishment? Of course not. The freedom of relations between the sexes does not contradict the ideology of Communism. The interests of the commonwealth of the workers are not in any way disturbed by the fact that marriage is of a short or prolonged duration, whether its basis is love, passion, or even a transitory physical attraction.

The only thing that is harmful to the workers' collective, and therefore inadmissible, is *the element of material calculation between the sexes,* whether it be in the form of prostitution, in the form of legal marriage,—the substitution of crassly materialistic *calculation for gain,* for a free association of the sexes on the basis of mutual attraction.

This factor is harmful, is inadmissible, will cut a breach in the feeling of equality and solidarity between the sexes. And from this standpoint we must condemn prostitution, as a trade, in all its shapes and forms, even that of the legal "wives", who maintain their sad part, so intolerable in the Workers' Republic.

But is this defining element sufficient to make it punishable by law? Can we prosecute before the law, and hold to account, persons engaging in a conjugal relationship if the element of "calculation" enters into the relation, in view of the instability and manifold nature of the forms of association now current and in spite of the absence of any declaration of the new responsible norms of conjugal morality in the working class? Where is the line now to be drawn between prostitution and marriage by calculation? In the Inter-departmental Commission the culpability of prostitutes, for prostitution, that is, for "purchase and sale," was rejected. There remained only to be decided the point that all persons wandering in the streets and deserting from work should be assigned to the disposition of the Commissariat of Social Welfare, and thence sent out, in accordance with general fundamental considerations, either to the Sections for the Distribution of Labor Power, of the People's Commissariat of Labor, or to courses, sanatoria, hospitals, and only after a repeated desertion by the prostitute, in other words, after evidence of malicious intent to desert, the individual should be subject to forced labor. There is to be no special culpability attached to the prostitutes. They are in no way to be segregated from the other bodies of deserters from work. This is a revolutionary and pregnant step, worthy of the first Workers' Republic of the world.

The question of the culpability of the prostitutes was formulated in point fifteen of our theses. When this question was brought up, there was also put before the Commission the other question as to the culpability of the *clients* of prostitution, in other words, of the men. There were advocates of this view in the commission. But this hopeless attempt had to be renounced, as it did not arise logically from our fundamental pre-suppositions. How shall we define the client of prostitution? And again where is the measure that will define the crime? The purchase and sale of female caresses? For in that case the husband of the most lawful wife might be subject to persecution. Who will undertake to define a client of prostitution? The proposition was put to the Commission, to establish institutions of "Sisters and Brothers of Social Investigation," which was voted down by the majority. The Central Organ came out sharply against this proposition. The representative of the People's Commissariat of Justice stated that as it is not even possible to define precisely the measure of the crime,—the question of the culpability of the clients is automatically precluded. The standpoint of the Central Organ was again victorious. But if the Commission recognized that the clients could not be punished by law, it nevertheless definitely expressed its moral condemnation both of those who desert to prostitution, and to those women who enter this occupation. We have still to point out those purely practical measures which will serve to decrease prostitution, in which the active and energetic participation of the Women's Sections will be required. There is absolutely no doubt that the poor, insufficient pay returned for female labor continues, in Soviet Russia, to serve as one of the real factors pushing women into prostitution in one or the other of its forms. Under the law, the earnings of the working men and working women are equal, but as a matter of fact the women engaged in work are in the great majority of cases unskilled laborers.

The question of making female labor skilled labor, of properly formulating this matter, of spreading a network of special courses all over the country, is an extremely urgent matter. The task of the Women's Sections is to influence the national instruction in this direction, to give impetus to the development of the vocational training of working women.

What Women Now Become Prostitutes

The second cause is the political backwardness of women, the absence of wide social points of view among them. Who is it that most frequently falls into the much-trodden path, the conscious working woman who has been organized in trade unions, or the colorless woman who has not been seized by the revolutionary wave, who has not been carried away by the great business of the construction of Communism? Of course it is the latter.

The task of the Women's Sections is to accelerate the work among the female proletariat. The best form of struggle against prostitution is to raise the political consciousness of the great masses of women, to attract them to the revolutionary struggle and the constructive work of Communism. Prostitution is also strengthened by the fact that the housing question in Soviet Russia is not yet solved. And in this matter the Women's Sections, together with the Commission for the Struggle against Prostitution, can and must say a decisive word. The Inter-departmental Commission is occupied with the drawing up of propositions for housing communes for the working young people, for an extensive network of houses for the temporary shelter of women arriving in town. But if the Women's Sections and the Commission to Aid Youth do not develop an active initiative and independent work in this matter, the whole thing will remain a mere paper prescription of the Commission, an excellent and beautiful paper set of wishes. But much can be done and much must be done!

The Women's Sections in the provinces also must enter into contact with the national educators, in order to push into the foreground the question of proper provision of sexual enlightenment in the schools. In addition, a number of conversations and lessons must be introduced, of social scientific or scientific hygienic character, as to questions of marriage, the family, the history of the form of the relationship between the sexes, the dependence of these forms, and of sexual morality itself, on purely economic, material causes.

... We know—I have said it several times today—that prostitution is a danger to the worker's commonwealth, corrupting the psychology of men and women, disturbing the feeling of equality, of solidarity between the sexes. Our task is to re-educate the psychology of the working commonwealth, to bring it into correspondence with the economic tasks of the working class. We must without reservation discard our old outlived conceptions, to which we are attached as to a bad habit....

Prostitution under Communism is passing into the domain of the forgotten past, together with the morbid forms of the present-day family. In its place there are growing healthy, joyful, and free relations between the sexes. A new generation is growing up to replace the old, with more developed social feelings, with greater mutual independence, with more freedom, health and courage. A generation for whom the welfare of the whole will stand higher than everything else.

Comrades! Together we have thus far only outlined the foundation for the beautiful building of the Communist future. But it is in our power to accelerate the construction of this magnificent and unprecedented edifice. In order to create Communism, we must strengthen the spirit of solidarity in the working class; in order to strengthen this spirit, we must wage a war against all the conditions that disintegrate the working class and foster a mutual estrangement. Prostitution interferes with the growth of this solidarity, and therefore we call upon the Women's Sections to start an immediate campaign for the eradication of this evil....

THE STRUGGLE FOR CULTURED SPEECH
L. Trotsky

I read lately in one of our papers that at a general meeting of the workers at the "Paris Commune" shoe factory, a resolution was carried to abstain from swearing, to impose fines for bad language, etc.

This is a small incident in the turmoil of the present day—but a very telling small incident. Its importance, however, depends on the response the initiative of the shoe factory is going to meet with in the working class.

Abusive language and swearing are a legacy of slavery, humiliation, and disrepect for human dignity—one's own and that of other people. This is particularly the case with swearing in Russia. I should like to hear from our philologists, our linguists and experts in folklore, whether they know of such loose, sticky, and low terms of abuse in any other language than Russian. As far as I know, there is nothing, or nearly nothing, of the kind outside Russia. Russian swearing in "the lower depths" was the result of despair, embitterment and, above all, slavery without hope, without escape. The swearing of the upper classes, on the other hand, the swearing that came out of the throats of the gentry, the authorities, was the outcome of class rule, slaveowner's pride, unshakable power. Proverbs are supposed to contain the wisdom of the masses—Russian proverbs show besides the ignorant and the superstitious mind of the masses and their slavishness. "Abuse does not stick to the collar," says an old Russian proverb, not only accepting slavery as a fact, but submitting to the humiliation of it. Two streams of Russian abuse—that of the masters, the officials, the polite, replete and fatty, and the other, the hungry, desperate, tormented swearing of the masses—have colored the whole of Russian life with despicable patterns of abusive terms. Such was the legacy the revolution received among others from the past.

But the revolution is in the first place an awakening of human personality in the masses—who were supposed to possess no personality. In spite of occasional cruelty and the sanguinary relentlessness of its methods, the revolution is, before and above all, the awakening of humanity, its onward march, and is marked with a growing respect for the personal dignity of every individual, with an ever-increasing concern for those who are weak. A revolution does not deserve its name if, with all its

Article from *Pravda*, May 16, 1923, reprinted by permission from *Problems of Everyday Life* by Leon Trotsky, Monad Press, New York. Copyright 1973 by the Anchor Foundation, Inc.

might and all the means at its disposal, it does not help the woman—twofold and threefold enslaved as she has been in the past—to get out on the road of individual and social progress. A revolution does not deserve its name, if it does not take the greatest care possible of the children—the future race for whose benefit the revolution has been made. And how could one create day by day, if only by little bits, a new life based on mutual consideration, on self-respect, on the real equality of women, looked upon as fellow-workers, on the efficient care of the children—in an atmosphere poisoned with the roaring, rolling, ringing, and resounding swearing of masters and slaves, that swearing which spares no one and stops at nothing? The struggle against "bad language" is a condition of intellectual culture, just as the fight against filth and vermin is a condition of physical culture.

To do away radically with abusive speech is not an easy thing, considering that unrestrained speech has psychological roots and is an outcome of uncultured surroundings. We certainly welcome the initiative of the shoe factory, and above all we wish the promoters of the new movement much perseverance. Psychological habits which come down from generation to generation and saturate the whole atmosphere of life are very tenacious, and on the other hand it often happens with us in Russia that we just make a violent rush forward, strain our forces, and then let things drift in the old way.

Let us hope that the working women—those of the Communist ranks, in the first place—will support the initiative of the "Paris Commune" factory. As a rule—which has exceptions, of course—men who use bad language scorn women, and have no regard for children. This does not apply only to the uncultured masses, but also to the advanced and even the so-called responsible elements of the present social order. There is no denying that the old prerevolutionary forms of language are still in use at the present time, six years after October, and are quite the fashion at the "top." When away from town, particularly from Moscow, our dignitaries consider it in a way their duty to use strong language. They evidently think it a means of getting into closer contact with the peasantry.

Our life in Russia is made up of the most striking contrasts—in economics as well as in everything else. In the very center of the country, close to Moscow, there are miles of swamps, of impassable roads—and close by you might suddenly see a factory which would impress a European or American engineer by its technical equipment. Similar contrasts abound in our national life. Side by side with some old-fashioned type of domineering rapacious profiteer, who has come to life again in the present generation, who has passed through revolution and expropriation, engaged in swindling and in masked and legalized profiteering, preserving intact all the while his suburban vulgarity and greediness—we see the best type of communists of the working class who devote their lives day by day to the interests of the world's proletariat, and are ready to fight at any given moment for the cause of the revolution in any country, even one they would be unable perhaps to locate on the map.

In addition to such social contrasts—obtuse bestiality and the highest revolutionary idealism—we often witness psychological contrasts in the same mind. A man is a sound communist devoted to the cause, but women are for him just "females," not to be taken seriously in any way. Or it happens that an otherwise reliable communist, when discussing nationalistic matters, starts talking hopelessly reactionary stuff. To account for that we must remember that different parts of the human consciousness do not change and develop simultaneously and on parallel lines. There is a certain economy in the process. Human psychology is very conservative by nature, and the change due to the demands and the push of life affects in the first place those parts of the mind which are directly concerned in the case.

In Russia the social and political development of the last decades proceeded in quite an unusual way, in astounding leaps and bounds, and this accounts for our present disorganization and muddle, which is not confined only to economics and politics. The same defects show in the minds of many people, resulting in a rather curious blending of advanced, well-pondered political views with moods, habits, and to some extent ideas that are a direct legacy from ancestral domestic laws. The correct formula for education and self-education in general, and above all for our party, beginning at the top, should be to straighten out the ideological front, that is, to rework all the areas of consciousness, using the Marxist method. But there again the problem is extremely complicated and could not be solved by schoolteaching and books alone: the roots of contradictions and psychological inconsistencies lie in the disorganization and muddle of the conditions in which people live. Psychology, after all, is determined by life. But the dependency is not purely mechanical and automatic: it is active and reciprocal. The problem in consequence must be approached in many different ways—that of the "Paris Commune" factory men is one of them. Let us wish them all possible success.

The fight against bad language is also a part of a struggle for the purity, clearness, and beauty of Russian speech.

Reactionary blockheads maintain that the revolution, if it hasn't altogether ruined it, is in the process of spoiling the Russian language. There is actually an enormous quantity of words in use now that have originated by chance, many of them perfectly needless, provincial expressions, some contrary to the spirit of our language. And yet the reactionary blockheads are quite mistaken about the future of the Russian language—as about all the rest. Out of the revolutionary turmoil our language will come strengthened, rejuvenated, with an increased flexibility and delicacy. Our prerevolutionary, obviously ossified bureaucratic and liberal press language is already considerably enriched by new descriptive forms, by new, much more precise and dynamic expressions. But during all these stormy years our language has certainly become greatly obstructed, and part of our progress in culture will show, among other things, in our casting out of our speech all useless words and expressions, and those which are not in keeping with the spirit of the language, while preserving the unquestionable and invaluable linguistic acquisitions of the revolutionary epoch.

Language is the instrument of thought. Precision and correctness of speech are indispensable conditions of correct and precise thinking. In our country, the working class has come to power for the first time in history. The working class possesses a rich store of work and life experience and a language based on that experience. But our proletariat has not had sufficient schooling in elementary reading and writing, not to speak of literary education. And this is the reason that the now governing working class, which is in itself and by its social nature a powerful safeguard of the integrity and greatness of the Russian language in the future, does not, nevertheless, stand up now with the necessary energy against the intrusion of needless, corrupt, and sometimes hideous new words and expressions.

When people say, "a pair of weeks," "a pair of months" (instead of several weeks, several months), this is stupid and ugly. Instead of enriching the language it impoverishes it: the word "pair" loses in the process its real meaning (in the sense of "a pair of shoes"). Faulty words and expressions have come into use because of the intrusion of mispronounced foreign words. Proletarian speakers, even those who should know better, say, for instance, "incindent" instead of "incident," or they say "instict" instead of "instinct" or "legularly" instead of "regularly." Such misspellings were not infrequent also in the past, before the revolution. But now they seem to acquire a sort of right of citizenship.

No one corrects such defective expressions out of a sort of false pride. That is wrong. The struggle for education and culture will provide the advanced elements of the working class with all the resources of the Russian language in its extreme richness, subtlety and refinement. To preserve the greatness of the language, all faulty words and expressions must be weeded out of daily speech. Speech is also in need of hygiene. And the working class needs a healthy language not less but rather more than the other classes: for the first time in history it begins to think independently about nature, about life, and its foundations—and to do the thinking it needs the instrument of a clear incisive language.

233

"THOU" AND "YOU" IN THE RED ARMY
L. Trotsky

In Sunday's *Izvestiya* there was an article about two Red Army men, named Shchekochikhin and Chernyshev, who had behaved as heroes on the occasion of a fire and explosion at Kolomna. As the article recounts it, the commander of the local garrison approached the soldier Shchekochikhin and asked:

"Do you *(ty)* know who I am?"

"Yes, you *(vy)* are the commander of the garrison."

I doubt that the dialogue has been recorded accurately in this case. Otherwise, one would have to conclude that the garrison commander does not use the proper tone in speaking to Red Army soldiers. Of course, Red Army personnel may use the familiar form in speaking to one another as comrades, but precisely *as comrades* and only as comrades. In the Red Army a commanding officer may not use the familiar form to address a subordinate if the subordinate is expected to respond in the polite form. Otherwise an expression of inequality between persons would result, not an expression of subordination in the line of duty.

Of course, the polite and familiar forms are only matters of convention. But definite human relationships are expressed in this convention. In certain cases the familiar form may be used to express close comradely relations. But in which? In those where the relationship is mutual. In other cases, the familiar form will convey disdain, disrespect, a looking down the nose, and a shade of lordly hauteur in one's relations with others. Such a tone is absolutely impermissible in the Red Army.

To some this might seem a trifling matter. But it is not! Red Army soldiers need to respect both themselves and others. Respect for human dignity is an extremely important element of what holds the Red Army together in terms of morale. Red Army soldiers submit to their superiors in the line of duty. The requirements of discipline are inflexible. But at the same time, the soldiers are conscious of themselves as responsible citizens

Article from *Izvestiya*, July 19, 1922, reprinted by permission from *Problems of Everyday Life* by Leon Trotsky, Monad Press, New York. Copyright 1973 by the Anchor Foundation, Inc.

In Russian, the second person plural, *vy* (you) is a polite form of address, while the second person singular, *ty* (thou), expresses intimacy. Under the old regime, however, *ty* was also used by persons of high rank towards their social inferiors, who were expected to respond with a respectful *vy*. The distinction is similar to that in French, German, and Spanish, and continues, despite efforts to the contrary, in contemporary Russian.

called upon to fulfill obligations of the highest sort. Military subordination must be accompanied by a sense of the civil and moral equality of all, and that sense of equality cannot endure if personal dignity is violated.

argument for soldiers

COMMUNISM AND RELIGION
S. Kheglund (Z. Höglund)

Is the Communist movement anti-religious? Must our party conduct a war with religion and must it refuse admittance to people with religious beliefs?

To all these questions we must answer decidedly no.

The Communist Party does not force its members to declare that they do not believe in god or in the afterlife. It does not demand that they abandon their present faiths, Christian, Buddhist or Jewish. It further does not declare that this faith is counter-revolutionary or an obstacle to participation in the proletarian class struggle. The Party demands only an acceptance—of a program of activities and organizational statutes. But this program and these statutes concern themselves only with the question of finding a method and means of liberating the proletariat from capitalist slavery, and do not attempt to give any explanation of the eternal mystery of life and death. Communism tries to create for all an environment of life on earth worthy of man. To establish what things will be like in heaven does not enter the realm of our tasks. Each can think about this as he wishes, as long as his concern about heaven does not interfere with the work of improving the condition of human life on earth.

It is another matter that the Communist Party uncompromisingly struggles against making religion into a class political institution, such as the state church. The state church is nothing but the spiritual police of the ruling class. It has nothing to do with real faith and even prefers to make short work of it. It is also another matter that we struggle with any church miracles of the type of the well known "and they began to speak in different languages" (Deeds of the Apostles, Ch. 2, p. 4) and other spiritual infections of an obviously harmful nature. And it is another matter that we protest against any attempt of one or another religion to defend slavery, the exploitation of the working masses, or injustice, or, speaking in a biblical tongue, to sanctify by religion the sins of the earth. . . .

There are people who look to Marxism for a defense of the position that our party should carry out anti-religious agitation. It is true that

Article from the journal *Molodaia gvardiia,* as republished in E. Yaroslavsky, ed., *Kakim dolzhen byt' kommunist,* Leningrad, 1925, pp. 61-64. A founder of the Swedish Communist party and an early supporter of Lenin during the World War, S. Kheglund (Zeth Höglund) was expelled from the Central Committee and the party in 1924 because of his independent-minded views.

Marxism as a world view, as a universalist philosophy, is not compatible with any religious system. This does not mean, however, that the materialist understanding of history sets itself the task of deciding the question of existence or other related questions. And although we Marxists see god as a creation of man and not the reverse, although we recognize paradise to be the dream of the enslaved for a better life, as the phantasmagoria of spiritual visions, as the idealist reaction against sad reality—it does not follow from all this that we must begin a war with religion. At the basis of the Marxist view is the position that current forms of ideas will change or disappear only with a change of the material base; therefore, it is less important to criticize the heavens than the earth, less important to struggle with the theology of the ruling class than with its politics, less important to subvert heaven than capitalism. This is a genuine Marxist chain of thought: Marx himself said that with the destruction of the false realism whose theory serves religion, religion itself will be destroyed. Therefore, it is first of all necessary to change the conditions of production, and then spiritual emancipation will begin. Just as physics destroyed the belief in miracles, and the lightning rod did more for the removal of prejudices than the most intensive propaganda, so will the social revolution toward which the Communist Party is striving free the people's souls from their hateful faith, in order to make their existence bearable. But the Communist Party does not demand a Marxist worldview from each of its members. We demand only that each fellow member take part in the revolutionary struggle with capitalism for the socialist organization of society. After all, the problem is one of a practical struggle, and not of philosophical or religious worldviews.

Therefore it is incorrect, to put it mildly, to consider Christianity or some other religious conviction as counter-revolutionary and to immediately stamp it as impermissible in the ranks of the Communist Party. If one could only be a revolutionary, if one shared the theoretical platform of Marxism, that would mean that there were no revolutionaries before Marx. If religious beliefs precluded revolutionary thoughts and actions, then there would never be religious insurrections or social uprisings under the guise of religion. History repudiates this nonsense by endless examples, and the experience of the present day gives new practical evidence that religious consciousness and revolutionary politics are not incompatible. And in our party and in fraternal Communist parties abroad there are many members-adherents of Christian and other persuasions who go hand in hand with us into the struggles.

An interesting piece of evidence that Christianity does not preclude, but in fact stimulates, thoughts of social revolution, is given to us by the well-known Swedish priest Herman Kutter in his book *They Must*. In his book Kutter declares that "the living god applies coercion." "The living god—is the most ardent revolutionary and the most daring insurrection-

237

ist." Thus the voice of the lord will cry out, "I am preparing to liberate my enslaved people, I will clean their limbs of the sores remaining from the tortures of Mamon. I will strike those who struck my poor people; I will extend my ire to those who wrathfully and unjustly condemned the meek. For I am the lord god." This, in the words of Kutter, is revolution; but in the revolution there is someone who directs and guides it: Mamon made the revolution a historical necessity.

Even if Kutter and his associates see in the revolution either the indirect or direct participation of god, it is a matter of their faith. The only important thing is that they are with the revolution. It is undoubtably rash on the part of the Communist Party that it publicly labels itself as anti-religious and in so doing scares away from us such elements as can be useful in our movement. We must remember that there exists the mass of workers, petty bourgeoisie, peasantry, who by their class essence sooner or later will come to a revolutionary point of view, that is, to our Party, but who will inevitably be held back in their approach to us by the "war with religion" carried out by the Party, since they remain stagnated in their religious tendencies. We must remember that there are many people indifferent to religion, who all the same are opposed to direct anti-religious propaganda. The Communist Party, like any militant movement, is hunting for the easiest path to victory. Therefore it must cautiously discard everything that might make the road more difficult, so long as it is not contradictory to its aims. Individual Communists, acting on their own, can engage in anti-religious propaganda—that is their right, and no one will interfere in this so long as it does not bring harm to the political program and activities of the Communist Party. But as soon as the Party declares atheism to be an indispensable element of the Communist world view, then it will un-doubtably fall to the level of a sect, just as surely as if it had declared itself Anabaptist or Ephriamist.

"True gods are those which help us to raise our head high in life's struggle," said a great thinker. We Communists are serving these gods, and it does not matter at all that some see them in the heavens and others in earthly garb. The main thing is that they help us hold our heads up high in life's struggle, that they teach us to struggle for social revolution; whether this is in the name of god or man is truly immaterial.

IS THE COMMUNIST MOVEMENT ANTI-RELIGIOUS?
(AN ANSWER TO KHEGLUND)
E. E. Yaroslavsky

In all likelihood, Kheglund's article, printed in the central organ of the Swedish Communist Party without any editorial comments, will evoke bewilderment, to put it mildly, and not only within the ranks of Russian comrades of the RKP, in whose program it is said that "the party strives toward the complete destruction of the tie between exploiting classes and organizations of religious propaganda, promoting the real liberation of the toiling masses from religious prejudices and organizing the widest scientific-educational and anti-religious propaganda." In all likelihood, this article will meet with a necessary rebuttal from French Communists, who publish a special journal for anti-religious propaganda among peasants and soldiers and who broke with the Franco-masons. Comrade Kheglund tries in this article to prove much more even than is needed, judging by the title. He has here a series of questions:

(1) Is the communist movement anti-religious?

(2) Should our party propagate a war with religion?

(3) Should it refuse admission to people with religious beliefs?

(4) Should communists have a Marxist-materialist world view, or can they be idealists? Or in other words, is it all the same to us whether members of the Communist Party are guided in their struggle by ideals of heavenly bliss or by human earthly aims? Is it all the same whether a Communist struggles in the name of god or in the name of man?

How—comrade communists will ask—can there still be arguments about this? In all likelihood comrade Kheglund has not been a communist for very long and has come to us from some alien environment, preserving vestiges of a papal world view which he is striving to advocate in the Communist Party. Or else he is a comrade with very low consciousness. But the comrades must know that Kheglund is a member of the Central Committee of the Swedish Communist Party, and that the entire party and entire working class in Sweden heed his voice. And if the central organ of the Communist Party of Sweden, *Politiken*, prints comrade Kheglund's

---

Article from the journal *Molodaia gvardiia*, reprinted in E. Yaroslavsky, ed., *Kakim dolzhen byt' kommunist*, Leningrad, 1925, pp. 65-78, and here abridged. A militant left communist and member of Agitprop, Yaroslavsky (M.I. Hubelmann) later became head of the League of Militant Atheists and an editor of *Bezbozhnik [The Atheist]*.

article without any comments, that means that the views of comrade Kheglund are not encountering any decisive rebuttal from Swedish communists. And since in this regard there exists confusion in the minds of not just a few Swedish comrades, then we consider it necessary to repudiate this type of uncommunist, unMarxist view, inherited entirely from the Second International. . . .

One feels awkward while writing about such things now in 1923. Let comrade Kheglund forgive this comparison which he unwittingly forces on the Russian reader. If one did not know that it was Kheglund who wrote this article, one might think that it was written by one of the leaders of the so-called contemporary Russian Ancient Apostolic Church, for example, Archbishop Vvedensky. At the church conference which was convened not long ago some extremely radical resolutions on political questions were accepted, and before that, at the congress of "The Living Church," resolutions still more radical. There could be heard the fullest avowal of communism, with priests declaring that they fully accepted the communist program, except the point on anti-religious propaganda. Priests coming to "partkoms" [party committees, ed.] with declarations of their desire to enter the RKP are common occurrences. If the party opened the door to such elements, there would probably be counted into its ranks some hundreds of priests and even priests' party organizations. According to the idea of comrade Kheglund's article, we must go this route and open wide our door to people who look upon capitalism as the vilest enemy of christianity. To comrade Kheglund it does not matter. He says, "In the name of god or the name of man—it's absolutely all the same."

No, it is not at all the same.

Our entire program is constructed on a scientific and materialist world view. And so the explanatory role of our program leads to an explanation of the real historical and economic roots of the religious fog. Consequently, the propaganda of atheism enters into our propaganda; the publication of a certain kind of scientific literature, which until now has been strictly forbidden and persecuted by the absolutist feudal government, must become an important activity of the party. In all likelihood, we need to follow the advice Engels gave once to German socialists: translate and spread as widely as possible French atheistic-enlightenment literature of the Eighteenth Century.

The lines below belong not to Comrade Kheglund, but to Comrade Lenin, and were published in December, 1905, in No. 28, the December third issue of the newspaper *Novaya Zhizn*. These lines were published when the working masses were rising in armed rebellion and when it was especially important to attract to our side the greatest possible number of workers. Comrade Lenin did not shy away from the fact, or doubt that it was necessary to attract workers, declaring honestly that our entire program was constructed on a scientific, clearly expressed, materialist world view, and that an integral part of our propaganda consisted of atheist propaganda.

"Religion is an instrument of spiritual oppression weighing everywhere on the common masses burdened by work and want. The helplessness of the exploited in their struggle with the exploiters also leads directly to a belief in a better afterlife, just as the impotence of savages in their struggle with nature leads to a faith in gods, devils, miracles and other such things. To those who work hard and experience want throughout their lives, religion teaches submission and patience, and promises consolation in a heavenly reward. And for those who live at the expense of the work of others, religion appeals for charity, offering them tickets for heavenly bliss at rather moderate prices. Religion is the opium of the people. Religion is spiritual alcohol, in which the slaves of capital drown out their human identity, their strivings for a life worthy of man.

"But the slave who recognizes his slavery, who rises up to battle for liberation, has already halfway ceased to be a slave. The conscious worker of our day, raised in the big factory, clears away from himself the darkness found in the service of priests and bourgeois hypocrites, in order to create for himself a better life here on earth. The proletariat of our day is becoming an advocate of socialism, which calls upon science to conduct a struggle with religious darkness, which frees the workers from faith in another life, which leads them to struggle for a better earthly life."

This description of religion corresponds entirely to the description given by Marx. It is an accurate one? Let comrade Kheglund prove that it is not. . . . If comrade Kheglund wants to say the Communist International does not need the theoretical platform of Marxism, then he must say so directly, because a revolutionary movement outside of time and space (which does not exist) is one thing, and the proletarian revolution which is unfolding before our eyes is another . . .

Now we can answer those questions posed in Comrade Kheglund's article. Is the communist movement anti-religious? Comrade Kheglund says decidedly, "No." But instead of proving that the communist movement is not anti-religious, he proves something completely different. He shows that in the past there were revolutionary movements with religious coloration; and going further, he shows that nowadays there are believers who sympathize with the struggle of our party. With surprising daring, Comrade Kheglund then rushes on to prove that the Communist Party is not hostile to religion. He writes, "It would be foolishness on the part of the Communist Party to call itself anti-religious and by this to alienate those elements which it could attract to its side. If the party as such declares atheism to be something necessary to the communist worldview of its members, then it will have fallen to the level of a sect just as surely as if it had declared itself to be a Baptist."

Is this really true? Of course it is completely false . . .

Comrade Kheglund feels that Marxism and religion cannot be combined. He labels himself a Marxist and writes, "It is possible and likely that Marxism as a world view, as a universal philosophy, is not compatible with any religious system, which does not mean, however, that the materialist conception of history sets itself the task of solving the question of existence and other related questions. But although we Marxists view god as the creation of man, and not the reverse, although we recognize paradise to be the dream of the enslaved for a better life, as a phantasmagoria of spiritual visions, as the idealist reaction against sad reality, from this it does not at all follow that we must conduct a war with religion." "Dream of the enslaved"—"phantasmagoria of spiritual visions," "idealist reaction," is how comrade Kheglund expresses it. "A type of spiritual drug," "the opium of the people, one of the forms of spiritual oppression"—is how Comrades Lenin and Marx characterize religion. But however it is characterized, by whatever words religion is called, for us it is absolutely clear that against this drug, against this opium, against this phantasmagoria, against this idealist reaction, each communist is obliged to struggle. . . .

But why . . . , since old productive relations have to give way to new ones, are the old religions still being preserved for so long?

It is necessary to give an answer to that question, because our opponents use that fact as an argument against us. The answer presents no difficulties.

First, the old means of production never dies out at once. In early centuries the dying out took place extremely slowly, and even now when heavy industry is so rapidly replacing the old technology, a very extended period of time is needed for petty production to disappear. Consequently, sufficient scope remains for the old religion for a very long time.

Second, the human spirit is characterized by inertia. Although the body already finds itself in a new relations of labor, the mind lags behind in grasping the new forms. Traditions, legends, have their hold on the brains of the living. . . .

Now we can briefly formulate our answer to comrade Kheglund.

Is the communist movement anti-religious? Yes. The communist movement, which is directed against the foundations of the bourgeois state, is anti-religious, because religion is one of the institutions of the bourgeois state for which there is no place in a communist society. And this must be recognized clearly.

Must our party wage a war with religion? Yes. It must conduct a war with religion by means of propaganda, agitation, the preaching of atheism, the uncovering of ties between religion and the exploiting ruling classes, with a replacement of the religious world view by a scientific, materialistic world view, by wide and deep natural-scientific and atheistic enlightening activity.

Should the communist party refuse admission to people with religious views? As a general rule, yes, because religious people will confuse and disturb the struggle of the working class, will introduce an idealist jumble where a clear materialistic conception of the world is needed. Individual proletarians who prove their loyalty to the proletarian revolution, but who still do not break with religion can be admitted to the party in particular instances. If such a proletarian, because of religion, does not go hand in hand with the party of the proletarian revolution, then this will mean that for him the proletarian revolution is not the chief thing.

Must communists have a Marxist materialist world view? Yes. Is it all the same whether a communist struggles in the name of god or of man? No, it is not all the same. A Marxist theory well mastered by the masses is in itself an enormous material strength. And people who do not even know in whose name they are fighting, that of god or of man, not only will not be able to become steadfast leaders of the vanguard of the proletarian revolution, but might in a decisive movement of the struggle seriously slow down the proletarian revolution.

243

ON ANTI-RELIGIOUS AGITATION AND PROPAGANDA AMONG WOMEN WORKERS AND PEASANTS
Central Committee, RKP

If one looks at how significantly the Revolution has decreased religious sentiment among workers and peasants, any observant person would agree that the Revolution has affected the female half of the Russian people much less in this respect. One has only to glance at any peasant procession, visit a church, listen to conversations on religious subjects, look at who attends sermons, and the preponderance of women immediately becomes obvious. During peasant processions, male figures appear solitary among masses of women. The principal reason for this is rooted in women's political backwardness. Women are less involved in the work of the Party, of the unions, of soviet establishments. They play a less prominent role in them. Economically they have still not been freed to the extent that men have by the Revolution. The economic-domestic tenor of a woman's whole life still keeps her in a backward existence, in the captivity of former attitudes which still survive from a time when hardly any ideology other than a religious one was available to her.

This, of course, is not peculiar to Russian women, female workers and peasants. West-European women as well represent a most rich soil for the growth of all kinds of religious organization. Everyone knows what a powerful influence the Catholic clergy has among women in France, Germany, Italy, Belgium, England, Holland and other European countries. It was not for nothing that Wilhelm, wishing to express the most apparent characteristics of conservatism, its narrowest limits, into which the life of women should be squeezed, said that women should know the three K's "Kuche, Kirche, Kinder" (kitchen, church and children). All clerical church organizations, monastic and Jesuit societies recruited their most fervent supporters among women. The so-called Catholic parties in European parliaments, as well as the Christian-Socialists—that is, in plain words, papists—depend in exactly the same way, to a great extent, upon the support of women, among whom they carry out intense work influencing them through their press, by means of sermons, and by different kinds of public ceremonies (mystery plays, church processions, special concerts, to which the greatest artistic talents are attracted), and

Vestnik agitatsii i propagandy, Sept. 15, 1921, as published in E. Yaroslavsky, ed., *Na anti-religioznom fronte. Sbornik statei, dokladov, lektsii, tsirkuliarov za piat'let, 1919-1924*, Moscow, 1924.

also through the individual influence of confessors. This influence of the Church in individual countries was so powerful at one time, that when the question was raised in Belgium about the extension of the general franchise to women, this threatened at first to strengthen the influence precisely of the Catholic party.

Of course, the Revolution caused an enormous change among us in attitudes towards religion and especially in attitudes to the former state church. Through agitation, the exposure of all kinds of frauds, the revelations concerning relics and other facts, the consciousness of masses of workers and peasants was cleared of the rubbish with which it had been choked for centuries. A significant number of women workers and some peasant women have completely broken with the Church. Those sectarian groups, who have not yet the strength to break completely with religion, but who have come a long way from the vulgar teachings to which, until very recently, the state church had still held them, have grown stronger. This can be said not only about Orthodox women, for this process is also going on among Muslim, Jewish and Catholic women, and others. The task of the Communist Party is to facilitate this process.

How to facilitate it is a question which is explained in the Party program. "Only the realization of balance and consciousness in all mass socio-economic activities will bring a total disappearance of religious prejudice." Thus, the more balance and consciousness we can bring into the socio-economic activity of the masses, the more quickly and more completely will this dying out process occur. Now, when we have still done so little to pull those masses out from under the influence of the spontaneous powers of nature and the disorganization of all our daily economic activities, we cannot count on the process of the disappearance of religious prejudice being a particularly rapid one.

Let us take as an example this year's crop failure, hunger, and food shortage. How do the priests explain them? They say that these calamities are a punishment, god's wrath against sin. It is necessary to plead with this god, pray to him to soften his anger. And because of these sufferings from hunger, a return to religious attitudes is appearing in the most backward sector of the peasantry and even in some workers, both male and female. Arguments of this kind can be heard: "Well, your hand won't fall off when you cross yourself, your head won't fall off after you bow, and god, perhaps, will take pity." Naturally, it is not difficult for us to make use of this kind of sermon to demonstrate all the evils of such an outlook on the world. We need to show only that people are capable of eliminating all these incredible sufferings by the systematic rebuilding of all our lives, by subordinating the forces of nature. Therefore, every possible resource should be used on behalf of our anti-religious agitation. Somewhere, they cleaned out a bog, turning it into a meadow. They built ditches for irrigation, introduced proper crop rotation and improved ground cultivation, or ran electricity into a village somewhere. We should freely use this to show that the matter has nothing to do with human sins or with the wrath of a non-existent god, but in how little we were able to introduce planning and organization into our lives.

What place should we allot to anti-religious propaganda today? Should it be the first order of business, as some Communists think? One should bear in mind that overcoming religious prejudices is generally an extremely slow process among women workers and peasants. By no means should we avoid answers to the questions brought forward by the masses in this area. It is absolutely necessary to use any appropriate moment to demonstrate the injuriousness of the religious outlook. For example, in that same question about hunger and drought it is certainly not difficult to show the working woman or peasant that belief in sin and punishment from god takes away a person's strength, makes him spineless, a toy in the hands of some sort of awe-inspiring punitive forces. It is not difficult to demonstrate that only the man who believes that he will attain freedom only "with his own hands" will be able to invest all his strength in the rebuilding of the economy, the rebuilding the whole of life.

But at the moment there is no point at all in putting anti-religious agitation in a place of first importance. There is no necessity for introducing this question as the order of the day at non-party conferences. It is perhaps much more useful to discuss it at Party conferences, because few Communists can distinctly outline to themselves the Party's program in this matter. Whereas at non-party conferences, which at the moment are examining economic questions for the most part, the question about religion should only be put when a significant majority of the conference demands it. Speeches on this issue should perhaps be as quiet and self-restrained as possible. They must be thoroughly prepared as much in the matter of organization as in form and content. Instead of petty attacks on priests, we have to touch upon the subject of the general outlook of women workers and peasants, to come out against religion as a world view, as a system, taking into account the attitudes of the majority of the assembly and its relationship with existing religious groups, church organizations, sectarians and others. It is especially important to connect questions of anti-religious propaganda with our economic measures. Without serious preparation for making a stand against religion, it is better to refrain from it (i.e., making a stand). This is particularly true for the organization of important anti-religious public debates in the provinces, which always attract the mass of the population, especially women. Such public debates must be treated in a particularly serious manner, and must be arranged only after thorough preparation.

The experience of our work has shown that sometimes we have success with anti-religious propaganda even among the most religiously inclined women if only we can connect that propaganda with issues which are vitally important for women.

Our propaganda was of this kind on the issue of religious freedom among women in the East, about their release from the tradition of bride price, from the harem and other forms of slavery. It was not difficult for the Eastern woman to understand our correctness, when on the one hand, the Communist Party came out against women's being sold from their very childhood for cattle, money, and other things, and on the other hand, the older order stood with its defender—the mullah.

Our anti-religious propaganda and agitation should be of precisely this sort: concrete, deeply thought-out, related to the vital issues of the masses, with their daily economic habits, with thoughtful work, and work accompanied by wide-ranging cultural enlightenment. Our task is to replace a religious explanation of the world with a scientific one.

"CALLING ALL BELIEVERS," "SCIENCE OR RELIGION?" "WITHOUT GOD, WITH MAN"
The Editors of *Bezbozhnik*

I. Calling All Believers

We are addressing this to all believers, be they of the "dead", the "living", or the "Tikhon" church. We invite them to test us, the non-believers, in an experiment.

You are frightening workers and peasants, who do not want to baptize their children in magical rites with the participation of "dunking" priests. You scare them by saying that children who are not christened by a priest will die more quickly than those who are. Not to mention that all this is rubbish which can be disproved by a simple reference—the children of heathens, Moslems and Jews live no less long and happily than Orthodox children. We propose, in any district, in any factory, to register christened and unchristened children separately and we will take it upon ourselves to show that the rates of death and illness among christened children are not only no lower, but, that in cases in which the font is not kept clean and the priest himself is not particularly concerned about cleanliness, the font is even a source of infection and sickness.

Further, we propose the following—let's take, for example, the Glasnoi Hospital (Tver St., 63) where doctors cure by science, without recourse to prayers, miracle-working icons, holy water, virgin's tears or other excretions of "holy bodies" (some monks healed with the virgin's milk, a kind of oil presumably excreted by dead heads of saints), and compare it with any holy monk who heals by holiness, prayers, icons, holy water—in a word, by faith. We are prepared to offer every assistance to believers in this test. We are prepared to help set up the experiment. The only thing is, will there be many fools who will submit themselves to this experiment? Don't the most ignorant of people understand that faith is powerless in the face of science?

We propose submitting holy water to a test. We claim that holy water gets musty and spoils, that the same rotten algae bacteria and microbes (tiny animals and plants, invisible to the unaided, ordinary eye) grow in it as grow in water that has not been blessed.

We are ready to allow the faithful an opportunity to use all the

From the journal *Bezbozhnik* (*Atheist*), No. 33, July 5, 1923.

microscopes, all the laboratories which are in the Republic. We will do our best to make this experiment as easy as possible for the believers. We are prepared to provide all necessary conditions for the accuracy of controls by the believers themselves over this test. And then you will see that microscopic creatures with hair, horns, and tails will grow in the holy water just as they do in unblessed water. We throw down this challenge to all believers. All the liars in the churches are tricking you. They are trying to show (as it was in the church at Myussa) that science and faith are compatible. And when they get caught in a lie they try to demonstrate that science is powerless in the presence of religion.

And we will take it upon ourselves to prove the opposite by experiment.

And the church of Tikhon, the "living" and "dead" church, the "renewed" and "revived" church—they are all tarred with the same brush. They still want to live at the expense of your lack of knowledge, your ignorance.

Let's see which is right, science or religion.

II. Science or Religion?*

Our repeated challenge to believers was answered by an outcry in various corners of our country and the editors of *Bezbozhnik* are receiving more and more answers from believers. These answers are all more or less similar, so that there is no possibility of publishing them all in their entirety. Some of them are so long they show the characteristics of those who write them, people who, in the first place, have lots of time and who, in the second place, have tongues that wag at both ends, for which reason the editors of *Bezbozhnik* will make room only for those answers which are distinguished by some originality. In this number, we print one such answer and at the same time we think it necessary to consider one question in particular which attracted the attention of all the believers who answered us. That is the question about holy water.

In its first answer to the question of the miracle of Archbishop Alexander Vvedensky, readers of *Bezbozhnik* could have read a priest's statement: "We will not deny that holy water can spoil, decay. So what? Religion did not promise to eliminate baccili in water."

The "Veryushchy" ["Believers," ed.] also writes, in an answer for which we make room, "Coming to the question of holy water, I suppose, that it can spoil and get musty, although those believers who base their faith solely on miracles and supernatural phenomena will assert the opposite. It seems to me that priests would not bless water in which the existence of dangerous microbes had been established by microscopes and laboratories, and they would probably advise that such water be boiled. In the texts of God's law,

* *Bezbozhnik*, No. 40, Sept. 23, 1923.

249

nothing says that holy water cannot get musty and spoil. I do not know where anything of the kind is asserted in any sacred writings. Even if it were said, it need not necessarily be the case, since, when the sacred books were written, there were neither microscopes nor laboratories and people did not have the slightest knowledge of bacteria and microbes. The conclusions about the spoilage of holy water can be confirmed since kulich blessed for Easter will dry out if it is not eaten in time, and an egg which has been blessed will go bad."

So "holy water in time will go bad, Easter kulich will dry out if not eaten in time and go musty just like unblessed kulich; an egg which has been blessed will rot just like one which has not been blessed."

Archpriest Vasily Arkhangelov (Ruzaev City Church, Penza province) in his very abusive letter, where he says above all that we, ignorant people, have no business in judging such wise matters as religion, "I am completely at a loss to understand where the editors got this information, that holy water does not spoil, that christened children live longer, and so on. You assert that holy water gets musty and spoils, and we not only do not deny it, but we confirm your opinion, that holy water spoils, and the length of its preservation in clean form depends solely on atmospheric conditions and on the quality of bottling. So what does this leave you with, your assertion and our confirmation of it? The essence of the matter lies in not whether the water spoils or not, but in that it is holy. I think that no priest, blessing water, would say that it would not spoil, for he knows (I have in mind an educated priest) that the water contains many microbes at the moment he blesses it. He knows as well that the act of blessing it is not an act of eliminating the microbes in it." And he continues, "In its prayers, read over the sanctified water, the Holy Church does not ask God to wipe out the microbes, but instead asks that the Lord send the Holy Spirit and move It to the cleansing of bodies and souls, to the healing of passions, to the blessing of homes and to any good purpose."

Priest Nechaev (Koroch, Kursk province) carefully avoids all of our clearly stated questions, and concentrates on philosophy, to which we will return in good time and to whose value we will testify.

Thus, we can conclude that our challenge to priests has come to at least one positive result. Orthodox priests, who have made fools of the people for centuries, as if water acquires some special properties because of their sorcery, have had to acknowledge that their secret blessings do not change the material characteristics of the water, kulich, eggs, and other objects they bless, that these objects rot, get musty, spoil, and decay the same as unblessed ones. And priest Arkhangelov puzzled in vain about where the editors got the idea that holy water does not spoil. There is no point in playing the fool. The editors do not believe this, but you, Father Arkhangelovs, Peering-Through-the-Fences, Holy Cross-Raisers, Annunciations and Makers-of-the-Sign-of-the-Cross with the Oil.

It is all the more revolting that you, priests, performing this sorcery, mocking Reason, the mind of humankind for centuries, now hypocritically try to demonstrate that there is no contradiction between science and religion. Aren't you ashamed to go through with this comedy, when you know quite well yourselves that there are no devils of any kind in a bottle of water, since there are none in any case? And you fool the simple folk into believing that if you make the sign of the cross, in this or that manner, over water, if you pronounce some kind of incantation or exorcism, then the devil, who is presumably sitting there in the water, will be frightened and run away, and the water will acquire some kind of special quality. And after this, some learned priest like Arkhangelov will shamelessly pronounce, "But the crux of the matter lies not in the water's ability to spoil, but in that it is holy." The priest Arkhangelov seems to foresee that this argument is not going to fool anyone.

"But you will say now," he writes, "that this is not sufficient for us, you will ask for facts, you will make endless appeals with requests for explanations—what does your holy water mean, your christening, and so on?" We will answer you then, but it is unlikely that you will understand, because your hearts, in the words of the prophet, are hardened; otherwise cassock-wearing priests have beaten into the heads of ignorant peasants, workers and petty bourgeois, that your spells give objects some kind of special properties. So now all believers have to know that they were fooled about this for centuries, and now, when they cannot be fooled any longer, when we propose proving everything by experiment, with microscopes and laboratories, then you all go back on your word.

So—your secret blessings do not drive away bacteria, but devils. In "Trebnika," the "status of holy water and the mystery of christening" is given a magic formula, how to drive devils out of water. For this the priest makes the cross over the water thrice, dipping his fingers in it (this dipping process is called, in their vernacular, dipping 'persty') then breathes on the water and says "may all evil forces be gone under the holy image of thy cross" three times. "We pray to you, Lord, to release from us all invisible apparitions and do not let this demon, this cunning, dark spirit, bringing about obscure thoughts and a revolt of mind, establish itself in the water." After this, he blows a little oil into the vessel and crosses it three more times so that the oil will make the water imperishable—an instrument of truth for the renewal of body and soul, and able to drive away all of the devil's doings. Then he has to read out hallelujah three more times with the people, and three times, although you listen, you do not hear.

Well, what is *true,* is true. It is very difficult to understand anything from your answer. Our hearts are hard, and yours, the priests, of course, are not—they are surrounded by a heavy layer of fat. Don't give us this line about hearts. All people's hearts are made in the same way, believers and unbelievers alike. The essential thing is that believers still cannot free

251

themselves from the narcotic with which you have confused them, whereas unbelievers have freed themselves, or are doing so.

Priest Alexander Vvedensky refers to a vulgar (that is, among the ordinary people) belief that holy water will not spoil. In parentheses he qualifies "although, it is true that this belief goes back even to Chrysostom," that is, to one of the most respected fathers of the Church. Here we ask the priest, is anyone of them courageous enough to tell the peasants in the church that the holy Chrysostom was wrong, that this is only a belief of the ordinary people, that it is a superstition. A priest would not say and does not say that in the church. He is afraid to say such a thing. He fears the light of science and prefers to it the shadow of religion. He prefers that people be fed on such superstitions.

"Where," asks the priest Vasily Arkhangelov, "where did you get this, as if a priest would confirm that christened children live longer than unchristened ones, and would frighten the people with this." It would be more appropriate if you asked where the people got this, that they justify the necessity for christening with it. And we know of hundreds and thousands of that kind of fact, when priests, especially village priests, spread such information on the sly as well as openly from the pulpit of the church.

So, your attempts to turn away from the question about holy water meant a total defeat for you. It appears that it is impossible to understand your explanations and as you yourselves admit, there is hardly anyone who does understand them, and that in the question of physical characteristics, you surrender your position altogether.

As regards the statement that a demon sits in a bottle of unblessed water, a dark demon, a cunning spirit who brings about obscurantism of thought and imaginations, and that you chase it out of that bottle, when you make the cross over it, sprinkle it with oil, breathe on it, then that is just the kind of charlatanism and sorcery which should make every honest person blush. But you do not blush, you continue to do this even in 1923, and will continue to do so, as long as ignorance exists among the people.

III. Without God, With Man*

It used to be like this: If they were building a church, or a palace, or a pub, or a brothel, where they traded in women on the spot, the first matter to be attended to was the placing of a cross on a post, and the priest sang prayers on the buildings' foundations. Without this, they did not build.

Without priests, without prayers, without crosses, a whole, beautiful city—our trade and agricultural exhibit—was built on putrid marshland in a single spring. The work continued day and night. We did not ask god, "God, give us the sun's light for night work." Without god, by force of will,

---

* *Bezbozhnik*. No. 43. Oct. 14, 1923.

work and the intelligence of humankind we lit up our own electric sun, leveled the earth, dried out the rotten bog, decorated it with flowers—in spite of a rainy summer, in spite of all adversity.

Without god, but with man, in human companionship—that's where the strength is here.

And now thousands of peasants from all parts of our land have seen what man can do. Looking at the running of trams, the flight of steel bird-airplanes over the Moscow River, at tractors crawling over the fields, at the electric sun and stars, at the tireless strength of movement, light, and heat that human work has produced, the peasant has understood that it is not in god but in humanity that one must place hope. We must rely on ourselves.

The worker built. The peasant saw the work. He understood that the worker would help him to create this light, this beauty, this wealth across the face of the earth. He will produce a machine—a tractor, a reaper, a mowing machine, a threshing-machine. He will save labor, increase the harvest, conquer the drought, drain the swamps.

This union of peasant and worker must be strengthened, the union of the hammer and scythe, the earth, village and city. And the priest is saying, "Have no faith in that union, have faith in god."

How can this be? That god has blessed wars, hunger, prostitution, and the endless, endless thousand-year sufferings of humanity.

And the peasant says, "I will get along without god. I will strengthen the union of man with man instead.

I will strengthen the union of hammer and sickle. Today it flies over our country, over one part of the earthly sphere. Tomorrow it will begin to sparkle over worker-peasant Germany, where its kingdom will arise out of the suffering and struggle of today. What if theirs is another faith, another language? Our thoughts, our feelings are with them, for them."

"A DAY OF TESTING IN THE COMMUNE"
Pravda, Agitprop Essay

Pravda, July 27, 1921

All the members of the Lenin commune—men, women, and teen-agers—were sitting around on the ground. They were waiting for a meeting.

The procedures for the day had not yet been announced, but everyone already knew about them. Everybody knew that the evening before, the party cell had met at the haystacks and decided to hold a general meeting to discuss the allotment of one hundred poods of rye for the starving, above the tax in kind. That evening, the cell made a decision and the same night in some families, "sawmills" were opened and the wives "took the bark" off their husbands.

—It is early to undertake anything risky. For two years the horsemen themselves have been eating grass. We couldn't slog our way out, no matter what we did. We barely manage to begin to crawl out from starvation, and you want to force us to eat grass again.

At the head of opposition to the cell was the chairman of the commune himself, a comrade who had recently left the Party, a good, honest worker, but one who sometimes could be easily carried away and then stubbornly persist in his errors.—"I'm going to speak against the cell's proposal," he said forthrightly. "The harvest isn't in yet, and the size of the tax is not yet clear. By my calculation, we're in this kind of a situation. We have to repay the seed debt with an additional percentage. That's the first thing. We borrowed grain to live on until the new harvest. We must return it immediately. That's second. The third thing is that we have to have some for seed. The fourth is that the tax will be about three hundred poods. The rest of the rye won't be enough to feed us. The question of donation should be postponed, until we harvest the grain, find out the size of the tax, and know our own strength. For the time being, I propose that we quickly mill several hundred poods of rye and send them as fast as possible to the grain collecting station as our seed and food debt, and on account for part of the tax. We have to look out for the commune or else it might perish because of one careless decision."

The floor is taken by the communard, an old Bolshevik.

"The commune won't die from showing that it is responsive to the needs of the State. Quite the opposite, the commune will perish precisely when it says, 'We have no concern for the people of Saratov, we have to feed ourselves up to standard.' We ourselves asked for help when we had neither seed nor grain, didn't we? How can we refuse help now? What kind of commune is this?"

An old Petersburg worker spoke up,

"Comrades, I remember 1918. We Petrograd workers had nothing but a small piece of bread a day, but the Saratov peasants ate their fill and would not give us any bread. We took them the last pair of trousers for bread. Then Comrade Lenin made an appeal, 'Organize detachments, Petrograd workers, and go to Saratov for bread.' Now there's a bad harvest in Saratov, and they turn to us for bread. What is to be done here?"

—You understand Lenin, but not completely. Lenin saw that the peasants of Saratov did not understand the needs of others. But Lenin never taught us to push away a fellow-worker in dire need. Quite the opposite. This is the time to show the Saratov peasants that one can't live on self-interest, that without brotherly love one cannot survive. They criticized the commune, but the commune comes to their aid. As far as the calculations of the chairman are concerned, they are incorrect. He only counted the rye. But we'll have oats, beef, potatoes, millet and buckwheat—though not a lot, but we'll have it. If there is not enough rye, we will put potatoes, beets, and cabbage leaves into the bread, and we will make it somehow. The chairman calculated seed based on the estimate to increase the sowing of winter grain by ten desiatins. That is laudable. But what's it going to be like along the Volga? Maybe there is a commune there just like ours sitting right now on similar rocks and thinking, 'where should we head for?' A desiatin brings us forty poods, but on the Volga, it might yield one hundred, two hundred. It's worth while to give them one hundred poods now or even more.

Let me say this. I am not a party member. I have my program and regulations— the conscience of an honest worker. We didn't unite in a commune to think only about ourselves. How are we different from a solitary peasant? We absolutely must help the State.

"I also think that we should help. It's quite possible that we'll turn to the State again for aid. If we don't help them, they won't help us."

The peacefulness of the proceeding was disturbed by women. The wife of one communist (an opponent of donation) attacked another, also the wife of a communist, for being too ready to "squander" bread.

Finally, the chairman calmed the women.

Another few words were exchanged. One person called someone else "Milyukov." The other returned the compliment.

It was very difficult for the ordinary members of the commune to agree on new limitations on bread. Two and a half whole years of devilish work, with deprivations and shortages, and the previous years' bad harvest— and all of a sudden, on the threshold of some sort of prosperity, they had to voluntarily skimp. And for whom? For some distant Saratov peasants, spoiled by their former plenty.

Still, at the vote, only one hand was raised against the donation. Everyone else was in favor of immediately setting aside one hundred poods above the tax, without even waiting for the end of the milling.

They had stood the test. The commune had come out of it honorably.

In two or three days two hundred twelve poods of rye in the commune's carts arrived at the grain collection point near station "Silver Ponds," Ryazan-Ural, Russian Republic (one hundred poods of seed debt, twelve as interest, and one hundred as donation).

On the road, the peasants greeted communards with mockery, "They even shook down the communists? They even got to you, huh?"

"No, friends, they didn't have to shake it loose from us. We were the first to bring in what was asked for us, and on top of it we allowed of our own accord, one hundred poods for the use of hungry people for sowing."

"No? where are you getting the grain?"

"From the same place you are. The ground's the same, Count Sheremetev's. Do your best, don't wait until they begin to shake you."

This was, as it turned out, the first grain from the new harvest at the grain collection point.

At home on the commune concern didn't die down so easily, especially among some of the women. But in the field, when the women began to gather sheaves from one plot where the harvest turned out to be higher than average, even the most violent protestor calmed down.

"What was I arguing about at the meeting? Look, there's a good crop this year. We'll make it somehow."

And in the commune's cell, the following proposals were prepared: about adopting several children from the hunger-stricken provinces to feed them; about taking some livestock from there for wintering (especially livestock from communes), and so on.

Even the chairman of the commune, who had come out against assigning the one hundred poods, agreed on the necessity of doing something else for those who were suffering from poor harvests.

The commune's party members were already mobilized by the District Party Committee to carry out agitation for the tax in kind in the district of Venevo. They will agitate for it not only in words, but also through deeds. Their sixteen families were the first in the district to set aside one hundred poods in addition to the tax, that is about six poods per family. Let all the peasants of the Venevo district do the same, as well as the other districts of Tula province and other provinces of the Republic. Then hunger will be overcome.

256

NOTES

Chapter I. What a Communist Ought to Be Like

1. E. Iaroslavskii, "Predislovie redaktora," in E. Iaroslavskii, ed., *Kakim dolzhen byt' kommunist,* Leningrad, 1925, p. 3.
2. V.I. Lenin, "Tasks of the Youth Leagues (Bourgeois and Communist Morality)," *Collected Works* (4th ed.), Vol. 31, Moscow, 1966, p. 293.
3. *Deviatyi s"ezd RKP(b). Mart-aprel' 1920 goda: protokoly.* Moscow, 1960, p. 90.
4. A. Kollontai, *The Workers' Opposition in the Russian Communist Party,* Chicago, 1921, pp. 35, 40.
5. *Ibid.,* p. 36.
6. F. Engels, *Anti-Dühring,* (2nd. ed.), Moscow, 1959, pp. 130-31.
7. See "Program of the Communist Party of the Soviet Union," adopted Oct. 31, 1961, Part II, Chapter V, in L. Schapiro, ed., *The USSR and the Future,* New York, 1962.
8. Krupskaya refers to the purge of party members which took place in 1921 at the close of the Civil War. This and subsequent purges during the 1920s were a routine way of expelling ineffective or undesirable members from the party's ranks, and involved arrest and imprisonment only in cases of criminal liability. See A.A. Solts' essay, below.
9. Subbotniks were "Volunteer Work Days," taken on Saturdays.
10. From "NEP" New Economic Policy, introduced in 1921, and involving a general relaxation from the economic, political, and ideological rigors of the civil war period (War Communism).

Chapter II. The New Man and the New Woman: Sex Roles, Marriage, and the Family

1. Cited in David Mitchell, *1919: Red Mirage,* London, 1970, p. 338.
2. See the discussion in Richard Stites, *The Women's Liberation Movement in Russia,* Princeton, 1978, chapter 8. At the first All-Russian Women's Congress in 1908, Bolshevik delegates passed resolutions from the Social Democratic Party program, rather than "non-partisan" ones. When the Congress rejected such "biased" appeals, they walked out, along with a number of women workers. (Stites, p. 252)
3. See also Trotsky's essay "Habit and Custom," in chapter V, below.
4. See Carol Eubanks Hayden, "The Zhenotdel and the Bolshevik Party," *Russian History,* Vol. 2, 1976, pp. 150-73.
5. See Clara Zetkin, *Lenin on the Woman Question,* New York, 1934, and Kollontai's essay "The Fight Against Prostitution," below, chapter V.
6. See Rudolph Schlesinger, ed., *The Family in the USSR, (Documents),* London, 1949, pp. 33-44.
7. See Stites, chapter 12.

Chapter III. Socialism and Social Welfare

1. H.E. Sigerist, *Medicine and Health in the Soviet Union,* New York, 1947, pp. 13-15, 34-35. The zemstvos were institutions of local government dominated by the gentry, established after the emancipation of the serfs in 1861.
2. N. Semashko, *Health Protection in the USSR,* London, 1934, p. 39.

Chapter IV. Proletarian Legality

1. Cited in David Mitchell, *1919: Red Mirage*, London, 1970, p. 89.
2. R. Schlesinger, *Soviet Legal Theory*, London, 1945, p. 73. See also John Hazard, *Settling Disputes in Soviet Society*, New York, 1960.
3. This incident is discussed more fully in Wm. G. Rosenberg, *Liberals in the Russian Revolution*, Princeton, N.J., 1974, pp. 278-81.

Chapter V. Religion, Language, and Other "Awkward Habits" of Everyday Life

1. The effort for language reform had actually begun, however, before the Bolsheviks came to power, during the Provisional Government in 1917. A new orthography was prepared, and efforts made to end the format style of address, particularly in the army.
2. See the discussion in R. Stites, *The Women's Liberation Movement in Russia*, Princeton, N.J., 1978, pp. 371–74.
3. K. Marx, *Contribution to the Critique of the Hegelian "Philosophy of Right"* (1844), Introduction.
4. *Tserkovnaia vedomosti*, Sept. 30, 1917.
5. As cited in A. I. Vvedenskii, *Tserkov i gosudarstvo*, Moscow, 1923, p. 105.
6. *Birzhevyia vedomosti*, Sept. 29, 1917.
7. See John S. Curtiss, *The Russian Church and the Soviet State*, Boston, 1953, chaps. 4 and 10.
8. See the discussion in Curtiss, p. 204.

SUGGESTIONS FOR FURTHER READING

Part 1

Since the first publication of this collection in 1984, several important new works on the cultural revolution in Soviet Russia have appeared. The most comprehensive is Abbott Gleason et al., eds., *Bolshevik Culture: Experiment and Order in the Russian Revolution* (Bloomington, Ind., 1985), a collection of essays by leading scholars drawn from a conference on "The Origins of Soviet Culture" sponsored by the Kennan Institute for Advanced Russian Studies, Washington, D.C. Of particular value here on the problem of cultural revolution as a whole is David Joravsky's essay "Cultural Revolution and the Fortress Mentality." *Bolshevik Culture* nicely complements the excellent collection edited by Sheila Fitzpatrick, *Cultural Revolution in Russia, 1928-31* (Bloomington, Ind., 1978), which covers important aspects of the revolution's "second phase." Richard Stites's superb study, *Revolutionary Dreams: Utopian Vision and Experimental Life in the Russian Revolution* (New York, 1989), investigates a number of the utopian aspects of the early cultural movement in depth, from revolutionary festivals and the rituals of a new, godless religion to communalism, notions of revolutionary justice, and the futurology of early Soviet writing. Stites's broad understanding of culture and his many insights into the varied dimensions of culture and cultural change in the early Soviet period make his book invaluable for students of the issues raised in *Bolshevik Visions*. Stites and Lars Kleberg have also edited a special issue of *Russian History* devoted to "Utopia in Russian History, Culture and Thought," (Summer–Fall, 1984), which contains a number of useful essays. Readers might also want to examine A. D. and A. S. Nakhimovsky, eds., *The Semiotics of Russian Cultural History* (Ithaca, 1985). For the broader intellectual context of cultural change in early Soviet Russia, Jane Burbank's new study, *Intelligentsia and Revolution: Russian Views of Bolshevism 1917-1922* (New York, 1986), is invaluable.

An early review of cultural change is R. Fülop-Miller, *The Mind and Face of Bolshevism: An Examination of Cultural Life in Soviet Russia* (London and New York, 1927), which, despite strong anti-Bolshevik biases, has interesting firsthand material. The institutions of Proletkult are studied by Lynn Mally, in *Culture of the Future: The Proletkult Movement in Revolutionary Russia* (Berkeley, 1989); and a number of related issues are explored in N. A. Nilsson, ed., *Art, Society, Revolution: Russia, 1917-1921* (Stockholm, 1979). Fitzpatrick's *The Commissariat of Enlightenment: Soviet Organization of Education and the Arts under Lunacharsky* (Cambridge, Eng., 1970), while focusing on Lunacharsky and education, has good treatment as well of Proletkult and other issues. See also Joseph Freeman, *The Soviet Worker: An Account of the Economic, Social and Cultural Status of Labor in the U.S.S.R.,* (New York, 1932), esp. chapter XI; and J. Freeman, J. Kunitz and L. Lozowick, *Voices of October* (New York, 1930), which focuses on the arts. A general, sympathetic eye-witness account may be found in Arthur Ransome, *Russia in 1919* (New York, 1919), although Ransome concentrates as much on politics as he does on cultural developments. James McClelland has reviewed the critical issues in the 1917-21 period in a superb essay, "Utopianism versus Revolutionary Heroism in Bolshevik Policy: The Proletarian Culture Debate," *Slavic Review*, 39:3 (Sept. 1980). For the "middle period," see S. Fitzpatrick, "The 'Soft' Line on Culture and Its Enemies: Soviet Cultural Policy, 1922-1927," *Slavic Review*, 33:2 (June, 1974), pp. 267-87. For those who read Russian the journal of the Proletkult organizations, *Proletarskaia kultura,* is indispensable.

Chapter I. What a Communist Ought to Be Like

Two good short studies on Marxism and ethics are Eugene Kamenka, *Ethical Foundations of Marxism* (New York, 1962), and *Marxism and Ethics* (London, 1969), by the same author. These books include chapters on the views of Marx as a young man, as an older scholar, and on such issues as alienation and the ethical aspects of human welfare questions. In *Marxism and Ethics* there is also a critical chapter on "Ethics in Soviet Philosophy." A dated but still useful treatise is V. Venable, *Human Nature: The Marxian View* (New York, 1946). Rufus Mathewson, Jr., explores the "prescriptive values" in early Soviet literature in his *The Positive Hero in Russian Literature* (New York, 1958); and Raymond A. Bauer's *New Man in Soviet Psychology* (Cambridge, Mass., 1952) is an analysis of "changing conceptions of human nature under conditions of social change," as well as an interesting analysis of Soviet psychology *per se*. See also Richard T. DeGeorge, *Soviet Ethics and Morality* (Ann Arbor, Mich., 1969) and the Soviet publication *Communist Morality* (Moscow, n.d.), which includes translated essays by Marx, Engels, Lenin, Dzerzhinskii, Krupskaya and others.

Chapter II. The New Man and the New Woman: Sex Roles, Marriage, and the Family

There are several excellent recent studies in this area. Richard Stites' *The Women's Liberation Movement in Russia: Feminism, Nihilism and Bolshevism, 1860-1930* (Princeton, N.J., 1978) will be the standard treatment for years to come, and contains an excellent bibliography. Gail Lapidus examines similar issues for the more recent period in her *Women in Soviet Society* (Berkeley, 1978), and has edited with Dorothy Atkinson and Alexander Dallin an excellent collection of essays by leading American scholars in *Women in Russia* (Stanford, 1977). Particularly valuable for the early period is Barbara Evans Clements, "The Birth of the New Soviet Woman," and Beatrice Farnsworth, "Village Women Experience the Revolution," both in *Bolshevik Culture*, Abbott Gleason et al., eds. (Bloomington, 1985). There are also three good biographies of Alexandra Kollontai: Barbara E. Clements, *Bolshevik Feminist: A Life of Alexandra Kollontai* (Bloomington, Ind., 1979), Cathy Porter, *Alexandra Kollontai: A Biography* (London, 1980), and Beatrice Farnsworth, *Aleksandra Kollontai: Socialism, Feminism and the Bolshevik Revolution* (Stanford, 1980). There is also a fine study of Bolshevik politics towards women in the Central Asian area by Gregory Massell, *The Surrogate Proletariat* (Princeton, N.J., 1974), which contains material on Zhenotdel and the Soviet Union more generally. The authoritative history of the family in Soviet Russia is Kent Geiger, *The Family in Soviet Russia* (Cambridge, Mass., 1968), and readers should also examine Rudolf Schlesinger, *The Family in the USSR: Documents and Readings* (London, 1949). The Stites, Lapidus, Clements, and Farnsworth volumes contain particularly good bibliographies. There are also a number of good article-length analyses, generally on specific issues. See, e.g., Carol Eubanks Hayden, "The Zhenotdel and the Bolshevik Party" *Russian History*, II:2, 1976, pp. 150-73; Beatrice Farnsworth, "Bolshevism, the Woman Question, and Alexandra Kollontai," *American Historical Review* (Summer 1976), pp. 292-316; and Anne Bobroff, "The Bolsheviks and Working Women, 1905-1920," *Soviet Studies*, XXVI:4 (Oct. 1974), pp. 540-67. An important general study with a chapter on Russia is Sheila Rowbotham, *Women, Resistance, and Revolution: A History of Women and Revolution in the Modern World* (New York, 1972). See also G. Browning, *Women and Politics in the USSR* (London and New York, 1987), Cathy Porter, *Women in Revolutionary Russia* (New York, 1987), and Mary Buckley, *Women and Ideology in the Soviet Union* (Ann Arbor, 1989).

Chapter III. Socialism and Social Welfare

A good general study of social welfare issues in the USSR is Bernice Madison, *Social Welfare in the Soviet Union* (Stanford, 1968), which concentrates on contemporary society, but has a good (if somewhat abbreviated) presentation of the historical background. This volume also has a comprehensive bibliography. The standard scholarly treatment on Soviet medicine is Mark G. Field, *Doctor and Patient in Soviet Russia* (Cambridge, Mass., 1957), but see also Henry Sigerist, *Medicine and Health in the Soviet Union* (New York, 1947), and Arthur Newsholme and John Adams Kingsbury, *Red Medicine: Socialized Health in Soviet Russia* (New York, 1934). In Manya Gordon, *Workers Before and After Lenin* (New York, 1941), there is a good section on social security, but pertaining mostly to the 1930s. See also Anna J. Haines, *Health Work in Soviet Russia* (New York, 1928), and the publication of the International Labour Office, *Labour Conditions in Soviet Russia: A Systematic Questionnaire and Bibliography* (London, n.d., but 1920), which includes documentary material on the 1917-20 period, and an entire chapter on "social insurance."

Chapter IV. Proletarian Legality

The best general study of the law during the "first phase" of Russia's cultural revolution is John N. Hazard, *Settling Disputes in Soviet Society: The Formative Years of Legal Institutions* (New York, 1960). This volume also has a good, if somewhat dated, bibliography. An excellent study of the entire post-1917 period is Harold J. Berman, *Justice in the U.S.S.R.* (Cambridge, Mass., 1966), a revised edition of a work first published in 1950. See also the excellent analysis by Peter Juviler, *Revolutionary Law and Order: Politics and Social Change in the USSR* (New York, 1976), and the brief but useful general study by Robt. Conquest, *Justice and the Legal System in the USSR* (New York, 1968). An important new study focusing on the bar is Eugene Huskey, *Russian Lawyers and the Soviet State: The Origins and Development of the Soviet Bar, 1917-1939* (Princeton, 1986).

An attorney in pre-revolutionary Russia, George G. Guins, has written an interesting study on *Soviet Law and Soviet Society: Ethical Foundations of the Soviet Legal Structure* (The Hague, 1954). Some of the issues he raises are also analyzed by Hans Kelson, *The Communist Theory of Law* (New York, 1955) which has material on Marx and Engels, Lenin, Stuchka, Reisner, Pashukanis, Vyshinsky and others. Vyshinsky's own treatise on Soviet law is also available in English (A. Vyshinsky, *The Law of the Soviet State*, New York, 1948). For an interesting analysis of criminal law in the 1920s, see Peter H. Solomon, "Soviet Penal Policy, 1917-1934: A Reinterpretation," *Slavic Review*, 39:2 (June, 1980). Two interesting eye-witness accounts of early Soviet justice in action are Walter Duranty, *The Curious Lottery and Other Tales of Russian Justice* (New York, 1929) and Mary S. Callcott, *Russian Justice* (New York, 1935). There is also good primary material in Rudolph Schlesinger, *Soviet Legal Theory* (London, 1945) and Hugh Babb, *Soviet Legal Philosophy* (Cambridge, Mass., 1951). Both Pashukanis and Stuchka await good full length biographies, but see Robt. Sharlet, "Pashukanis and the Withering Away of Law in the USSR," in S. Fitzpatrick, *Cultural Revolution in Russia, 1928-31* (Bloomington, Ind., 1978), and his "Pashukanis and the Rise of Soviet Marxist Jurisprudence, 1927-1930," *Soviet Union*, 1:2 (1974).

Chapter V. Religion, Language, and Other "Awkward Habits" of Everyday Life

Most of the material on questions of habit and custom focuses on religion, but see Bernard Comrie and Gerald Stone, *The Russian Language Since the Revolution* (Oxford,

1978), which includes chapters on "Modes of Address and Speech Etiquette," and "Sex, Gender, and the Status of Women," and contains additional references to these issues. Discussion of habits and customs can also be found in such general studies as John Maynard, *Russia in Flux,* (New York, 1951) and G. Gorer and J. Rickman, *The People of Great Russia* (New York, 1957).

The best general study of the church after 1917 is still John S. Curtiss, *The Russian Church and the Soviet State, 1917-1950* (Boston, 1953), but see also David E. Powell, *Anti-religious Propaganda in the Soviet Union* (Cambridge, Mass., 1957) and Richard H. Marshall, Jr., ed., *Aspects of Religion in the Soviet Union 1917-1967* (Chicago, 1971). The Marshall volume contains a good essay by John Delaney "The Origins of Soviet Anti-religious Organizations" and Zvi Gitelman, "The Communist Party and Soviet Jewry: The Early Years." A collection of useful documents has been pulled together by Boleslaw Szczesniak, *The Russian Revolution and Religion: Documents Concerning the Suppression of Religion by the Communist, 1917-1925* (Notre Dame, Indiana, 1959).

Part 2

Chapter I. United Labor Schools: The Nature of a "Communist Education"

Of the vast amount of material available on Soviet educational policy, the best studies are Fitzpatrick's on the *Commissariat of Enlightenment,* noted above, and James C. McClelland's excellent articles, "Bolshevik Approaches to Higher Education, 1917-1921," *Slavic Review,* 30:4 (Dec. 1971), pp. 818-31, and "The Utopian and the Heroic: Divergent Paths to the Communist Educational Ideal," in *Bolshevik Culture,* Abbott Gleason et al., eds. (Bloomington, Ind., 1985). Although primarily on the 1930s, there is also interesting material on the training of specialists in Kendall E. Bailes, *Technology and Society under Lenin and Stalin: Origins of the Soviet Technical Intelligentsia, 1917-1941* (Princeton, N.J., 1978), which contains as well a good, current bibliography. See also the essay by Nicholas DeWitt, "The October Revolution and Soviet Education," *Canadian Slavonic Papers,* Autumn, 1968. On the youth league (Komsomol) see Ralph Fisher, *Pattern for Soviet Youth* (New York, 1959).

A sympathetic eye-witness account of the early reforms is Scott Nearing, *Education in Soviet Russia* (New York, 1926), and a somewhat similar viewpoint is reflected in Albert Pinkevitch, *The New Education in the Soviet Republic* (New York, 1929), translated from the Russian, and written by a professor at Moscow University. Robt. H. McNeal has written a good general biography of Krupskaya, one of the leaders of Soviet educational affairs after the revolution, in *Bride of the Revolution* (Ann Arbor, Mich., 1972), and readers might also want to examine Lucy L. Wilson, *The New Schools of New Russia* (New York, 1928), another sympathetic eye-witness account. General studies like Maurice Shore, *Soviet Education: Its Psychology and Philosophy* (New York, 1947), cover broad issues, but see James Bowen, *Soviet Education: Anton Makarenko and the Years of Experiment* (Madison, Wisc., 1962). There is also, of course, an extensive range of journal articles. See the bibliographies in Fitzpatrick and McClelland.

Chapter II. Vodka, the Church, and the Cinema: Workers' Films and the Proletarian Theater

There is an extensive literature on art, film, and the visual arts. On film, see in particular Jay Leyda, *Kino: A History of Russian and Soviet Film* (New York, 1959, 1971), which is illustrated and extensively annotated: and L. Schnitzer et al., eds., *Cinema in Revolution: The Heroic Era of Soviet Film* (London, 1973), which includes essays from victorious people who worked in the period. Essays by Eisenstein, Pudovkin, and other prominent Soviet film figures are also available in English (e.g. V.I. Pudovkin, *Film Technique and Film Acting*, London, 1929, 1958; S. Eisenstein, *Film Essays and a Lecture*, New York, 1970). Eisenstein's essay "Soviet Cinema" can also be found in J. Freeman, et al., *Voices of October* (New York, 1930), for which it was originally written. See also Peter Dart, *Pudovkin's Films and Film Theory* (New York, 1974), S. Eisenstein, *Film Form* (Cleveland, 1957, 1968), Paul Babitsky and John Rimberg, *The Soviet Film Industry* (New York, 1955), and Richard Taylor, *The Politics of the Soviet Cinema* (New York, 1979). Peter Kenez, *The Birth of the Propaganda State* (Cambridge, Eng., 1985), has an extensive discussion of early Soviet film as well as an analysis of the political use of books, films and posters, and other agitational activities.

There are also several good general studies on Soviet theater. See esp. Marc Slonim, *The Russian Theater* (Cleveland, 1961), and the superb volume by K. Rudnitsky, *Meyerhold* (Ann Arbor, 1981). Robert C. Williams, *Artists in Revolution,* has sketches on Meyerhold, as well as other avant-garde figures. See also the materials listed under chapter IV, below.

Chapter III. Architecture and City Planning: Constructing the New Socialist Collective

The best general survey of Soviet architecture and city planning is Anatole Kopp, *Town and Revolution: Soviet Architecture and City Planning 1917-1935* (New York, 1970). Kopp's book is enthusiastic and lavishly illustrated. See also Maurice Parkins, *City Planning in Soviet Russia* (Chicago, 1953), and the special issue of *Russian History*, 11:2-3 (Summer-Fall, 1984), devoted to "Utopia in Russia: History, Culture, and Thought," especially the essay by Claes Caldenby on "The Vision of a Rational Architecture." Perhaps the best illustrated volume on early city planning is Selim Chan-Magomedow (Khan-Magomedov), *Pionere der sowjetischen Architektur* (Vienna, 1983), translated from the Russian. S. Frederick Starr, "Visionary Town Planning During the Cultural Revolution," in *Cultural Revolution in Russia, 1928–1931,* S. Fitzpatrick, ed. (Indiana, 1977) is an important contribution, although concentrating on the later period. See also K. Frampton, "Notes on Soviet Urbanism, 1917-1932," *Architects Yearbook* (London), XII (1968). A detailed general bibliography, now somewhat dated, is Anatole Senkevitch, ed., *Soviet Architecture, 1917–1956* (Charlottesville, 1973). Senkevitch is also completing a new, comprehensive volume entitled *The Modern Movement in Soviet Architecture.*

On Melnikov and early Soviet architecture in general, S. Frederick Starr's *Melnikov: Solo Architect in a Mass Society* (Princeton, 1978) is indispensable and contains a detailed bibliography. Important works by individual figures in translation include N. A. Miliutin, *Sotsgorod: The Problem of Building Socialist Cities* (1930) (Cambridge, Mass., 1974); Moisei Ginzburg, *Style and Epoch* (1924) (Cambridge, Mass., 1982); L. Sabsovitch (L. M. Sabsovich), *L'U.R.S.S. dans dix ans: plan général de la construction du socialisme: hypothèse* (Paris, 1930), and M. Ilin, *New Russia's Primer: The Story of the Five Year Plan* (Boston, 1932). On Tatlin, see the chapter in Robert C. Williams, *Artists in Revolution: Portraits of the Russian Avant-Garde* (Bloomington, Ind., 1977), and especially John Milner, *Vladimir Tatlin and the Russian Avant-Garde* (New Haven, 1983), which also surveys the period more broadly.

Chapter IV. Creating Proletarian Cultural Forms: Art, Music, and Literature

On Soviet aesthetics generally, an interesting essay by Margaret M. Bullit, "Toward a Marxist Theory of Aesthetics: The Development of Socialist Realism in the Soviet Union," can be found in *Russian Review*, January 1976, pp. 53-76. This subject is also treated by Camilla Gray, in her extensively illustrated *The Russian Experiment in Art, 1863-1922* (London, 1962). See also John Bowlt, ed. *Russian Art of the Avant-Garde* (New York, 1976), a collection of documents and materials; and his "Russian Art in the 1920s," *Soviet Studies*, 22:4 (April, 1971), pp. 574-94. Bowlt's book has an excellent, comprehensive bibliography.

On poster art, see especially the lavishly illustrated M. Guerman, *Art of the October Revolution* (New York, 1979). An interesting article on "agitprop" is Richard Taylor, "A Medium for the Masses: Agitation in the Soviet Civil War," *Soviet Studies*, 22:4 (April, 1971), pp. 562-75. See also Stephen White, "The Political Poster in Bolshevik Russia," *Sbornik*, 8 (1982). Readers might also want to look at the superb illustrations in Harrison Salisbury, *Russia in Revolution, 1900-1930* (New York, 1978), which includes some excellent examples of early Soviet posters, as well as the Guerman volume just cited. Robt. C. Williams, *Artists in Revolution: Portraits of the Russian Avant-Garde* (Bloomington, Ind., 1977), contains informative chapters on several figures of the period, including Malevich. A special issue of the journal *Soviet Union*, Vol. 3, pt. 2 (1976), has been devoted to Constructivism. See also Christina Lodder, *Russian Constructivism* (New Haven, 1983), and the interesting collection of essays edited by N. A. Nilsson, *Art, Society, Revolution: Russia 1917-1921* (Stockholm, 1979). *Art into Production: Soviet Textiles, Fashion and Ceramics, 1912-1935* (New York, 1984), handsomely illustrates decorative arts of the period.

There are also several good general studies on Soviet music. See James Bakst, *A History of Russian and Soviet Music* (New York, 1962); and the thorough study by Boris Schwarz, *Music and Musical Life in Soviet Russia 1917-1970* (New York, 1972). Israel Nestyev and Victor Scroff have written biographies on Prokofiev which touch on the 1920s, although briefly.

Much has been written about the effect of the revolution on Russian literature from a political as well as cultural perspective, and the reader interested in exploring this area might best begin with one of the general surveys: Edward J. Brown, *Russian Literature since the Revolution* (New York, 1963); Robt. A. Maguire, *Red Virgin Soil: Soviet Literature in the 1920s* (Princeton, N.J., 1968); Helen Muchnik, *From Gorky to Pasternak: Six Writers in Soviet Russia* (New York, 1961); or Gleb Struve, *Russian Literature under Lenin and Stalin, 1917-1953* (Norman, Okla., 1971). Brown's book has a good bibliography. Muchnik's volume concentrates on Gorky, Blok, Mayakovsky, Leonov, Sholokhov and Pasternak, but has much to say of interest about the period generally. Gleb Struve's study heavily emphasizes the 1920s. Brown has also written an excellent study of the proletarian cultural revolution in its "second phase," *The Proletarian Episode in Russian Literature, 1928-1932* (New York, 1953). See also H. Stephan, *"Lef" and the Left Front of the Arts*, Munich, 1981. There is also a wide array of periodical literature, both in scholarly and literary journals, as well as memoirs. See especially I. Ehrenburg, *First Years of the Revolution, 1918-1921* (London, 1962), and the journals *Slavic Review, The Slavonic and East European Review*, and of course, *Russian Literature Triquarterly*, especially issues number 2, 7, 12 and 13, on "The Twenties," "Russian Theater and Film," and "Futurism and Constructivism." *Russian Literature of the 1920s: An Anthology*, Carl Proffer et al., eds. (Ann Arbor, 1987) is an important new collection of writings from the early Soviet period. Additional material from the period in translation can be found in Anna Lawton, ed., *Russian Futurism through Its Manifestoes* (Ithaca, 1988).

CONTENTS OF PART 2

IV.   **Creating Proletarian Cultural Forms: Art, Music, and
      Literature**

Ann Arbor Paperbacks

Waddell, *The Desert Fathers*
Erasmus, *The Praise of Folly*
Donne, *Devotions*
Malthus, *Population: The First Essay*
Berdyaev, *The Origin of Russian Communism*
Einhard, *The Life of Charlemagne*
Edwards, *The Nature of True Virtue*
Gilson, *Héloïse and Abélard*
Aristotle, *Metaphysics*
Kant, *Education*
Boulding, *The Image*
Duckett, *The Gateway to the Middle Ages*
   (3 vols.): *Italy; France and Britain;*
   Monasticism
Bowditch and Ramsland, *Voices of the*
   Industrial Revolution
Luxemburg, *The Russian Revolution* and
   Leninism or Marxism?
Rexroth, *Poems from the Greek Anthology*
Zoshchenko, *Scenes from the Bathhouse*
Thrupp, *The Merchant Class of Medieval*
   London
Procopius, *Secret History*
Adcock, *Roman Political Ideas and Practice*
Swanson, *The Birth of the Gods*
Xenophon, *The March Up Country*
Trotsky, *The New Course*
Buchanan and Tullock, *The Calculus of*
   Consent
Hobson, *Imperialism*
Pobedonostsev, *Reflections of a Russian*
   Statesman
Kinietz, *The Indians of the Western Great*
   Lakes 1615–1760
Bromage, *Writing for Business*
Lurie, *Mountain Wolf Woman, Sister of*
   Crashing Thunder
Leonard, *Baroque Times in Old Mexico*
Meier, *Negro Thought in America,*
   1880–1915
Burke, *The Philosophy of Edmund Burke*
Michelet, *Joan of Arc*
Conze, *Buddhist Thought in India*
Arberry, *Aspects of Islamic*
   Civilization
Chesnutt, *The Wife of His Youth and*
   Other Stories
Gross, *Sound and Form in Modern Poetry*
Zola, *The Masterpiece*
Chesnutt, *The Marrow of Tradition*
Aristophanes, *Four Comedies*
Aristophanes, *Three Comedies*
Chesnutt, *The Conjure Woman*
Duckett, *Carolingian Portraits*
Rapoport and Chammah, *Prisoner's Dilemma*

Aristotle, *Poetics*
Peattie, *The View from the Barrio*
Duckett, *Death and Life in the Tenth Century*
Langford, *Galileo, Science and the Church*
McNaughton, *The Taoist Vision*
Anderson, *Matthew Arnold and the Classical*
   Tradition
Milio, *9226 Kercheval*
Weisheipl, *The Development of Physical*
   Theory in the Middle Ages
Breton, *Manifestoes of Surrealism*
Gershman, *The Surrealist Revolution in*
   France
Burt, *Mammals of the Great Lakes Region*
Lester, *Theravada Buddhism in Southeast Asia*
Scholz, *Carolingian Chronicles*
Wik, *Henry Ford and Grass-roots America*
Sahlins and Service, *Evolution and Culture*
Wickham, *Early Medieval Italy*
Waddell, *The Wandering Scholars*
Rosenberg, *Bolshevik Visions* (2 parts in 2
   vols.)
Mannoni, *Prospero and Caliban*
Aron, *Democracy and Totalitarianism*
Shy, *A People Numerous and Armed*
Taylor, *Roman Voting Assemblies*
Goodfield, *An Imagined World*
Hesiod, *The Works and Days; Theogony; The*
   Shield of Herakles
Raverat, *Period Piece*
Lamming, *In the Castle of My Skin*
Fisher, *The Conjure-Man Dies*
Strayer, *The Albigensian Crusades*
Lamming, *The Pleasures of Exile*
Lamming, *Natives of My Person*
Glaspell, *Lifted Masks and Other Works*
Wolff, *Aesthetics and the Sociology of Art*
Grand, *The Heavenly Twins*
Cornford, *The Origin of Attic Comedy*
Allen, *Wolves of Minong*
Brathwaite, *Roots*
Fisher, *The Walls of Jericho*
Lamming, *The Emigrants*
Loudon, *The Mummy!*
Kemble and Butler Leigh, *Principles and*
   Privilege
Thomas, *Out of Time*
Flanagan, *You Alone Are Dancing*
Kotre and Hall, *Seasons of Life*
Shen, *Almost a Revolution*
Meckel, *Save the Babies*
Laver and Schofield, *Multiparty Government*
Rutt, *The Bamboo Grove*
Endelman, *The Jews of Georgian England,*
   1714–1830